NEW FORMATIONS

EDITOR:
Judith Squires,
in association with *Signs of the Times*

CONSULTING EDITORS:
James Donald
Erica Carter

EDITORIAL BOARD:
Homi Bhabha
Lesley Caldwell
Tony Davies
Simon Frith
Jim Grealy
Stuart Hall
Dick Hebdige
Graham Murdock
Ali Rattansi
Denise Riley
Jenny Bourne Taylor
Valerie Walkerdine

OVERSEAS EDITORS:
Ien Ang
Angelika Bammer
Tony Bennett
Jody Berland
Victor Burgin
Hazel Carby
Iain Chambers
Joan Copjec
Lidia Curti
Ian Hunter
Cora Kaplan
Noel King
Colin Mercer
Kobena Mercer
Edward Said
Renata Salecl
Gayatri Chakravorty Spivak
John Tagg

New Formations is
published three times
a year by
Lawrence & Wishart
144a Old South Lambeth Road
London SW8 1XX
Tel 071–820 9281
Fax 071–587 0469

ADVERTISEMENTS
for enquiries/bookings contact
Ruth Borthwick, Lawrence & Wishart

SUBSCRIPTIONS
For 1995, subscription rates to Lawrence &
Wishart are, for 3 issues
UK: Institutions £55, Individuals £35.
Rest of world: Institutions £58; Individuals
£38.
Single copies: £14.99

CONTRIBUTIONS, CORRESPONDENCE
AND BOOKS FOR REVIEW
should be sent to
The Editor, *New Formations*,
Dept of Politics, University of Bristol,
12 Priory Road, Bristol BS8 1TU

Prospective writers are encouraged to contact
the editors to discuss their ideas and to obtain
a copy of our style sheet.
Manuscripts should be sent in triplicate. They
will not be returned unless a stamped,
self-addressed envelope is enclosed.
Contributors should note that the editorial
board cannot take responsibility for any
manuscript submitted to *New Formations*.

ISSN 0 950-2378
ISBN 0 85315 812 6

Text design by Jan Brown Designs, London
Photoset in North Wales by
Derek Doyle & Associates, Mold, Clwyd
Printed in Great Britain
at the University Press, Cambridge

NOTES ON CONTRIBUTORS

David Macey is a translator and the author of *The Lives of Michel Foucault* (1993). He is currently preparing a biography of Frantz Fanon.

John Rajchman lectures in philosophy at the Collège de Philosophie, Paris.

Kate Soper is a Senior Lecturer in Philosophy at the University of North London. She is author of *On Human Needs* (1980), *Humanism and Anti-Humanism* (1986) and *Troubled Pleasures* (1990).

Alan D. Schrift is Associate Professor of Philosophy at Grinnell College, USA. He is the author of *Nietzsche and the Question of Interpretation: Between Hermeneutics and Deconstruction* (1990). His latest work, *Nietzsche's French Legacy: A Genealogy of Postructuralism*, is to be published in 1995.

Sue Golding is a writer on ethics, sexualities, and radical democratic theory. She is also a director of avant-garde erotic art and theatre, and is a Senior Lecturer in Political Philosophy at the University of Greenwich, London. Her new book *The Cunning of Democracy* is forthcoming.

James Miller is Director of Liberal Studies and Professor of Political Science at the New School for Social Research, New York. He is author of *The Passion of Michel Foucault* (1993).

Robert J.C. Young lectures in English at Wadham College, Oxford. He is author of *White Mythologies* (1990) and *Colonial Desire: Hybridity in Theory, Culture and Race* (1995).

John Marks lectures in the Department of European Studies, Loughborough University of Technology and is currently completing a book on Gilles Deleuze.

Wendy Wheeler is a Senior Lecturer in English and Critical Theory at the University of North London.

Nick Couldry recently completed his MA at Goldsmiths College, London, and is now researching issues of public space and media space. He is also active as a musician and performance artist.

CONTENTS

NUMBER 25 SUMMER 1995

Michel Foucault: J'Accuse

MICHEL FOUCAULT: *J'ACCUSE*

What might we do with Foucault's philosophy? To what new uses might it yet be put? These two questions, raised by John Rajchman in his 'Foucault Ten Years After', seem to capture the underlying concerns of the contributions in this collection.

25th June 1994 marked the tenth anniversary of the death of Michel Foucault. To reflect upon this moment a one-day conference was organised in London by *Signs of the Times*, exploring the legacy of Foucault's work ten years on.[1] *Signs of the Times* is an open and independent discussion group based in London. In the words of their founding statement they are 'committed to developing an understanding of the profound changes which are redrawing the political and cultural map. We aim to chart this new landscape and shape new agendas for the nineties.'[2] A selection of the most stimulating and provocative papers from this staggeringly well-attended conference are brought together in this issue of *New Formations* (along with other more general pieces) as our contribution to the continuing debates sparked by the memory of Michel Foucault.

These essays embody a range of different answers to Rajchman's question: what might we do with Foucault's philosophy? Clearly what we might choose to do with it will be influenced, as David Macey argues, by the political landscape and the theoretical climate of the day. I take it as a rather positive 'sign of the times' that the contributors to this issue of *New Formations* have all resisted the tendency to commemorate and revere Foucault, in favour of a more dissonant and experimental *use* of his thought to pursue varied agendas of current concern. The issues of new technologies, feminism, subjectivity, the philosophical life, race, sexuality and space are all contemplated in the light of Foucault's philosophy.

These various contemplations are premised by David Macey's political cry of 'j'accuse': the democratic state challenged in the name of democratic values. The demand for the 'clearing of a non-party space for an ethically governed politics', thereby represents, both within this collection and more generally, the context and the consequence of the art of philosophical experimentation. In answer to our opening question then, perhaps we might respond positively that the most significant use to which the philosophical life of Michel Foucault might yet be put is in providing both a reminder of the importance of the philosopher engaging in the political, and a model for its possibility.

Whatever our response, it would seem that, in the words of Alan Schrift: '... although Foucault himself may have been "erased, like a face drawn in sand at the edge of the sea", the discursivity founded by his analytics of power have established possibilities whose end we are far from reaching.'

Judith Squires
January 1995

1. The Conference was sponsored by *New Formations*, the journal *Economy and Society*, and the publisher Lawrence & Wishart. In addition it also received valuable financial assistance from the Barry Amiel and Normal Melburn Trust, and the Lipman Trust.

2. The group organises seminars, produces discussion papers and in 1994 published, in association with Lawrence & Wishart, the book *Altered States: Postmodernism, Politics, Culture*. For details of *Signs of the Times* seminars, publications and 1 July 1995 'Postmodern Times' Conference write to Signs of the Times, 28 Wargrave Avenue, London N15 6UD.

MICHEL FOUCAULT: *J'ACCUSE*

David Macey

This conference marks the tenth anniversary of an event we would all prefer not to be commemorating: the death of Michel Foucault. It also coincides with a number of other anniversaries that are worth noting for their symbolic and political importance. June 1993 saw the murder in Algiers of Tahar Djaout. Djaout was a journalist and poet, and possibly one of the finest Algerian novelists of his generation.[1] And that is why he was killed at the age of thirty-nine on the orders of the Front Islamique du Salut by two men who were paid the equivalent of £30 for the murder. Asked why they had killed Djaout, one of them allegedly replied: 'Because he was a good writer. He knew how to influence the Muslim people.'[2] I recall Djaout's death because I feel confident that, were he alive today, Foucault would be working with Pierre Bourdieu and the Comité International de Soutien aux Intellectuels Algériens. It was, of course, together with Bourdieu that Foucault protested so strongly and so effectively about the French government's silence over the establishment of martial law in Poland in the winter of 1981–82.[3]

A second anniversary will come at the end of the year: the beginning of the Dreyfus Affair. All communities appear to require a foundation myth and the Dreyfus Affair is that of the French intellectual tribe. It is probably not in fact true that, as has often been claimed, the noun 'intellectual' was coined during the affair and it is not true that it marks the first use of a petition as a weapon: the first petition in the modern sense was directed against the building of the Eiffel Tower.[4] It is, however, true to say that the Dreyfus Affair signals the emergence of a phenomenon characteristic of French political life over the last century. It provoked, that is, a collective act of protest – the *Manifeste des intellectuels* of 1897 – on the part of men – and the word is used advisedly – incarnating an intellectual-moral authority. The Dreyfus Affair inaugurates or cements a tense and contradictory relationship between the Republican State and intellectuals – many of them employed by the state itself, others in what Althusser terms Ideological State Apparatuses. It should be recalled that any French philosopher working within the educational system – even at the Collège de France – is, technically, a *fonctionnaire*, a civil servant. In the tradition inaugurated by the Dreyfus Affair, the Republican State is challenged in the name of Republican values deriving from the founding moment of 1789.

The paradigmatic form of that challenge is defined by the title of Emile Zola's open letter to the President of the Republic: *J'accuse*. Significantly, the Dreyfusards were not members of any one political party and the Dreyfus/anti-Dreyfus division was not, in any simple sense, a left/right divide. Indeed, for a significant section of the institutionalized left, the case of a Jewish

1. See in particular his satirical *Les Vigiles*, Seuil, Paris 1991.

2. Rachid Mimouni, 'Tuez-les tous!', *Le Monde*, 4 June 1993, p11; Catherine Seddon, 'Letter from Algiers', *New Statesman and Society*, 3 December 1993, p28.

3. David Macey, *The Lives of Michel Foucault*, Hutchinson, London 1993.

4. Jean-François Sirinelli, *Intellectuels et passions françaises: Manifestes et pétitions au XXième*, Seuil, Paris 1990.

officer accused of treason was of no concern to the proletariat and his defence was, in what has become the time-honoured phrase, a diversion from the class struggle. The *Manifeste des intellectuels* clears a non-party space for the expression of an ethnically-governed politics. From the mid-1930s onwards, a further factor is introduced into the State-intellectual relationship as the Parti Communiste Français inscribes itself in the national tradition during the Popular Front and indeed claims to be the legitimate heir to 1789. In the early 1950s, Sartre relates to it as a critical fellow-traveller; in the 1970s Foucault will situate himself in opposition to it. In both cases, the PCF is an essential player; this is not a situation that will apply for much longer.

J'accuse is a cry that has often been repeated throughout this century. It could serve as a generic title for the clandestine publications of the Resistance. It punctuates the tormented history of the Algerian War of Independence. When, in 1957, Maurice Audin, a mathematician and communist who taught at the University of Algiers, was captured, tortured and finally 'disappeared' by the 1er Régiment de Chasseurs Parachutistes, a pamphlet entitled *Nous Accusons* was published by an ad hoc 'Audin Comité'. Like the Dreyfus manifestos, it took the form of an open letter to the President of the Republic.[5] After the war, Jules Roy's denunciation of an *a posteriori* retrospective attempt to justify the routine use of torture during the Battle of Algiers was entitled *J'Accuse le Général Massu*.[6] A reserve officer, that is, accuses a serving brother officer and presses charges against the military in the name of the republican values of the army. More significantly, *J'Accuse* was the title of a short-lived Maoist newspaper published in the early 1970s. *J'Accuse* merged with a second paper known for a while by the dual title *J'Accuse/La Cause du peuple*, which combines a direct reference to the Dreyfusard tradition with what sounds like an allusion to Marat's *L'Ami du peuple*. Michel Foucault was an occasional contributor.

5. Pierre Vidal-Naquet, *L'Affaire Audin (1957-1978)*, Minuit, Paris 1989, p122.

6. Seuil, Paris 1972.

Before going on to more specific points, mention should perhaps be made of one final anniversary. On 6 April 1993, a young Zairean was shot dead in a police station in Paris. He was the second young man to die at the hands of the police that week. The following day a young Algerian was shot and seriously wounded by a police officer. All these incidents occurred within days of the election of Balladur's right-wing government and the appointment of Charles Pasqua as Minister of the Interior – a minister with a harsh line on immigration and law and order. In 1972, the death of an Algerian lorry driver in police custody received widespread press coverage and led to effective protests organised by Foucault and others. In 1993, there were spontaneous protests and disturbance, but there was no cry of *J'accuse*. It would be interesting to speculate as to why that was the case.

The 1970s – and particularly the early 1970s – were the most politically active period in Foucault's life. Indeed, although he was briefly a member of the PCF in his youth, Foucault was basically a non-political animal until the late 1960s or the early 1970s. If we wish to understand anything of his politics and political activity during these years, we have to begin by looking at the political landscape in which he was operating. Only then can we begin to look at the lessons, if any, that are to be learned from Foucault. It is not in fact easy to reconstruct this landscape. Whilst the literature on May 1968 is very extensive, that on the subsequent period of political turbulence is less abundant, though significant studies are now becoming available.[7]

Foucault returned to Paris in the autumn of 1968 after a two-year stay in Tunis which appears to have done a lot to politicise him. He had not taken part in the May 'events' in Paris, though he evidently viewed them as announcing a revolution in everyday life. At times he could also be very scathing about May: the students he had known in Tunis risked fifteen years in prison for opposing their government, and no *soixante-huitard* risked such penalties. The events of that May were, however, something that shaped the political world in which Foucault was to operate. In terms of the political geography of France, the PCF was for many to the right of the political spectrum, an 'objective ally', as the saying goes, of the Gaullist state. The Party, for its part, predictably argued that the new left was in alliance with the Gaullist state against the working class. Quite aside from the widespread disenchantment with the Soviet Union that developed from 1956 onwards, there were a number of more immediate reasons for the sapping of the Party's authority. Firstly, there was still recent memory of its less than enthusiastic support for the struggle for Algerian independence from 1954 onwards.[8] As Foucault put it in 1978, the Algerian War marked the end of the long period in which it had been possible to believe 'a bit naively' that 'the Communist Party, just struggles and just causes were one and the same.'[9] Secondly, there was a widespread feeling that the PCF had undermined – or at least failed to support – the May movement.[10] And thirdly, there came accusation from the far left that it was 'revisionist', that it had abandoned the basic principles of Marxism in favour of a peaceful coexistence with the status quo. Hence the many pamphlets and leaflets that referred scornfully to '*l'ex-Parti Communiste*' or the '*Parti "Communiste" Français*'.

Most of the emergent movements of the day, many of them ephemeral, defined themselves in opposition to the sclerosis of the PCF. Neither gay nor feminist groups were likely to ally themselves with a party that could still talk of the values and virtues of the proletarian family. Vociferous opposition to the PCF was expressed by a number of Maoist groups, though the most important were not the tiny parties 'officially' recognized by Peking. In terms of Foucault's politics, the most important group was the Gauche Prolétarienne, the product of a fusion between elements of the Union des Jeunesses Communistes (marxiste-léniniste) and the Mouvement du 22 mars that occurred in late 1968. Described by many of its members as 'Maoist but not Leninist', it was reliant upon a vision of spontaneous action on the part of the 'masses' and strongly influenced by a romantic interpretation of Mao's Cultural Revolution. It was apocalyptic and by 1969 was openly calling for civil war.[11] Foucault was never a Maoist – he certainly had no patience with the notion of studying Mao-Tse-Tung thought – and does not appear to have endorsed the 'civil war' line, but saw himself as working alongside Maoists. The intellectual,

7. See, for example, F.M. Samuelson, *Il était une fois 'Libé'* …, Seuil, Paris 1979; Hervé Hamon and Patrick Rotman, *Génération*, Seuil, Paris 1987, two vols.; Sunil Khilnani, *Arguing Revolution: The Intellectual Left in Postwar France*, Yale University Press, New Haven 1993.

8. For an account of disillusionment with the Communist and Socialist parties during the Algerian War see Michel Winock, *La République se meurt*, Seuil, Paris 1978.

9. Michel Foucault, *Remarks on Marx: Conversations with Duccio Trombadori*, tr. R. James Goldstein and James Cascaito, Semiotext(e), New York 1991, p111.

10. Richard Johnson, *The French Communist Party Versus the Students: Revolutionary Politics in May–June 1968*, Yale University Press, New Haven 1972.

11. Michèle Manceaux, *Les Maos en France*, Gallimard, Paris 1972; Michèle Manceaux and Jacques Donzelot, *Cours, Camarade, le PCF est derrière toi*, Gallimard, Paris 1974.

that is, seeks allies but refuses to enter the space occupied by a party or organised movement.

Working alongside the Maoists was no easy option, not least because of their militant anti-intellectualism. One strand in the movement had, even before 1968, co-ordinated two attempts on the part of young intellectuals to 'establish' themselves as factory workers – preferably at the Renault or Citroën car plants. They were to be, it was hoped, part of a growing revolt at shop-floor level, though in most cases the long-term result was no more than great personal hardship and lasting depression.[12] Of more immediate concern to Foucault, who was trying to establish a philosophy department at the new University of Vincennes (founded in late 1968), was the wonderfully named 'Base Committee for the Abolition of the Wage-System and the Destruction of the University'. This could lead to some strange conflicts: the Foucault who had taken part in the violent occupation of the campus in January 1969 occasionally found himself locked out of his own lecture rooms, or was reluctantly obliged to take part in endless General Meetings. For these elements, he was the most dangerous thing of all: a liberal, and therefore unreliable, ally.

If the political landscape had changed, so too had the theoretical climate. In 1965–66 (a period which saw the publication in rapid succession of Althusser and Balibar's *Lire le Capital*, Foucault's *Les Mots et les choses* and Lacan's *Ecrits*) it had seemed possible that a tripartite alliance could be formed – despite the obvious disagreements signalled by Foucault's jibe that 'Marxism exists in nineteenth-century thought like a fish in water: that is, it is unable to breathe anywhere else.'[13] May 1968 in some ways signalled the end of a certain emphasis on theory. As a graffiti seen at the Sorbonne put it: 'Structures do not take to the streets' (though Lacan argued that they had done precisely that). The post-1968 period saw the emergence of a plethora of groups and of new forms of militancy: the Front Homosexuel d'Action Révolutionnaire, the early feminist movement, the Groupe d'Information sur les Prisons and, most exotic of all, Vive La Révolution. The latter's slogan, borrowed from Lotta Continua in Italy, was 'What do we want? Everything.' Combine that with a line from a song by The Doors, 'We want the world and we want it now', and you go some way to capturing the heady atmosphere of the beginning of the 1970s.

The change of climate had its inevitable effects on the reception of Foucault's work, and even on his own perception of it. *Histoire de la folie* was in 1961, an academic thesis that was successfully submitted for a doctorate; by 1969, it had, to its author's surprise, become part of an anti-psychiatry movement which easily mutated into a positive celebration of madness, and its author could actually be accused of 'psychiatricide' by the very academics and clinicians who had taught him in the 1940s and 1950s.[14] By 1972, Guy Hocquenghem, a friend of Foucault's and probably the first gay activist to attain a degree of media stardom, could identify gays with the excluded and confined populations described by Foucault.[15] This is a reminder that it is not only individuality that is an unstable category – and that surely is the fundamental lesson to be learned from Foucault, not to mention Lacan; texts too have an

12. Virginie Linhart, *Volontaires pour l'usine: Vie d'établis 1967-1977*, Seuil, Paris 1994.

13. Michel Foucault, *The Order of Things*, Tavistock, London 1970, p262.

14. See the conference papers published in *Evolution Psychiatrique*, April-June 1971 under the generic title *La Conception idéologique de 'l'Histoire de la folie' de Michel Foucault*.

15. Guy Hocquenghem, *Le Désir homosexuel*, Editions Universitaires, Paris 1972.

unstable meaning and can undergo metamorphoses. Their destiny is not preordained for all time. As Foucault himself put it in 1974 when he was interviewed by an Italian journalist:

> The boundary of politics has changed, and subjects like psychiatry, confinement and the medicalisation of a population, have become political problems. With what has been happening over the last few years, political groups have been obliged to integrate these domains into their action, and they and I have come together, not because I've changed ... but because I think I can say with some pride ... that it is politics that has come to me.[16]

In May 1970 the Gauche Prolétarienne (GP) was proscribed by the government and the editors of its newspaper *La Cause du peuple* were in jail, soon to be joined by a fair number of its militants. On the night of the GP's proscription, a 5000-strong meeting called for their release and then took to the streets in violent protest. The jailed Maoists almost immediately demanded political status, citing as a precedent the Algerian War, when prisoners belonging to both the Algerian Front de Libération Nationale and the clandestine neo-fascist Organisation Armée Secrète were granted that status. Before long, the political prisoner/common-law prisoner distinction had been dropped; the whole question of the carceral system could now be politicised.

It is this that leads to the beginning of Foucault's main political project of the period: the Groupe d'Informations sur les Prisons (GIP). The GIP emerged from the suggestion put forward by Foucault's partner Daniel Defert that a commission of some kind should be established to investigate and publicise the 'political prisoners' conditions of detention. On 8 February 1971 Foucault read out the founding statement:

> None of us can be sure of avoiding prison. Less so than ever today. Police control over our day-to-day lives is becoming tighter: in the streets and on the roads; over foreigners and young people; it is once more an offence to express an opinion; anti-drug measures are leading to increasingly arbitrary arrests ... They tell us that the prisons are over-populated. But what if it were the population that were being overimprisoned?[17]

Some twenty years after the event, this may sound something of a melodramatic exaggeration. Not at the time. If, for example, you had gone to Foucault's inaugural lecture at the Collège de France on 2 December 1970, you would have had to make your way past coachloads of riot police in the Latin Quarter, even though nothing in particular was happening in the streets. You would have found similar coaches outside the venue for virtually any rock concert. For young people, the threat of police violence was very real, and it was commonplace to speak of 'anti-youth racism'. A much higher level of violence prevailed within the prison system: the period 1971–73 was punctuated by a series of mutinies, hunger strikes, suicides, hostage-taking

16. Michel Foucault, 'Prisons et asiles dans le mécanisme du pouvoire' in *Dits et ecrits, Volume Two, 1970-1975*, Gallimard, Paris 1994, p524.

17. Jean-Marie Domenach, Michel Foucault and Pierre Vidal-Naquet, 'Manifeste du GIP', *ibid.*, pp174-75.

incidents and very violent repression. Involvement with the GIP at any level was no game.

The GIP was not a reform group. Originally a reflection of the Maoist prisoners' demand for political status, it became a denunciation of the prison system as such, and its main task was to obtain and spread information about its realities: 'The GIP interviews prisoners, former prisoners, their families, all those who have had experience of prisons. After all, we might all go to prison: by what right are we prevented from knowing what prison really is?'[18] Nor was it an organisation that spoke on behalf of prisoners – as Foucault once remarked to Gilles Deleuze, there is something shameful about speaking on behalf of others.

18. Michel Foucault, 'La Prison partout', *ibid.*, p193.

Organisationally, the GIP was unstructured, informal (there were no membership cards, no official constitution) and remarkably effective at mobilising its supporters and publicising its actions. With great efficiency, it produced a series of pamphlets dealing with accounts of prison life, an account of a model prison, of suicides in prison, and of the George Jackson case in the United States, that still make for chilling reading. The generic title given to them – *Intolérable* – captures the general tone and echoes the old cry of *J'Accuse*.

The founding statement of the GIP was signed by Foucault and two other men: Jean-Marie Domenach and Pierre Vidal-Naquet. The former was at the time the editor of the left-Catholic monthly *Esprit* and once a youthful member of the wartime resistance. Vidal-Naquet was a very distinguished classicist, but more significantly he was one of the first intellectuals to denounce France's policies in Algeria – especially the use of torture.[19] *Esprit* had been one of the main vehicles for criticisms of the war. Neither Vidal-Naquet nor Domenach were Communists; in their different ways, they represent an ethical social-democratic tradition. The Resistance and Algeria were constant references for those I spoke to about the GIP when I was researching my *Lives of Michel Foucault*. They are part of a powerful political memory or 'imaginary', even for those who are too young to have been involved in either. Foucault himself had not been part of the 'Resistance' movement that opposed the Algerian War,[20] yet he saw those who dared to denounce abuses of the prison system and to name individual abusers as the political successors to those bold enough to have gone beyond generic denunciations of torture in Algeria and to have named specific officers.[21]

19. Pierre Vidal-Naquet, *Torture: Cancer of Democracy*, Penguin, Harmondsworth 1963. The text was written in 1962; censorship ensured that the French version did not appear until 1975. See also Vidal-Naquet, (ed), *Les Crimes de l'armée française*, Maspero, Paris 1977.

20. Hervé Hamon and Patrick Rotman, *Les Porteurs de valises: la résistance française à la guerre d'Algérie*, Seuil, Paris 1979.

21. Michel Foucault, 'Le Discours de Toul', *Dits et écrits, Volume 2.*, p237.

22. Steven Lukes, *Emile Durkheim*, Penguin, Harmondsworth, 1992, p333.

Certain of the individuals involved with the GIP were quite literally the incarnation of the political tradition of ethical resistance to the intolerable that underpins the memory of the Resistance and Algeria. Pierre Halbwachs, for instance, was the son of Maurice Halbwachs, who died in a German concentration camp in 1945. Maurice Halbwachs studied with Durkheim, for whom the Dreyfus Affair was *un moment de la conscience humaine* that introduced a 'high degree of moral seriousness into political life.'[22] And listen to voices from the other side: 'The great culprits who should be punished, are the "intellectuals", the "anarchists of the lecture platform", the "metaphysicians of sociology". A band of arrogant madmen. Men who take a criminal self-satisfaction in their intellegence, who treat ... our social institutions as absurd and our tradition as unhealthy ...' This is not the voice of the Communist trade-unionist who described the GIP as a hooligan's union, nor that of the police spokesman who, amazingly, described the prison riots of 1971–72 as the work of 'outside agitators', but that of Maurice Barrès commenting on the Dreyfusards in 1902.[23]

23. *Ibid.*, p335.

We have therefore, on the one hand, an alliance with Maoists and, on the other, a deliberate invocation of a non-Communist tradition of resistance and insubordination: *J'accuse*. In varying combinations, this provides the basis for Foucault's other political interventions of the period: involvement in anti-racist campaigns, in support for journalists beaten by the police and so on. It was not really a question of asserting or defending rights, but of revealing the oppression of power and providing a vector for resistance. I think it important to stress that no theory was being applied: for some of those involved in the GIP – Hélène Cixous, for instance – 'Why are we doing this?' was a question that came after the event. They were acting because this or that situation or event was intolerable. This is the kind of politics that is determined, not by some manifesto, but by the telephone call last night, by the news on television. Not so much what is to be done, but what are we going to do. Now.

Although effective in many senses, the GIP was in constant danger of being isolated. Even some of its Maoists allies argued against publicising prison mutinies – on the grounds that those involved were, like Alfred Dreyfus, insufficiently proletarian. Political parties shunned it, and it was impossible for it to work with trade unions: most prison officers were members of PCF-affiliated unions. At the opposite extreme, there was the danger that an intellectual such as Foucault would be trapped within a neutral space defined by the State and would become a 'Voltaire', a symbolic figure to be tolerated. As De Gaulle put it referring to one of Sartre's more provocative exercises (urging conscripts to resist their call-up for service in Algeria): '*On n'arrête pas Voltaire*' ('You don't arrest Voltaire').[24]

24. Ronald Hayman, *Writing Against: A Biography of Sartre*, Weidenfeld and Nicolson, London 1986, p352.

There were attempts to use the GIP as a model in other sectors: a Groupe d'Information Santé attempted to radicalize discussion of health issues, especially in industry. There was also an attempt to transfer the model to the psychiatric sector with a Groupe d'Information sur les Asiles. The latter existed in fairly shadowy form but without any assistance from Foucault, whose experience at one of its first public meetings convinced him that its members were quite insane and therefore impossible to work with (sic). This period of hyper-activity could not and did not last. The GIP was dissolved at the end of 1972 to make way for the Comité d'Action des Prisonniers; it was argued that it was now up to former prisoners, and not intellectuals, to organize their own campaign.

This hyper-active period, which seems to contrast with the deep pessimism of many of Foucault's works, may allow us to explore the basis for his actions. As I have said, the work of the GIP was not an application of theory, though it obviously feeds into the writing of *Surveiller et punir*: the growl of revolt and rebellion is clearly audible in the final pages. Although the GIP and its members were involved in direct confrontations – many of its actions, such as demonstrations outside prisons, were met with brutal force – the methods used were in many ways very traditional: the carefully placed press release in *Le Monde*, the collective petition, the well-publicized arrest and the decision to challenge it in court. The support base is new – the radicalized post-1968 class – but not really the methods. In other areas too, Foucault was operating in a fairly traditional mode. I am thinking of the pro-abortion literature produced by the GIS, of the 'Great Encyclopedia of Homosexualities' that was banned (thus provoking brisk under-the-counter sales of the remaining stock) ... all this using the 'cover' of the name Michel Foucault (and others), daring the State to arrest Voltaire. Asked what the results of the GIP's actions might be, Foucault replied that there were two possibilities. Either the Ministry of Justice would have to recognize that the criticisms of the system was justified, or Michel Foucault, Gilles Deleuze and Jean-Marie Domenach would go to prison.[25] They did not.

And ultimately who is that says '*J'Accuse*'? What is or was the role of the intellectual? In a discussion with a worker identified as José published in *Libération* in 1973, Foucault remarks that the role of the intellectual is to bring together ideas and goes on: 'but his knowledge is always partial compared to the knowledge of the workers. What we know about the history of French society is very partial, compared to the massive experience that the working class has.'[26] This is obviously very close to the Maoist notion of 'serving the people', but it masks some problems, as does Foucault's notion of the 'specific intellectual', who is supposed to speak on the basis of specific knowledge relating to particular areas of struggle. The elaboration of this notion is no doubt in part an attempt to shrug off the mantle of the intellectual who speaks in the name of universal values: the named targets being Voltaire and Zola, the real one probably being Sartre, so prompt to support a multiplicity of causes as to become almost a parody of the committed intellectual. It is a healthy reaction against the arrogance that all too often characterizes the stance of intellectuals who espouse political causes. The struggle against universals is also the intellectual's struggle against part of himself. Yet as one of the best historians of 'the French intellectual' makes clear, the 'specific nature' of Foucault's intellectuality is precisely its 'universality': 'He can represent these specific intellectuals ... only by betraying his own position as universal; conversely, his betrayal, which necessarily depends upon his status as a universal intellectual, is his only way of being the kind of specific intellectual he himself has mandated.'[27] Take the example of Serge Livrozet. Livrozet has served time for theft and burglary, and was deeply involved in prison 'disturbances' of 1971–72. For many years, he was an active and effective leader of the CAP and is the author of a number of books, both fictional and non-fictional, on the prison system.[28] In other words, he appears to be a highly specific intellectual with a much more massive experience of the system than Foucault. But he did not write *Surveiller et punir*. Michel Foucault did so, on the basis of his archival

25. Michel Foucault, 'Je perçois l'intolérable', *Dits et écrits, Volume 2*, p205.

26. Michel Foucault, 'L'Intellectuel sert à rassembler les idées mais son savoir est partiel par rapport au savoir ouvrier', *Dits et écrits*, Volume 2, p422.

27. Allan Stoekl, *Agonies of the Intellectual: Commitment, Subjectivity and the Performative in the 20th-Century French Tradition*, University of Nebraska Press, Lincoln 1992, p197.

work and his scholarship. That, together with the prestige attached to being a professor of the history of systems of thought, is the basis for his intellectual power. And his intellectual power is his political base. The preconditions for the effectiveness of Foucault's interventions also establish their limitations. It is not easy to give up being Voltaire.

The passing of the moment of the GIP did not put an end to Foucault's political activities, but they did tend to take a different form, and one more in keeping with the traditional definition and role of the committed intellectual. To take only the most obvious instances: an attempt to prevent executions taking place in Spain ... the defence of Klaus Croissant, who was the lawyer for Germany's Baader-Meinhof group (combined with a refusal to justify their terrorism) ... a surprisingly modest role in gay politics ... the defence of Soviet dissidents and Vietnamese boat-people ... support for Solidarity in Poland ... In very general terms, this is a trajectory taken by many on the French left. In all cases, Foucault displayed remarkable commitment and courage; he is quite possibly the only French philosopher to have had his ribs broken by the CRS riot police. And in all cases, he is exploiting a very traditional power base. If it is not easy to stop being Voltaire, it was certainly difficult to cease being Michel Foucault, Professor Militant, but also Professor of the History of Systems of Thought at the Collège de France. Whether or not all this offers a model for a general politics is, I think, open to debate, though it certainly exemplifies an honourable tradition.

To close, it is worth citing Foucault once more. The text was written in June 1981 and read out at an international conference on piracy in Geneva, the immediate referent being the plight of the boat people:

> There exists an international citizenship which has rights and duties and which commits us to rising up against all abuses of power, whoever their author and whoever their victims ... One of the duties of international citizenship is to reveal human misery to the eyes and ears of governments, as it is not true that they are not responsible for it. Human misery must never be the silent residue of politics. It founds an absolute right to rise up and to address those who hold power.[29]

So stark in their terrible beauty, the words of Tahar Djaout as he reacted to the intolerable alternative of authoritarian state repression and fundamentalism, surely embody certain of Foucault's rights and duties, as well as the attendant dangers: 'Silence is death, and if you say nothing you die, and if you speak you die, so speak and die.'[30]

28. Serge Livrozet, *De la prison à la révolte*, Mercure de France, Paris 1973; *La Rage des murs*, Mercure de France, Paris 1975; *Aujourd'hui la prison*, Hachette, Paris 1976.

29. 'Face aux gouvernements, les droits de l'homme', *Dits et Ecrits Volume 4, 1980-1988*, Gallimard, Paris 1994, pp707-8.

30. Cited, Juan Goytisolo, 'Algeria in the eye of the Storm', *New Statesman and Society*, 19 August 1994, p25.

FOUCAULT TEN YEARS AFTER

John Rajchman

In what ways and in what sense ten years after his untimely death is Foucault a 'sign of the times'? The question is complicated since so much of what he thought now comes absorbed, packaged, labelled; it is often difficult to disentangle what he said from what he 'represented' to people. Foucault was not a prophet or a social scientist. He was an historian who tried to think in terms of 'signs of the times' that are neither prophetic nor predictive, but tell of unknown problematic forces knocking at the door, unforeseen untried possibilities in our history. But what kind of activity was this; and is it one that is still possible or desirable for us to engage in today? Foucault's motto, applied to Nietzsche, was 'don't just interpret, use!' But what then might we *do* with his philosophy, to what new uses might it yet be put?

EXPERIMENTS

Foucault advanced many new conjectures and unearthed novel facts in many domains. But this historical research was inseparable from a new sense of what it is to *do* philosophy, and of its social and political roles. He had a very practical view of this activity, of which he left a number of images.

He conceived of thought as a kind of experimentation with questions that are prior to agreements and interpretations. He spoke of theory as a tool-box of concepts. But in talking about concepts as tools, he did not have in mind an 'instrumental' relation to struggles; it was rather the zones of 'problematisation' the struggles introduced with which he thought we should experiment. Indeed he tried to extract the notions of means, techniques and strategies from the neo-Kantian dichotomy between instrument and communication or between instrumental reason and practical reason, and to regard the pure noumenal (or communicational) subject as only the product of one 'technology of the self' among others. He was very interested in *how* things are done, and how people participate, body and soul, in the ways things are done, and hence in how they might come to refuse to do so. Thinking for him was a *Versuch* – an attempt or essay – in relation to such manners of being and doing; and even his last works were 'attempts on himself', as, he came to see, all of his previous ones had already been.

This experimentalist image of his thought has often been misunderstood. His history has been called functionalist, and his outlook instrumentalist. I think it is better termed a *pragmatism*. For it fits with Peirce's attempt to move away from a picture where things are governed by a unique and total set of laws, and from the Kantian notion of freedom as self-legislation, derived by analogy from such 'determinism'; it is a philosophy that lives instead in a universe of chance, pecularity and risk, in which freedom becomes associated with experimentation, or with what Kant had called 'the pragmatic point of view'.[1] And yet Foucault's 'pragmatism' differs from that of Dewey, or Dewey updated by Rorty. It is more disobedient or dissident.[2] For Foucault wanted to experiment with questions that are prior to consensus or solidarity. He thought of an intellectual as someone who works with such questions, rather than with organic ties or ready-made theories or ideologies. In relation to gay struggles, for example, what he tried to work with were the 'zones of problematisation' they created, obliging us to rethink the ways things are done and how we participate in them.

Foucault's discussion of the 'enlightenment-question' that Kant introduced into philosophy is a story of the emergence and recurrence of that question in different times and places, leading up to his own version. His own formulation was tied up with his sense of what transpired in 1968, when, in an unexpected manner, new questions arose 'about women, about relations between the sexes, about medicine, about mental illness, about the environment, about minorities, about delinquency...'[3] It is such questions that were for him 'signs of the times'; and his sense of the political role of the intellectual is linked to them. He observes that these questions emerged in different places, in relation to different kinds of economy, government, and today one might add, to different 'cultures'. They arose in Prague as well as in Paris, where they led to the specific form of resistance known as 'dissidence'. In western countries, they gave rise to 'social movements' outside party-organisations, which served to introduce new questions into law or jurisprudence. In this manner, they showed that there is more to justice than fairness in distributing goods, or equality in the consensus as to how they are distributed – more to the *question* of justice than a 'theory of justice'.

One of Foucault's 'attempts' was to try to articulate such questions in and for the gay and women's movements. What was important in these movements, he thought, was not the assertion of rights to a given identity, community or culture, but, on the contrary, the kinds of question which arise when community or identity are *not* given, when they are up for grabs, when they become a sort of open question with which one must experiment.[4] For his part, he focused on how people in those movements were moving away from the ways things had been done under the aegis of the category of Sexuality, which had come to be taken for granted, though in fact it was only an invention of the last century and its mad preoccupation with the Normal. What relations can we have with ourselves and one another once we are no longer willing to accept this dominant view of sexuality, for example, in work or law? It was questions like this Foucault thought the movements were posing to society as well as to government, and which he in turn made the object of the 'attempts' of his historical research.

Working with such questions, Foucault came to some views about free-speaking (*dire-vrai*), the role of the 'public' in democracy, and therefore of

1. On this change from law to chance, and its relation to the anti-determinism of the pragmatist philosophers see Ian Hacking, *The Taming of Chance*, Cambridge, 1990.

2. John Dewey took 'experimentalism' to differ from 'empiricism' in not being based on laws or generalisations; thus it belongs to his version of the pragmatist departure from determinism. At the same time he takes 'experimental philosophy' to belong to a consensus of experts (see his *German Philosophy and Politics*, pp200ff).

3. *The Foucault Reader*, Paul Rabinow (ed), Pantheon, New York 1984, p386. Thus there was a 'plurality of questions posed to politics rather than the reinscription of the act of questioning within the framework of a political doctrine'. The role of the intellectual would change correspondingly.

4. See *Power/ Knowledge*, Colin Gordon, p219.

democracy itself. And perhaps what is singular about democracy as a complex historical invention is its capacity to experiment with its own concept. In Foucault's case, we see an attempt to make 'questioning' or 'experimenting with questions', rather than consensus or agreement, a basic part of the practices of democracy, and the role of intellectuals in it. Thus he differed from those who would base its concept in parliamentary representation or popular participation alone. We see this in his rejection of contractualism, of Hobbesian notions of subject and sovereignty, and of the attempt to find in 'rational communication' a substitute for the contract. For he tried to work instead with the 'movement' of things that cannot yet be 'represented', and which require a kind of 'non-participation' in the ways things emerge. To formulate the questions, the 'problematisations', which such movement introduces concerning the ways things are done, and especially, the ways people govern themselves and one another – that is what Foucault took to be his way of taking up the enlightenment question and of trying it out anew.

QUESTIONS

In the ten years since Foucault's death, I think we have rather lost touch with this art of experimenting with questions, or zones of problematisation, that are 'signs of the times'. Instead we are fed empty abstractions and pious 'values' which satisfy the 'craving for generality' that Ludwig Wittgenstein so loathed. The result has been a decline in the political intelligence of philosophy, a tendency to revert to a kind of verbose journalism that discredits philosophy in the eyes of the intelligent public.

I think one source has been the bad influence of Habermas on Rorty, or on people like Peter Dews in Britain. Foucault has been buried in a liberalism, for which the decline of the left serves as a blackmail, and which is focused on consensus – on how one comes to an agreement, or the meta-norms of doing so. Another source is the culturalism that imagines that people come divided into different 'communities' each competing with the others for resources, and so are obliged to come to some agreement with one another. The philosopher is then called upon either to 'represent' some such community, or else to be the guardian of some highly general notions as to the 'values' communities must share in order to be able to agree. Thus everybody is trying to agree and agree in the right way, but who is asking any questions anymore?

There is no doubt that obtaining a consensus can be important in democratic politics. But it is less central in philosophy, where, as Wittgenstein said, 'the philosopher is a citizen of no group of ideas; that's just what makes him a philosopher'; and indeed a political *dissensus* can become the source of a philosophical questioning that transforms the 'wide reflective equilibrium' in unexpected and unpredictable ways. Thus, we need some resistance to our new consensus about consensus in order to find again the fresh air to pursue the odd multiple paths of those attempts which question things. We need again sceptical, disobedient, dissident or cynical styles in philosophy, like those of

Foucault or Wittgenstein.

It is then that we will better be able to see what Foucault was trying to do. In particular we can note how this image of philosophy as experiment or attempt was interconnected with his view of history and of event. As he sought an experimental rather than an instrumental relation to the 'movements' of the 1960s, so he took the aim of his historical work not to 'contextualize' everything others talk about, but to 'eventalise' certain things that are taken for granted in the ways people talk about themselves, and therefore the ways they deal with themselves and one another.

EVENTS

One thing that has been difficult to understand about Foucault is his departure from the notion that the historian is concerned to explain the events of history, and, on that basis, to make predictions. He started instead with the problem of 'objects of discourse' – of why some things rather than others are talked about at a given time and place, and of how the changes come about. This led him to a peculiar notion of what an event is. In the Introduction to *The Archaeology of Knowledge*, he looks at how Annales historians and Bachelardian epistemologists had discovered events in domains where there were previously thought to be none, thereby transforming our views of history and of knowledge. But such events – things like a change in demography, or in the way bone structure was looked at in different times – are occurrences of a particular kind, unlike the narrative sequences one was accustomed to. Foucault then asks: what must 'discourse' be in order for there to arise in it events of this kind?

In the course of answering this question, he thought he had come upon a strange characteristic of 'discourse' itself unlike those isolated by philologists, linguists, logicians, speech-act theorists, and today, one might add, cognitive neuroscientists: an *énoncé* he said is *'always an event that neither the language (la langue) or the meaning (la signification) can ever quite exhaust'*.[5] Conversely one might say that events are those occurences of discourse that go beyond the meanings given to them, or the languages in which they occur, opening them to strange unpredictable mutations. We can never *infer* such events from their 'contexts', since just what makes them events is the unforeseeable 'movement' that they introduce into those 'contexts'. Thus in *The Archaeology of Knowledge*, Foucault describes certain 'regularities' of discourse, that cut across different groups, that come from many different sources and places, such that they cannot be said to belong to anyone or any one 'community', regularities that govern discourse by controlling its circulation, and specifying who can engage in it. His argument is then that it is just because it is 'dispersed' and 'anonymous' in this way that discourse is open to 'events', that it always *is* an event that goes beyond meaning and language.

Discussing *Discipline and Punish* with some French historians, Foucault later returns to this idea drawing out its practical or political consequences. He talks of 'eventalising' history, by breaking with the assumptions on which 'our

5. *The Archaeology of Knowledge*, p xx.

6. *L'impossible prison*, Michelle Perrot (ed), Seuil, Paris 1980, pp43-46.

knowledge, our agreements, our practices' rest, and using this 'virtual break' to go back and examine how things ever came to 'function with self-evidence'.[6] History is thus not what vouchsafes consensus; on the contrary it is always disrupting our agreements and assumptions in unexpected ways. Events are just those occurences that show that history is *not* determined or lawlike, total or finalised. That there exist events in thought thus became Foucault's 'principle of singularity'.[7] And he thought that it is neither possible nor desirable to rid history of such events, and so of its zones of problematisation, of its 'singularities', for they are the conditions of freedom in relation to history, of the new possibilities of our 'attempts with ourselves'. We are thus rather far from a picture of history as tradition, context, cultural background; those are only negative conditions for our questions, and our attempts or experiments. That is why the art of thinking 'historically' doesn't consist in finding contexts or backgrounds for everything, but in being attentive to those events that we can't predict or explain since they require us to imagine other categories than the ones through which we make our predictions or explanations – 'to be respectful when something singular arises', as Foucault put it. Is it then possible for us to continue this art of 'eventalising' our history, this attempt to experiment with those events that question how we conceive of ourselves and our possibilities, that 'resingularize' our ways of being?

7. *The Foucault Reader*, op.cit. p335.

CULTURES AND MACHINES

Today everyone in the US knows that we are living in the age of diversity or 'difference'. That is something people now take for granted, whether they like it or not; it has come to form part of the habitual views they have of themselves, and their possibilities. But what is this 'diversity'? We might pause a moment on the now ubiquitous category of culture, and on the view that diversity consists in many different distinct cultures.[8]

8. See *The Identity in Question*, John Rajchman (ed), (forthcoming from Routledge), especially the essays of Etienne Balibar and Fredric Jameson.

Foucault was of course not himself a 'culturalist'. He tried to divide up what are called 'cultures' into other analytic categories like 'discursive practices' with regularities that cut across the views of different, often opposing groups. In this sense he was not a 'multiculturalist'. His view was not that there are many cultures, but that what is called 'culture' is itself many things, and because of this multiplicity is open to events that cause or allow it to go off in other directions. In particular he took racist discourse to be many different things, of which the modern or 'biologizing statist form'[9] was only one kind, with a specific historical genealogy.

9. *The History of Sexuality I*, p149.

In the US today much is made of 'cultural justice' in the curriculum or the gallery. But some have also seen the emergence of a new 'culturalist' kind of racism, or of racist discourse tied up with the new patterns of immigration that have made the presence of 'foreigners' such an explosive issue, and which has in turn insinuated itself into the 'counter-racism' of the marginalized groups.[10] What sorts of relations does such culturalist discourse have with the 'statist biologism' of the last century; is it a new formation with a different genealogy?

In the US at least, talk of 'culture' comes with many therapeutic categories, as when it is said that one's relation to one's 'culture' derives from good 'role models' and the endless problem of 'self-esteem'; experts in 'sensitivity to difference' now do very good business. On the other hand, some people want to give up the nineteenth century notion that 'homosexuality' is an abnormality, and view homosexuals instead as a kind of immigrant group – perfectly normal but with a 'different' kind of 'culture', to which we need to do justice. Thus homosexuality finds other non-pathological connections with biology, as when it is said that our sexual 'orientations' are doled out to us by our brains and not by our 'personalities' in the form of a 'lifestyle', which, depending on how we are oriented, we must work out 'culturally' in order to compete and survive. How cruel it now seems to have ever talked in terms of sexual 'preferences' or 'choices'!

We then find another departure from the great meta-category of the nineteenth century, the normal. It is based in brain-machines rather than language-cultures, and the way they figure in a discourse is based less on norms and deviations than on more or less testable achievement skills of just the sort which information-machines can also perform, what are called 'smart' machines, weapons or environments. One philosophical expression of the idea is the popular debate over the proposition that our minds are nothing but the information-programmes of our brains – the achievement skills that come wired in the brain, placed there by evolution. What matters in this sort of discourse is not language but 'information'. Speaking is only one 'cognitive' skill among others, and while it is cerebral, it is also compatible with other physical media that manipulate information. Today there is nobody to defend the once popular views of Whorf and Sapir that the mind depends on language; now it is the reverse, language depends on the mind – the mind that is the cognitive programme of the brain. And, as everyone can see, linguistics is waning and neuroscience is flourishing.

It is thus quite striking to look back to *The Order of Things*, when linguistics was thought so crucial that people wondered if we were not living in a 'prison-house of language'. In 1966 when Foucault wrote his unexpectedly popular 'archaeology' of the 'human sciences', Freud and Saussure were heroes of the day. But now it would seem that our 'brains' have triumphed over our more or less Freudian 'personalities', and our cognitive skills over our language practices. It is becoming difficult to even understand what Wittgenstein was up to in his rambling, deliberately non-explanatory 'investigations' of our language uses, and the forms of life in which they are embedded. In the place of Wittgenstein and Freud, we have Alan Turing (who showed what can be computed in a finite number of steps using any procedure whatsoever) and John Von Neumann (whose team built the first electronic digital computer). For the questions of who we are and of the computational machines we use have become inseparable from one another, and apparently more important to us than the language we speak or the Oedipal complexes from which we suffer.

One rather less Darwinian thing we might do with our brains today is to

10. Etienne Balibar examines one version of the thesis of a new 'culturalist' racism in *Nation, Race, Class*. On the importance and specificity of white 'biologising statist racism' in the United States, and its relation to the Emancipation, see Barbara Fields 'Racism in America', *New Left Review* May 1990.

analyse this formation, investigating its 'genealogies', and exposing its 'zones of problemisation'. To do this, we need to dispense with the notion that machines are simple protheses of natural abilities; we must instead analyse how 'discourse' intervenes in the ways we think about our relations with machines, and in how it thus helps determine the ways we conceive of our selves and our world. We may then note that our enthusiasm over the achievements of brain-machines comes at a time marked by competing world-market economies in which information-technology plays a central role – much as our earlier enthusiasm for 'behaviour' came at time of Taylorism in industry. We may then further notice that these same global information-economies are not unrelated to the new geographies which have helped to make the question of 'other cultures' and of 'others' in our culture, such an explosive one.

Foucault devised a use of history to save us from the progressivism and the historicism invented by the sociology of the last century. But who will continue it today along new lines to save us from our current obsessions with cultures and new technologies, our 'techno-culturalism'? Who will formulate questions in the face of these new assurances, these new 'signs of the times'?

At the end of *The Archaeology of Knowledge*, Foucault carried on a curious conversation with himself that ends with a much-quoted remark: 'do not ask who I am and do not ask me to remain the same'. Perhaps it is worth recalling this remark when we today ask what we might yet do with his philosophy. For it suggests another way of 'remembering' what he did than internalising, commemorating or contextualising his image – a free experimental *use* of his thought, which might offer it a chance of other new futures.

FORGET FOUCAULT?

Kate Soper

Of Foucault it has been remarked, that he combines 'a kind of secret apocalyptic ultra-leftism with a dry-eyed, pragmatic political reformism' in a manner that protects him from appearing either reactionary, on the one hand, or naively romantic, on the other.[1]

If I open on this note, it is not so much to endorse the point – though I think there is a good measure of truth in it – but because of the bearing it has on the risk run by those directing a critical gaze upon Foucault's work of appearing either gullible or boringly virtuous. Foucault is one of those thinkers who has the art of making those who problematise his thought all too conscious of the pieties they may be bringing to it. Yet if we are not to lapse into hagiography the irreverence of some of these pieties may be needed, and it is those associated with feminist critique I propose to moralise about here.

Let me note, however, as a preliminary that there should be no critique of Foucault that does not proceed from an acknowledgement of the gestalt shift he has achieved in our intellectual perception of modernity. He possessed that rare capacity as a thinker to open us to an optic, or should I say panoptic, whose perspective now seems so familiar that it is difficult to see how we previously failed to bring it to bear. But having acknowledged his unique contribution in this respect, I think one must also pay tribute to the more collectively achieved impact of feminism upon the contemporary *Zeitgeist*, since this has also been responsible for a repatterning of our thought of a kind which now seems indispensable. This makes it only appropriate, when approaching the work of the single author to assume that there ought to be some reciprocity of influence and to judge it in the light of that assumption.

In a formal sense it is indisputable that Foucault engages quite closely with feminist issues and perhaps he nowhere more obviously does so than as a theorist – along with feminists themselves – of the conceptions of power implicit in the practices of 'new social movement' politics. In reconceptualising power as a dispersed and ramifying network unamenable to monocausal explanation, Foucault's work was bound to figure as a potential resource of those in the feminist movement frustrated by the orthodox socialist insistence that the oppressions of gender were ultimately rooted in relations of class exploitation and must await their correction upon a revolution at that level.

Foucault, moreover, is an anti-naturalist thinker, a genealogist of sexuality and a theorist of bio-politics, and in all these respects his concerns chime with those of feminism. The instituting moment of feminism is, after all, its challenge to the supposed naturality of male supremacy; much of its critique is targeted on the role played by the discourses of sexuality and their norms of

1. Terry Eagleton, *Ideology of the Aesthetic*, Blackwell, Oxford 1991, p386.

conduct in protracting female oppression; and the body has inevitably been a focus of feminist attention – both as the instrument and manipulated effect of patriarchal power, and because of its symbolic association with the feminine. If the first task of any feminist philosophy is to seek to expose the role played by the traditional hierarchy of mind over body in the devaluation of the female, then Foucault's rethinking of the status of reason in western thought, together with his return to the body – his readiness to further the programme invited by Nietzsche's reappraisal of the history of western philosophy as being a history of renunciation of the body – might be said in a formal or symbolic sense to figure as a supportive move. In the recent period, moreover, we have seen all these potential Foucaldian resources for feminism concretely realised in the large and varied array of feminist studies drawing on his argument, some of them working sufficiently under his sign to allow us to speak of a distinctively Foucaldian feminist formation.

Yet we would also have to say, I think, that at this more concrete level the lines of influence have not been as reciprocal as they might have been, and that there are dimensions of Foucault's argument which severely complicate any feminist rapprochement with it. On the one hand, I suggest, there are the difficulties which its more nihilist or anti-progressivist aspects present for any attempt to yoke it to an emancipatory programme of the kind which feminism represents, and which must necessarily put a question mark over the political coherence of a Foucaldian feminism. On the other hand, there are the strains and stresses placed on any such synthesis as a consequence of the androcentric perspective which infects Foucault's work at a number of different levels.

2. Judith Butler, *Bodies that Matter: On the Discursive Limits of 'Sex'*, Routledge, London 1993, see esp. pp32-5, Cf. *Gender Trouble*, Routledge, London 1990.

3. Susan Bordo, 'Anorexia Nervosa: Psychopathology and the Crystallisation of Culture' in I. Diamond and L. Quinby (eds), *Feminism and Foucault: Reflections on Resistance*, Northeastern University Press, Boston 1988, p90.

4. M.E. Bailey, 'Foucauldian Feminism: Contesting Bodies, Sexuality and Culture' in Caroline Ramazanoglu (ed), *Up Against Foucault*, Routledge, London 1993, pp106-7.

Feminists have drawn on Foucault's accounts of the objectivising and dividing practices of medical and psychiatric knowledge in historical studies of the 'masculine' gaze of science, and its appropriative constructions of 'femininity' and the female body. They have appreciated the attention he has paid to the collusive role of the 'self-policing' subject in the maintenance of the regimes of bio-power, and have offered a number of studies in the light of it of the voluntary modes of bodily discipline and surveillance through which stereotypical conceptions of gender appearance and behaviour are sustained; and they have seized on his conventionalism in support of an extreme constructivist position which would proclaim not simply that there is no 'natural' gender, but that sex difference is no more than a normative, hence arbitrary, support of the binary gender system and the body itself to be viewed as the construct of culture. Judith Butler interprets Foucault as arguing, in *Discipline and Punish*, that the materiality of the body is effectively brought into being by power relations, rather than merely invested by them, and has drawn on this argument to reinforce her claim that the body, and specifically the sexed body, is materialised through power.[2] 'There is no "natural" body,' Susan Bordo has argued in her influential Foucauldian treatment of anorexia nervosa.[3] One must question, writes another of his followers, 'whether it is possible to use biological "sex" without being trapped in some notion of "nature" ',[4] and these claims are echoed in the rhetoric of other feminist theorists working under his influence.

But while one can readily agree that we do not have experience of the body other than as symbolically and culturally formed, and agree, too, that the Foucaldian feminists have been instructive about the forms of that mediation, there is surely something inherently self-defeating about adopting so radically anti-essentialist a position. At the very least we need to ask what is meant by these rhetorical denunciations of the 'natural' body and whether they are not the vehicle of some considerable confusion or vacillation in the discourse theory conception of the self. For if they are meant to deny the existence of the body as a natural organism subject to processes of a continuous and constant kind – to processes which allow us through dieting, or surgery, for example, to alter bodily shape and appearance in accordance with norms of beauty and gender identity – then it is difficult to see the force of any political critique of the disciplinary effects of power. In other words, we must surely acknowledge the existence of the body in this extra-discursively constituted sense if we are to render coherent the idea of its being constructed by discursive formations and social and sexual norms and powers – and in fact some such notion of the body would seem to be recognised by Foucault himself insofar as he speaks of this as a site of forces, energies, sensations and pleasures upon which cultural practices are inscribed. It may be true that Foucault's own position on the body hovers between a realism which acknowledges the formative influence of an extra-discursive nature upon which culture goes to work, and an idealist dismissal of any determinations at this level; but this is a vacillation which any feminist appropriation of his argument needs to address rather than reproduce. They need to make clear, that is, whether they are really denying that there is any dialectic or interaction between nature and culture; for if they are, they have removed the grounds for challenging any construction of gender as merely 'normative' or conventional. If they are inviting us to view the nature-culture distinction as entirely politically constructed and reinforced, and thus denying that there are any instincts, needs, pleasures or sensations which are not simply the effects of culture but impose their own conditions upon its 'constructions', then it is difficult to see what sense we can make of the notion of feminist reclamations of the body or selfhood from the distorting and repressive representations to which they have been culturally subjected. A Foucaldian feminist critique of the 'disciplined' body would seem caught in an internal contradiction between its reliance on a naturalist ('back to the non-normalized body!') ethic and its denial of the 'natural' body.

In fact, it would be only consistent with Foucault's own emphasis on the non-Hegelian dialectic governing the successive investments of discursive power in the body for this feminist discourse to treat itself as an instance of that 'control by stimulation' ('be your authentic self, eschew gender stereotypes!') with which power is said to respond to 'control by repression' ('look and behave like a woman!')[5] – which in effect would be to adopt a position which acknowledged from the outset the provisional and equivocal nature of its forms of resistance to patriarchal power.

In this connection one might add that Foucault's emphasis on the discursive

5. Michel Foucault, *Power/Knowledge*, Pantheon, New York, pp56-7.

construction of sexuality – his tendency to present the discourses of sexuality as moral panics analysable without reference to any precipitating extra-discursive features of existence – has very problematic implications for the status and significance of the discourse of feminism itself, insofar as it suggests that there was no obvious rationale for its emergence: no condition of oppression prior to the discourse which might explain and justify its production. Foucault is very good at revealing the discursive 'machinery for speechifying, analyzing and investigating' which goes into the making of the 'events' in the history of sexuality.[6] But insofar as he would have us view the significance of these 'events' as exhaustively constituted in these discursive explosions, his analysis in itself offers us no reason either to applaud or condemn any particular discourse. His account of eventuation within the history of sexuality is just as consistent with dismissing the 'speechifying, analyzing and investigating' which goes into the making of feminism as a discursive fuss about nothing, as it is with treating it as the emergence of a highly significant discourse of resistance. I am not suggesting that Foucault himself ever dismissed it as being of no account. My point, rather, is that his analytics of power can be put to the service of multiple political ends, and carries no obvious prescriptive force either in favour or against the project of female emancipation. Those insisting on the purely 'normative' status of the body and sexuality might consider what comfort they methodologically offer to anyone inclined to dismiss feminism on the grounds that there was never any justification in 'reality' for any of its garrulous protestation.

6. This is the phrase used by Foucault to describe the response to the 'child abuse' incident at Lapcourt 1867, which he relates in the course of his discussion of the 'repressive hypothesis' (see *The History of Sexuality Vol.1: An Introduction*, Penguin, Harmondsworth 1978, p148, pp31-2). For a much fuller discussion of the implications of Foucault's conception of the significance of this response for the emergence of feminist discourse, see my 'Productive Contradictions' in Caroline Ramazanoglu, *op.cit.* pp42-8.

To make these points is not to deny the importance of Foucault's emphasis on the discursive formation of sexuality and corporeal existence, but only to suggest that this ceases to be productive if it is pressed at the expense of proper recognition of the impossibility of dispensing with any reference to a pre-discursive reality. This may be a complex and difficult dialectic to register, but that is no reason to deny the underlying reference to the humanist subject which sustains the critical force of the constructivist argument.

At the same time, it may be said that there is something problematic in focusing on the body and sexuality as the key sites of inscription of gender power, and that in the end a Foucaldian feminism can offer us only a phenomenology of the effects of this power at the level of subjective experience: it may be illustrative of the ways in which women are co-opted by the discursive regimes of power and actively involved in enacting their disciplines upon the self, while leaving us very unclear about the ultimate source or reason for the existence of these forms of coercion in the first place; in short while failing to offer any clear picture of the relations between the bio-political and the socio-economic dimensions of female subordination. With this failure we may link the Foucaldian feminist inclination to adopt an individualist and elitist approach to liberation, where the stress falls on the politics of 'gender choice', 'self-making' and the aesthetic of the self at the cost of any sustained engagement with those structural features which deny most women the option of that kind of gender self-styling in the first place.

I recognise, of course, that I am here only echoing the complaints of other critics that Foucault fails to offer any anchorage for his conception of power, which he presents as both all encompassing yet curiously bereft of any rationale, direction or purpose of a kind which might explain and justify his pejorative descriptions of its effects; and that this is reflected in the tension between his activist critique of power and his pessimist emphasis on the inevitability of domination. On the one hand, we have the normative-critical Foucault who aspires to an anarchic freedom from governance, on the other, the theoretical-analytical Foucault who reminds us always that there can be no exit from it, and while the anarcho-existentialist dimension of his argument might seem to coincide with the emancipatory and utopian logic of feminism; the analytical dimension invites us to accept the futility of its aspirations.

Now two points might be made here: firstly that Foucault himself acknowledges and addresses these tensions insofar as he allows the relations between power and resistance to be in some sense mutually implicative; and secondly, that it is precisely the value of Foucault's work that it asks us to confront this ambiguous and unresolved dialectic between the libertarian and oppressive aspects of any emancipatory project. But the problem, I think, is whether we *can* confront this dialectic in the terms which Foucault invites us to – since the libertarian impulse is sustained only through an autotelic or existentialist conception of the subject which is belied by the radical anti-humanism of the account which is given of social process.

Let me only add here that how we respond to these tensions will fundamentally depend on the view we take of his overall project: is Foucault still working ultimately within a conventional framework of thinking about human progress and amelioration, but revealing how much less unitary, more troubled and equivocal any advance towards these goals is likely to prove than we had previously supposed? Or is he questioning the very conceptions of freedom and happiness which motivate the emancipatory programme – exposing the 'humanism' of those aspirations as dependent upon norms of thinking about pain and pleasure, self and other, even life and death, which are in some sense confining and inherently revisable? If we take the former view, then we might claim, as various critics, including some of his feminist critics, have, that the value of his work lies precisely in the attention it draws to the vexed and ambiguous quality of human progress. But to view him in this light is necessarily to invite comparison with other thinkers who, from Gramsci through to Sartre, Thompson, Williams and the Frankfurt School have rejected simplistic accounts of the dialectic of progress, and thus to pose a question about Foucault's originality – about how far he definitively advances our thinking about the relations of agency and process. If, on the other hand, we view Foucault as attempting to think beyond the ethics of progress itself – the position represented, for example, in his denunciations of the quest for happiness and his advocacy of an ethic of cruelty[7] – then he emerges as an altogether different kind of thinker, but also as a far more dangerous and problematic ally of leftwing causes than is often supposed.

7. This is the Foucault who argues that 'humanism, at least on the level of politics, might be defined as every attitude that considers the aim of politics to be the production of happiness. Now, I do not think that the notion of happiness is truly thinkable. Happiness does not exist – and the happiness of men exists still less' (interview with *La Fiera Litteraria*, 39, 28 September, 1967, cit. James Miller, *The Passion of Michel Foucault*, Harper Collins, London 1993, p173).

But whatever line one takes on these issues; and whatever one thinks about the adequacy of Foucault's portrayal of the relations between agency and process, the picture seems skewed from any feminist point of view by Foucault's tendency to presuppose the masculinity of the subject – by what I earlier termed his androcentric perspective. One of the more frequently voiced complaints in this connection is that Foucault presents power as an essentially neutral rather than gendered force, and nowhere shows much interest in relating his account of the power/knowledge axis to the feminist critique of phallocracy. Thus, Foucault has rather little to say on the links between patriarchal power and the dominion of science and instrumental reason which many feminists have wanted to emphasise; and he tends not only to ignore those highly specific forms in which power is exercized in any sexually hierarchical society, but also to overlook the differential impact of the general 'disciplining' modalities to which he does attend on the lives of men and women. In this sense, his critique of the liberal and Marxist accounts of power may be said to retain that same universalising and gender-blind conception of the human subject which for feminists has been a central failing of those theories.

Nor, indeed, is one encouraged to think otherwise by some of Foucault's more casual asides – such as his comment in the course of an interview on his *History of Sexuality* that 'in our society the main field of morality, the part of ourselves which is most relevant to morality, is our feeling (you can have a girl in the street or anywhere, if you have very good feelings towards your wife)'[8] – where the offence lies not so much in the crassness of the sexual ethics imputed to the moral majority, but in the donnish assumption that wherever we are talking about 'our' morality we are talking about 'his'.

But what is perhaps most discouraging is the fact that when Foucault does finally 'return to the subject' in the later volumes of his *History of Sexuality*, it is to offer us a treatment of Greek, Greco-Roman and early Christian ethics which is systematically abstracted not only from the female but from any relational conception of the person. My charge here is not that Foucault is blind to the sexism and elitism, and hence limited social reference, of the ideas about sexuality and the 'aesthetics' of the self with which he is concerned in these studies, since he himself draws attention to these and is critical of them. It relates rather to the behaviourism of his approach: his tendency to treat the history of ethics as a registering of the differential modes in which the subject experiences his desires, sets rules of conduct for the self, and conceives his purposes in life. For this, rather oddly in some ways for the genealogist, inevitably abstracts from the history of those more subterranean changes responsible for these stylistic shifts – changes which Foucault himself describes as taking place in 'marriage, society and so on' – but which matter to Foucault only in their impact on this masculine ethics of self-comportment. The account is confined to a documentation of effects at the level of the man's personal conception of his duties and appropriate modes of self-care, which means that we are offered a history whose primary object of study is the male perception

8. Michel Foucault, 'On the Genealogy of Ethics: An Overview of Work in Progress', in Paul Rabinow (ed), *The Foucault Reader*, Penguin, Harmondsworth 1984, p352.

of ethical developments – developments for example in the emotional relations between men and women – which remain almost entirely unexamined. Foucault acknowledges changes in the marital relationship, and in the degrees of reciprocity, intimacy and dependency between the sexes, but only in the form of noting their influence at the level of male behaviour and self-regulation – the more 'austere' requirements they impose, for example, on the husband's fidelity. This is itself an austere and clinical ethics, conducted as far as possible without reference to affectivity, which cannot bring itself to speak of 'love' but only of the development of a 'stylistics of the individual bond',[9] and which would have us rethink sentiment as essentially a matter of technique.[10] It is not only that Foucault offers a story of sexual ethics which is more or less devoid of any reference to the feelings of women and sees no reason to speculate on the influence these may have had on the changes he charts; but that emotional responses drop out of the picture altogether. The ethical is here defined in terms of personal style, self-mastery and authorial creation.

Moreover, as Jean Grimshaw has pointed out, insofar as Foucault suggests we might have something to learn from this classical ethics or aesthetics of the self, he seems curiously ready to present modes of self-regulation which his earlier work had problematised as being the internalised policing effects of 'panoptical' power, as witness to our autonomous powers of artistry upon the self.[11] It is as if when he goes in quest of the lost subject, Foucault himself complies with that injunction to 'forget Foucault'.

This brings me to a last point. For I think it would be regrettable if we were to follow suit in this 'forgetting' by approaching the later work as if it offered the resolution to the earlier tensions of his thought. It may be tempting to view it as the site of his most considered instruction on our times, but it can also be regarded as their philosophic reflection. For could we not also say that these current discourses which would have us focus on the self as the site of political governance and aesthetic order are the stimulated product of the new norms of social anarchy and economic deregulation; and that we need to respond with something more transgressive than Stoicism, personalism or egoism if we are seriously to resist these newly circulating forms of power/knowledge? At any rate I think this is not the time to forget what Foucault in his work as a whole forcibly reminds us of: that there is a danger in every form of resistance, and a self-deception lurking within every assertion of the truth of the self. Those reminders, I have suggested, are problematically contradictory, but they are also, as Habermas put it, 'productively' contradictory, and the better way to remember Foucault, so it seems to me, is as their producer.

9. Cf. Michel Foucault, *The History of Sexuality Vol. III: The Care of the Self*, Penguin, Harmondsworth 1988, p148.

10. Cf. Terry Eagleton, *Ideology of the Aesthetic, op.cit.*, p395.

11. Jean Grimshaw, 'Practices of Freedom' in Ramazanoglu, *op.cit.*, pp61-7.

RECONFIGURING THE SUBJECT AS A PROCESS OF SELF:
FOLLOWING FOUCAULT'S NIETZSCHEAN TRAJECTORY TO BUTLER, LACLAU/MOUFFE, AND BEYOND

Alan D. Schrift

The breakdown of philosophical subjectivity and its dispersion in a language that dispossesses it while multiplying it within the space created by its absence is probably one of the fundamental structures of contemporary thought. Again this is not the end of philosophy, but rather, the end of the philosopher as the sovereign and primary form of philosophical language.

Michel Foucault, 'A Preface to Transgression'

If Foucault is a great philosopher, this is because he used history for the sake of something beyond it: as Nietzsche said: acting against time, and thus on time, for the sake of a time one hopes will come.

Gilles Deleuze, 'What is a *dispositif?*'

There is perhaps no name more closely associated with the recent critique of the subject than that of Michel Foucault. In his earliest works, he was aligned, perhaps precipitously, with those structuralist theorists who proclaimed the 'death of the subject.' And even when reading his later works – *Discipline and Punish* and the first volume of *The History of Sexuality* – there is a tendency to be seduced by the force of Foucault's narratives into dispensing altogether with any notion of agency as one comes to view human beings merely as nodes through which institutionalized power relations are transmitted. But when using a Foucaldian framework to analyse concrete political situations, care is required if one is to avoid overreacting to and overcompensating for Foucault's diagnosis of the juridico-discursive focus on power as a sovereign possession. For by moving too quickly toward dispensing with everything that pertains to the individual human subject, one fails to attend to the final development in Foucault's thought, where he suggests several ways in which we might reconfigure our understanding of the relationships between power and subjects. In what follows, I will examine Foucault's return to the question of the subject. I will argue, moreover, that he does not complete the project he set for himself of recuperating a positive notion of the subject. And I will conclude by suggesting that we can see how his project might be developed in the work of two increasingly influential voices on the contemporary scene.

Before turning to these tasks, however, it will be helpful first to review quickly Foucault's earliest, and perhaps better known position on the subject.

Foucault concluded his 1960 *thèse complémentaire* on Kant's anthropology with the following remark: 'The trajectory of the question *"Was ist der Mensch?"* in the field of philosophy culminates in the challenging and disarming response: *der Übermensch.*'[1] In *Les mots et les choses* [*The Order of Things*], Foucault pursued this trajectory as he linked the death of God with the end of man, an end punctuated by the laughter of the *Übermensch* that closes *The Order of Things*.[2] Examining Foucault's initial response to the question of the subject will allow us to see how his reconfiguration of the subject within an analytic of power exceeds this initial Nietzschean trajectory; at the same time, we will have prepared the way for showing how the final turn in his thinking remains within what is perhaps best viewed as a different but yet still Nietzschean trajectory.

In *The Order of Things*, Foucault raises the question of the subject in terms of what he refers to as the Nietzschean question, 'who is speaking?' (*OT*, p305). This question appears in the context of Foucault's crediting Nietzsche for opening up language as 'an enigmatic multiplicity that must be mastered'. Foucault writes:

> For Nietzsche, it was not a matter of knowing what good and evil were in themselves, but of who was being designated, or rather *who was speaking* when one said *Agathos* to designate oneself or *Deilos* to designate others. For it is there, in the *holder* of the discourse and, more profoundly still, in the *possessor* of the word, that language is gathered together in its entirety (*OT*, p305).

In drawing the genealogical distinction between the noble's 'good', operating as it does within the couplet 'good-bad,' and the slave's 'good,' which functions within the very different couplet 'good-evil,' Foucault remarks that Nietzsche was perhaps the first to notice that words had 'ceased to intersect with representations and to provide a spontaneous grid for the knowledge of things' (*OT*, p304). This recognition that the faith in the representational accuracy of language had been eclipsed led Nietzsche to shift the focus of his critical attention away from *what* was said, turning this attention instead toward a genealogical critique of *who* said what was said, and on what the *reasons* were which had given rise to what was said.

Foucault had already made this point in the underappreciated essay 'Nietzsche, Freud, Marx', his contribution to the 1964 Colloquium on Nietzsche held at Royaumont. In his concluding remarks on the obligation of interpretation to interpret itself to infinity, he noted that 'interpretation will be henceforth always interpretation by the "who?": one does not interpret what there is in the signified, but one interprets, fundamentally, *who* has posed the interpretation. The origin [*principe*] of interpretation is nothing other than the interpreter, and this is perhaps the sense that Nietzsche gave to the word "psychology".'[3] In other words, to ask '*who* interprets?' or '*who* speaks?' does not produce an answer taking the form of a subject's name, as Foucault indicates when he inscribes the question 'who?' within 'psychology', which we must recall

1. Michel Foucault, 'Introduction à l'*Anthropologie* de Kant,' photocopy of *thèse complémentaire*, Université de Paris, Faculté des Lettres, 1960, Centre Michel Foucault p128.

2. See Michel Foucault, *The Order of Things*, Random House, New York, 1973, p385. Hereafter cited parenthetically as *OT*.

3. Michel Foucault, 'Nietzsche, Freud, Marx', trans. Alan D. Schrift in *Transforming the Hermeneutic Context: From Nietzsche to Nancy*, Gayle L. Ormiston and Alan D. Schrift (eds), State University of New York Press, Albany 1990, p66.

was defined by Nietzsche in *Beyond Good and Evil* (§23) as 'morphology and *the doctrine of the development of the will to power*'. For Nietzsche it is not a subject but will to power which speaks and interprets, and rather than eliciting the name of a subject, for Nietzsche the question 'who?' calls for a genealogical inquiry into the type of will to power (life-affirming or life-negating) that manifests itself in speech or interpretation.

In his earliest works, Foucault gave two distinct responses to the Nietzschean question 'who speaks?' In *The Order of Things*, the response to Nietzsche's question was drawn from Mallarmé:

> what is speaking is, in its solitude, in its fragile vibration, in its nothingness, the word itself – not the meaning of the word, but its enigmatic and precarious being ... Mallarmé was constantly effacing himself from his own language, to the point of not wishing to figure in it except as an executant in a pure ceremony of the Book in which the discourse would compose itself (*OT*, pp305-306).

And when he returned to the question in 'What Is an Author?', Foucault now responded with Beckett's indifference: 'What does it matter who is speaking?'[4] Within these two answers, we locate Foucault's earliest position on the question of the subject – the subject appears as an ideological product, a functional principle of discourse rather than its privileged origin. The subject thus stands as an obstacle, an impediment that distracts one from the discourse.

Nietzsche too, by the way, had noted that a good book 'is harmed by its living author if he is celebrated and much is known about him'.[5] 'As soon as the author announces himself on the title-page, the reader dilutes the [book's] quintessence again with the personality, indeed with what is most personal, and thus thwarts the object of the book.'[6] While Foucault, in his early work, had already remarked that the author was 'the principle of thrift in the proliferation of meaning' ('WA'. p118), he echoed Nietzsche's sentiments in one of his final interviews (April 25, 1984), noting in response to a question concerning the diverse, often polemical readings of his works, that the knowledge of an author frequently stands as a barrier to the reading of their books. He went on to speculate about the sort of reading his works might provoke if they did not appear as the latest work by the famous philosopher at the Collège de France, Michel Foucault: 'it would be better if my books were read for themselves, with whatever faults and qualities they may have.'[7]

Of course, this was not to say that the subject was to be entirely abandoned, however, as Foucault's transformation of the author in 'What Is an Author?' from a 'natural subject' to a constructed 'author-function' makes clear. Instead, it was for Foucault a matter of depriving the subject of its role as originator and analyzing the subject as a variable and complex function of discourse and power. To do so meant giving up the questions: 'How can a free subject penetrate the substance of things and give it meaning? How can it activate the rules of a language from within and thus give rise to the designs which are

4. Michel Foucault, 'What Is an Author?' trans. Josué V. Harari in *The Foucault Reader*, Paul Rabinow (ed), Pantheon Books, New York 1984, p101; cf. p 120. Hereafter cited parenthetically as 'WA'.

5. Friedrich Nietzsche, *Human, All-Too-Human*, Volume Two: *Assorted Opinions and Maxims*, trans. R.J. Hollingdale, Cambridge University Press, Cambridge 1986, Section 153.

6. *Ibid.*, Section 156.

7. Michel Foucault, 'An Aesthetics of Existence,' trans. Alan Sheridan in Lawrence D. Kritzman (ed), *Michel Foucault: Politics, Philosophy, Culture, Interviews and other Writings 1977-1984*, Routledge, New York, 1988, p53.

properly its own?', replacing them, instead, with the following questions: 'How, under what conditions and in what forms can something like a subject appear in the order of discourse? What place can it occupy in each type of discourse, what functions can it assume, and by obeying what rules?' ('WA', p118).

This was not to be Foucault's final position on this matter, however. Nor was it to mark his final appeal to Nietzsche in grounding this issue. In displacing the question of the 'free subject's' endowing things with meaning, it is clear that Foucault was distancing himself from the phenomenological-existential and, in particular, the Sartrean subject.[8] By returning to a Nietzschean account of the subject, Foucault replaces the Sartrean project of an authentic self with the Nietzschean project of creatively constructing oneself.[9] In so doing, he both displaces the valorized free existential subject and retrieves a more ambivalent subject whose constitution takes place within the constraints of institutional forces that exceed its grasp and even at times its recognition.

This is the subject whose genealogy Nietzsche traced in *On the Genealogy of Morals* (I, §13). In an analysis that exhibits the traits Foucault noted in his early essay 'Nietzsche, Genealogy, History', Nietzsche focuses not on the valorization of origins (*Ursprung*) but on a critical analysis of the conditions of emergence (*Entstehung*) and descent (*Herkunft*). Pursuing the task of 'history as a curative science',[10] Nietzsche locates the subject not as a metaphysical given but as a historical construct; a construct, moreover, whose conditions of emergence are far from innocent. The 'subject' is not only a superfluous postulation of a ' "being" behind doing', a 'doer' fictionally added to the deed; in addition, the belief in this postulate is exploited by 'vengefulness and hatred' to convince the strong that they are *free* to be weak, resulting in the consequence that they are to be held accountable for their failure to be weak. Prompted by the instinct for self-preservation and self-affirmation which sanctifies self-serving lies, Nietzsche writes:

> the subject (or, to use a more popular expression, the *soul*) has perhaps been believed in hitherto more firmly than anything else on earth because it makes possible to the majority of mortals, the weak and oppressed of every kind, the sublime self-deception that interprets weakness as freedom, and their being thus-and-thus as a *merit*.[11]

In this remark, we see that it is not simply the subject's ignoble origin that comes under genealogical scrutiny. In addition, Nietzsche directs his genealogical gaze to the life-negating uses to which the idea of the subject has been put in a further effort to challenge the subject's privileged status. Foucault comments that a genealogy of *Herkunft* 'is not the erecting of foundations: on the contrary, it disturbs what was previously considered immobile; it fragments what was thought unified; it shows the heterogeneity of what was imagined consistent with itself.'[12] This is precisely what Nietzsche does as his genealogy of the subject demonstrates the oppressive use made of the principle of subjectivity as a principle of domination in the service of a

8. See Michel Foucault, 'The Ethic of Care for the Self as a Practice of Freedom', trans. J.D. Gauthier, S.J., *Philosophy and Social Criticism*, special issue 'The Final Foucault', vol.12, no.2-3, Summer 1987 p121. Hereafter cited as 'ECS'.

9. See Michel Foucault, 'On the Genealogy of Ethics: An Overview of Work in Progress,' *The Foucault Reader*, p351.

10. Nietzsche, *Human, All-Too-Human, Volume Two: The Wanderer and His Shadow*, Section 188.

11. Friedrich Nietzsche, *On the Genealogy of Morals*, trans. Walter Kaufmann, Random House, New York 1967, Essay I, Section 13.

12. Michel Foucault, 'Nietzsche, Genealogy, History', trans. Donald F. Bouchard and Sherry Simon in *The Foucault Reader*, p82.

13. Friedrich Nietzsche, *Twilight of the Idols*, trans. R.J. Hollingdale, Penguin Books, Harmondsworth, 1968, 'The Four Great Errors' Section 7.

14. Michel Foucault, 'Why Study Power: The Question of the Subject' in Hubert L. Dreyfus and Paul Rabinow, *Michel Foucault: Beyond Structuralism and Hermeneutics*, Unviersity of Chicago Press, Chicago, 1982, p212.

15. Michel Foucault, 'How is Power Exercised?', trans. Leslie Sawyer in Dreyfus and Rabinow, *op.cit.*, p216. Emphasis added.

16. See Michel Foucault, *Discipline and Punish: The Birth of the Prison*, trans. Alan Sheridan, Random House, New York 1978, p29.

'hangman's metaphysics'.[13] And it is this account of the subject that leads Foucault to link the modern form of power with subjects and subjection: 'It is a form of power that makes individuals subjects. There are two meanings of the word *subject*: subject to someone else by control and dependence, and tied to his own identity by a conscience or self-knowledge. Both meanings suggest a form of power which subjugates and makes subject to.'[14]

This linkage sets the stage for the final turn in Foucault's thinking, namely, his return to ethics as the inquiry into the self's relationship to itself. 'For let us not deceive ourselves,' he writes, 'if we speak of the structures or the mechanisms of power, it is only insofar as we suppose that certain *persons* exercise power over others.'[15] From the publication of the first volume of *The History of Sexuality* in 1976 until the end of his life, Foucault focused his attention upon the ways in which 'techniques of power' are exercised on and resisted by persons as he inquired into the link between contemporary power relations and the construction of the modern subject. While this turn toward the subject is associated with the *History of Sexuality*, and especially the second and third volumes, we can already see indications of Foucault moving in this direction in *Discipline and Punish*. In this, his most Nietzschean text, Foucault notes the link between power and the subject while arguing that the history of the micro-physics of punitive power would be an element in the genealogy of the modern 'soul'.[16] Foucault addresses this soul most explicitly in the discussion of the construction of the delinquent as a responsible subject, arguing that there is a subtle transformation in the exercise of power when punishment no longer is directed at the delinquent's *actions*, but at his very person, his 'being' as (a) delinquent. Yet throughout the discussion in *Discipline and Punish*, Foucault's attention remained focused not on the subject constructed but on the power-knowledge relations that made possible this construction. Because power and knowledge directly implicate one another, power-knowledge relations are to be analyzed

17. *Ibid.*, pp27–28.

> not on the basis of a subject of knowledge who is or is not free in relation to the power system, but, on the contrary, the subject who knows, the objects to be known and the modalities of knowledge must be regarded as so many effects of these fundamental implications of power-knowledge and their historical transformations.[17]

18. See Dreyfus and Rabinow, *op.cit.*, pp143-183.

Insofar as Foucault's discussion links the genealogy of the modern, disciplined subject with the genealogy of the carceral system, one might accept Dreyfus and Rabinow's suggestion that the move from *Discipline and Punish* to the first volume of the *History of Sexuality* is a move from a genealogy of the modern individual as *object* to a genealogy of the modern individual as *subject*.[18] But to accept their characterization is not to accept that Foucault has returned to a philosophy of the subject. Rather, as Deleuze correctly notes, 'Foucault does not use the word subject as person or form of identity, but the words "subjectivation" as process and "Self" as relation (relation to itself [relation à soi]).'[19]

When Foucault attends to the problematics of the subject, he is not rediscovering a principle of subjectivity which marks a rupture with his earlier reflections on the 'end of man'. Instead, he remains insistent in his belief

19. Gilles Deleuze, *Pourparlers*, Éditions de Minuit, Paris 1990, p127.

> that there is no sovereign, founding subject, a universal form of subject to be found everywhere. I am very sceptical of this view of the subject and very hostile to it. I believe, on the contrary, that the subject is constituted through practices of subjection, or, in a more autonomous way, through practices of liberation, of liberty, as in Antiquity, on the basis, of course, of a number of rules, styles, inventions to be found in the cultural environment.[20]

20. Foucault, 'An Aesthetics of Existence', pp50-51.

It is by retrieving the subject in the form of questions concerning the process of subjectivation that Foucault adds the third axis of his genealogical project. In the Introduction to the second volume of the *History of Sexuality*, Foucault speaks of his 'new' project as operating now along three axes: an archaeological axis that will analyze forms of knowledge, a genealogical axis that will focus on systems of normativity, and an ethical axis that will examine forms of subjectivation. When he thus projects these three axes onto the experience of 'sexuality', for example, it produces an analysis constituted in terms of '(1) the formation of sciences (*savoirs*) that refer to [sexuality], (2) the systems of power that regulate its practice, (3) the forms within which individuals are able, are obliged, to recognize themselves as subjects of this sexuality.'[21]

Elsewhere, he makes this same point as he discusses his project in terms of the four types of technologies at work in the human sciences: technologies of production, of signification, of domination, and of the self. While acknowledging that the technologies of domination were his fundamental focus prior to his analysis of sexuality, he does not introduce the technologies of the self in order to exclude the other technologies. Instead, a 'genealogy of the subject' will have to 'take into account the interaction' of all these technologies and, in particular, the interaction of the technologies of domination and of the self 'where the technologies of domination of individuals over one another have recourse to processes by which the individual acts upon himself. And conversely, he has to take into account the points where the techniques of the self are integrated into structures of coercion or domination.'[22] The contact point between these technologies is what Foucault calls 'government' and his emphasis on the care and cultivation of the self is a tacit admission that his earlier genealogies of the subject had placed too great an emphasis on domination by others as the sole form of governing.[23]

21. Michel Foucault, *The Use of Pleasure*, trans. Robert Hurley, Random House, New York, 1985, p4.

22. Michel Foucault, 'About the Beginning of the Hermeneutics of the Self: Two Lectures at Dartmouth', *Political Theory*, May 1993, p203.

23. *Ibid.*, p204.

This being the case does not, however, warrant the conclusion that Foucault's thinking is marked by discontinuity. Nor should we view each subsequent analytic dimension explored by Foucault as a dialectical supercession of his previous analyses. This is to say, it is important to note that the introduction of the ethical axis or the technique of the self does not take the place of an earlier analytic level. Rather, the care of the self is *added* on as a *supplément* in the Derridean sense of that term, deepening the analysis by adding a dimension – the self's relations to itself (in terms including but not limited to relations of power and knowledge) – that had been insufficiently attended to in the earlier analyses. In other words, the move from one axis or technique to the next has a *cumulative* effect, as they work together toward establishing the analytic grids that make possible genealogical critique.

Drawing attention to the ethical dimension that he calls the care of the self was momentous for Foucault's project, as he could no longer finish the initial plan for the *History of Sexuality*, opting instead to begin again with a history of the construction of the self as a sexual subject from Greek antiquity through early Christianity. Like Nietzsche before him, in one final tragic analogue between their respective careers, Foucault's final project was never completed, cut short not by madness but by Foucault's untimely death. And what Foucault left to us were several thoughts on the self or subject in terms of an aesthetics of existence which resist easy integration into the power analytics of his earlier works, a self that at times appears autonomous and able to extricate itself from the normalizing practices that work to construct disciplined and docile subjects.

Foucault left to us the task of thinking a notion of a subject that is both autonomous and disciplined, both actively self-forming and passively self-constructed, as he left us to think about the emergence of a modern state whose exercising of pastoral power both totalizes and individualizes.[24] I would like to conclude by examining several directions for future thinking about the subject and power that follow the general itinerary indicated by Foucault. For while Foucault's own suggestions as to how we should set up our initial analytic grid seem to me to be a fruitful place to begin our local projects of resistance, they are only a beginning. Deleuze, in his remarks at the 1988 Colloquium on Foucault organized by the newly formed Centre Michel Foucault in Paris, noted that Foucault's analyses of apparatuses (*dispositifs*) are comprised of two lines: 'the lines of the recent past and those of the near future: that which belongs to the archive and that which belongs to the present; that which belongs to history and that which belongs to the process of becoming; *that which belongs to the analytic and that which belongs to the diagnostic*.'[25] Deleuze goes on to claim that in his books, Foucault addresses his attention primarily to the first of these lines as he specifies the archives he analyses with great precision. But for whatever reason (Deleuze suggests 'confidence in his readers'[26]), Foucault does not formulate the other line, the one which addresses the present. And here we find our task: we need to develop Foucault's suggestions and explore the interlaced technologies of subjects and power, recognizing, as Foucault reminds us, 'not that everything is bad, but that everything is dangerous'[27] as we work to tilt the balance of power towards the forces of production rather than those of repression.

Relations of power are inevitable, but we need not accept as inevitable the particular forms in which those relations have emerged. There is, in other

24. See Foucault, 'Why Study Power: The Question of the Subject', pp213-216.

25. Gilles Deleuze, 'What is a *dispositif*?', trans. Timothy J. Armstrong in *Michel Foucault, Philosopher*, Routledge, New York 1992, p164.

26. *Ibid.*, p165.

27. Foucault, 'On the Genealogy of Ethics', p343.

words, an emancipatory dimension of Foucault's analytic insofar as the understanding of how power relations function in the local arenas in which we act can aid us in diagnosing and resisting the more repressive exercises of these relations. The omnipresence of relations of power, therefore, does not lead to a resigned acceptance of the fact of domination, as a nihilistic reading of Foucault often concludes. To the contrary, in one of his final interviews, Foucault remarks that when he rejects as utopian Habermas's idea that 'there could be a state of communication which would be such that the games of truth could circulate freely, without obstacles, without constraint and without coercion', his alternative is not a dystopian vision of inevitable oppression:

> relations of power are not something bad in themselves, from which one must free one's self. I don't believe there can be a society without relations of power, if you understand them as means by which individuals try to conduct, to determine the behavior of others. The problem is not of trying to dissolve them in the utopia of a perfectly transparent communication, but to give one's self the rules of law, the techniques of management, and also the ethics, the *ethos*, the practice of self, which would allow these games of power to be played with a minimum of domination' ('ECS', p129).

In this remark, Foucault makes clear that it is a mistake to regard his power-analytic as leading to a quietist acceptance of the inevitability of oppression. Far from producing a neo-conservative acceptance of the status quo, we see the potential usefulness of the Foucaldian analytic for a strategy of liberation in two recent works which have justifiably attracted a great deal of attention. Judith Butler's *Gender Trouble: Feminism and the Subversion of Identity*, offers one of the most sophisticated, thought-provoking and potentially valuable accounts of the 'subject' to have appeared following the structuralist 'death' and post-structuralist 'decentring' of 'subjectivity'. And while her account of the subject as a performative is far more than an 'application' of the Foucaldian analytic, it remains nevertheless a profoundly Foucaldian enterprise. In fact, she acknowledges at the start of her text the political import of Foucault's emphasis on the productive power of law for a subversion of identity.[28] She also acknowledges, albeit less frequently, the importance of Nietzsche for a critical project that seeks to rethink gender (and) identity insofar as Nietzsche's challenge to a metaphysics of substance opens the possibility for a performative account of identity. Drawing upon Foucault and Nietzsche both, Butler challenges the language of interiority or internalization, offering in their stead the language of performativity in which 'the gendered body [as] performative suggests that it has no ontological status apart from the various acts which constitute its reality' (*GT*, p136).

While critical of some of Foucault's positions on sexual difference and the body, the political dimension of Butler's conclusions that identity is a practice and gender a performative remains profoundly Foucaldian as it articulates the alternative gender possibilities produced within the repressive and

28. Judith Butler, *Gender Trouble: Feminism and the Subversion of Identity*, Routledge, New York 1990, p2. Hereafter cited parenthetically as *GT*.

constraining practices of our compulsory heterosexist culture. Arguing that 'all signification takes place within the orbit of the compulsion to repeat,' Butler locates ' "agency" ... within the possibility of a variation on that repetition' (*GT*, p145). In order to be intelligible, cultural forces compel certain repetitions, but at the same time, these forces *produce* possibilities of alternative performances. The task for a subversion of identity, therefore, 'is not whether to repeat, but how to repeat or, indeed, to repeat and, through a radical proliferation of gender, *to displace* the very gender norms that enable the repetition itself' (*GT*, p148). By keeping in view the Nietzschean-Foucaldian dimension of her thinking on the question of the subject, one can thus avoid the precipitous misreading of 'performative' as 'performance,' an all-too-common misreading that produces the view that Butler in *Gender Trouble* articulates a voluntaristic notion of a subject who wilfully decides one day to adopt one gender position, with the implication that it could just as wilfully adopt a different gender position the next day.

This point bears repeating, for the Nietzschean dimension of Butler's position here is rarely noted, and it is precisely in terms of this dimension that she avoids the voluntaristic position she is mistakenly accused of holding. In *Gender Trouble*, when arguing for a nonsubstantive notion of gender, Butler quotes (p25) Nietzsche's remark, cited above, from *On the Genealogy of Morals* (I, §13): 'there is no "being" behind doing, effecting, becoming; "the doer" is merely a fiction added to the deed – the deed is everything.' While this remark is not cited in her latest work, I would argue that insofar as Nietzsche's 'metaphysics of the subject' offers neither a traditional metaphysical account (since there is no 'being') nor a position that allows for a substantive subject, it continues to serve as a resource for Butler's performative account of gender identity. We see this Nietzschean dimension clearly, I think, in the following remark from the concluding pages of *Bodies That Matter*:

> One might be tempted to say that identity categories are insufficient because every subject position is the site of converging relations of power that are not univocal. But such a formulation underestimates the radical challenge to the subject that such converging relations imply. For there is no self-identical subject who houses or bears these relations, no site at which such relations converge. This converging and interarticulation *is* the contemporary fate of the subject. In other words, the subject as a self-identical identity is no more.[29]

29. Judith Butler, *Bodies That Matter: On the Discursive Limits of 'Sex'*, Routledge, New York, 1993, pp229-230.

While it would take us too far afield to demonstrate in detail the Nietzschean character of Butler's position, I would like here to simply note that one could easily show that Nietzsche's account of a non-substantive self as a convergence of relations of will to power confronts a traditional metaphysics of the subject with the same radical challenge.

Before leaving Butler, it is worth noting that in her recent work, she develops her position through the Derridean notion of iterability; what she earlier discussed in terms of performative repetition, she now recasts as a subversive re-iteration which re-embodies subjectivating norms while at the same time redirecting the normativity of those norms. Even in this Derridean incarnation, however, her position remains, it seems to me, more congenial to a Foucaldian than a Derridean politics, a fact Butler herself seems to acknowledge as she re-iterates her Foucaldian sympathies in a recent discussion of Drucilla Cornell and Ernesto Laclau. She concludes her discussion of 'Poststructuralism and Postmarxism' by posing a Foucaldian alternative to 'the Derridean approach pursued, for the most part, by both Laclau and Cornell'.[30] And for those who are willing to see, one must also note that this Foucaldian alternative is itself couched in the language of Nietzschean genealogy, language which calls for a shift in the focus of critical inquiry. Leaving the question 'what kinds of political practices are opened up now that Emancipation and the Good have proven their unrealizability', Butler suggests we move 'to the more Nietzschean query: "how is it that the unrealizability of the Good and/or Emancipation has produced a paralyzed or limited sense of political efficacy, and how, more generally, might the fabrication of more local ideals enhance the sense of politically practicable possibilities?" '[31] In so doing, she displays her continued affinity for operating out of a Foucaldian grid, framed within the ambivalence of production and repression, an affinity she recalls in the concluding chapter of *Bodies That Matter*:

30. Judith Butler, 'Poststructuralism and Postmarxism,' *Diacritics* Winter 1993: pp3-11.

31. *Ibid.*, pp10-11.

> the question for thinking discourse and power in terms of the future has several paths to follow: how to think power as resignification together with power as the convergence or interarticulation of relations of regulation, domination, constitution? How to know what might qualify as an affirmative resignification – with all the weight and difficulty of that labor – and how to run the risk of reinstalling the abject at the site of its opposition? But how, also, to rethink the terms that establish and sustain bodies that matter?[32]

32. Butler, *Bodies That Matter*, p240.

While Butler in *Gender Trouble* develops a Foucaldian position that primarily addresses politics at the level of individual agents enacting their genders while subjected to various cultural constraints,[33] Ernesto Laclau and Chantal Mouffe in *Hegemony and Socialist Strategy* have argued for a radical democratic politics that is dependent in part upon reconfiguring subjectivity in terms of a multiplicity of subject positions. Laclau and Mouffe make a strong case for the necessity of reconfiguring subjectivity; yet they fail to see how Foucault's turn toward the subject in his last works can serve as a resource that will help facilitate a radical and plural democratic leftist politics. That is to say, Foucault showed how the discursive practices of modernity served to construct the modern docile and disciplined subject. In so doing, he demonstrated the historically contingent character of the subject's construction while showing as well the possibility of alternative constructions. This is the sense in which Foucault's works can be regarded as a 'critical ontology of the

33. While I cannot discuss this here, it should be noted that in *Bodies That Matter*, Butler herself addresses some of the implications of her theory of performativity for democratic and coalition politics.

present': insofar as the subject position delivered to us by modernity is not an ontological necessity, other subject positions will be historically possible in terms of the contingencies of the present moment.

Acknowledging the multiple positions which 'subjects' occupy helps to explain both the current resistance to enduring political allegiances and the attractiveness of a model of coalition politics that will allow temporary alliances among various groups in response to contingent developments which call for these groups to mobilize collectively. Foucault's genealogy of the subject provides a theoretical articulation of this account of a multiple subject positioning insofar as it frames the subject not as a substance but as a form, a form, moreover, that is not always identical to itself. Quoting Foucault:

> You do not have towards yourself the same kind of relationships when you constitute yourself as a political subject who goes and votes or speaks up in a meeting, and when you try to fulfill your desires in a sexual relationship. There are no doubt some relationships and some interferences between these different kinds of subject but we are not in the presence of the same kind of subject. In each case, we play, we establish with one's self some different relationship. And it is precisely the historical constitution of these different forms of subject relating to games of truth that interest me ('ECS', p121).

Like Foucault, Laclau and Mouffe advocate a dispersion of a fixed and unified subjectivity, but they also claim that the moment of dispersion cannot exist in theoretical isolation. Instead, a second analytic moment is required, as 'it is necessary to show the relations of overdetermination and totalization that are established among these [moments of dispersion].'[34] It is precisely this second moment which Foucault's last works sought to articulate as he began his 'hermeneutic of the self.' For Laclau and Mouffe, the hegemonic relations established among the discursively dispersed subject positions are what provide the conditions for their notion of a 'radical and plural democracy' (HSS, pp166-167). While they do acknowledge Foucault's importance in terms of his concept of 'discursive formation' (HSS, pp105-107), they fail to acknowledge the profoundly Foucaldian character of their own identity politics. That is to say, democracy requires a fluid, transformative and historically contingent notion of identity:

34. Ernesto Laclau and Chantal Mouffe, *Hegemony and Socialist Strategy: Towards a Radical Democratic Politics*, Verso, London 1985, p117. Hereafter cited parenthetically as *HSS*.

> For there to be a 'democratic equivalence, something else is necessary: the construction of a new 'common sense' which changes the identity of the different groups in such a way that the demands of each group are articulated equivalentially with those of the others – in Marx's words, 'that the free development of each should be the condition for the free development of all.' That is, equivalence is always hegemonic insofar as it does not simply establish an 'alliance' between given interests, but modifies the very identity of the forces engaging in that alliance (HSS, pp183-184).

For this reason, there can be no foundational, unified discourse. Instead, 'discursive *discontinuity* becomes [for Laclau and Mouffe] primary and constitutive' (*HSS*, p191) inasmuch as the 'identity' of the democratic subject is always *in process*, producing itself in response to and being produced by the contingent antagonisms and alliances that constitute the social.

As we have already seen, this view of self as a process of socially constrained subjectivation is one way that the Nietzschean trajectory followed by Foucault might develop. With Laclau and Mouffe's call for discursive discontinuity and the multiplicity of subject positions, as with Butler's bringing to the fore of the productive resistances called forth by the repressive constraints of contemporary gender/identity politics, we can thus hear clearly the echoes of Foucault. Which is only to say, in conclusion, that although Foucault himself may have been 'erased, like a face drawn in sand at the edge of the sea' (*OT*, p387), the discursivity founded by his analytics of power has established possibilities whose end we are far from reaching.

THE POLITICS OF FOUCAULT'S POETICS, OR, BETTER YET: THE ETHICAL DEMAND OF ECSTATIC FETISH

Sue Golding

Seduction is *not* a passive form of incitement.

M. Foucault, *The History of Sexuality*, pp95-6

Toward the end of his third volume on *The History of Sexuality*, where he expressly links the 'art of living' with the care of oneself, Foucault invites us to think through the moral and ethical implications of such a connection. It is a troubled connection, indeed, a dangerous path, and we are forewarned of the trouble ahead. '...[A]s the arts of living and the care of the self are refined,' says Foucault, 'some precepts emerge that seem to be rather similar to those that will be formulated in the later moral systems.'

> But one should not be misled by the analogy. Those moral systems will define other modalities of the relation to self: a characterization of the ethical substance based on finitude, the Fall, and evil; a mode of subjection in the form of obedience to a general law that is at the same time the will for a personal god; [...] a mode of ethical fulfilment that tends toward self-renunciation.[1]

1. Michel Foucault, *The Care of the Self: The History of Sexuality, Volume Three*, trans. by Robert Hurley, Vintage Books, New York 1988, p239-40.

At the risk of too rapidly citing these dangers or stating their implications in too coarse a way, here is what lies at the heart of the matter: on the face of it, comparisons of apples and oranges do not – because they cannot – yield the same fruit. But why not? What is it that makes this comparison untenable?

It is not enough to point out the obvious, says Foucault; to wit, that there is no over-arching archimedean point, no 'outside' that makes the comparison empty. It is not enough to say, in other words, that these 'latter [Judeo-Christian] systems', these 'modalities' may sound like, might even appear similar to, earlier modalities touching upon body and soul and the relations therein or thereabouts ascribed – but now, given a 'different' socialized horizontal history we might call 'the Law' (be it God, evil, goodness, renunciation, selfhoodedness, enlightenment, or whatever), that these comparisons must come to an abrupt halt.

No.

These comparisons cannot be made, as such, because something else or something other is at play in Foucault's work, an elsewhere or otherness that he often locates or points to by way of insisting on its 'techné' or 'use'. This something else or something other is not simply a 'trace' of the not-nameable representation standing before, beyond or beside the Law. Nor for that matter is it 'difference', if, by difference, we mean to say 'not-the-same'. Apologies to Baudrillardians (and Lacanians) on this score, but this something else or something other is not a trace at all; nor is it an abyss, a lack, a shame, a disappointment, an embarrassment or void. For we are not dealing with representation, as in metaphor, in any of its symbolic order or symbolic disarray. Nor are we dealing with a representational identity around which an x or y can be reproduced or deduced or induced, leaving, in its wake, a remainder as such.

Something much more excessive, ungrateful and greasy, something much more melancholic, subtle, and in some ways, more dangerous, is nagging at the skin of our so-called, and seemingly not comparable, fruit. Rather than the bold and sweeping morass of contradiction (subjectivity v. objectivity, and the transcendentalism that this implies, be damned!), this 'other' is a something else whose creation or invention, whose actuality, is contoured by the very nature of its having been, actively, perhaps event relentlessly, *seduced*, and, in its seduction, *used*. Over and over again. The endlessly compelling attraction, the concrete infinity, of techné. Let there be no mistake about it, we are speaking here of the 'being used', in all the profane and corrupting senses of the verb: to use. The physicality of this terrain (if, indeed, there is one), its 'materiality' is, in this case, the 'inbetween' of the stitched together discourse, the fleeting inbetween of an infinitely beating strange-time called 'the present' (despite the fact this entire remark rests upon pre-the Christian martyrdom).

In philosophic prose, it is a mimetic re-presenting of the present around which a something else or something other is at stake – indeed, is created by virtue of its being there (as in: 'over there'). Its 'use' does not – because it cannot – presuppose binaric polarities, contradictions, oft times posed as self in relation to the not-of-self, the so-called 'outside' of self. Rather, this 'other' self/identity self becomes, simply, the expression of multi-particled selfnesses, made meaningful, made into a something else, due precisely to its having been attracted/seduced, and therewith, sutured, into a oneness (of sorts) though not because of beauty (per se) or desire (per se) or even magnetism (per se) but precisely because it *can* be – and must be – used. Techné. Cohesive relations, processes, wanderings, traditions, fleeting nodal points, dreams, even the sweat (or especially the sweat) of the body loins, are all grist for the mill, all 'props' for establishing the multiple-as-a-singular-unity, establishing, in other words, the that which lies around us, the elsewhere or otherness, *as us*; but an 'us' as 'selfhood' quite distinct from the wholly-formed Truth of the Cartesian ego-I, self-reflexive sense of self. Foucault writes:

> In Epictetus there are 2 exercises: sophistic and ethical. The first borrowed from school: question-and-answer games. [...] The second are ambulatory exercises. In the morning you go for a walk and test your reactions to that walk. The purpose of both exercises is control of representations, not the deciphering of truth. They are reminders about conforming to the rules in

the face of adversity. [...] For Epictetus, the control of representations means not deciphering but recalling principles of acting and thus seeing, through self-examination, if they govern your life. It is a kind of permanent self-examination. [But in the end] *You have to be your own censor.*[2]

2. Michel Foucault, *Technologies of the Self*, p38 my emphasis.

This 'kind of permanent self-examination' and 'self-censorship' is what Foucault shorthands as 'technologies of the self'; i.e., the 'logic of the techné,' the logic of seductions (plural) of the self to the self which creates the necessary distance or path for a *conversio ad se*, a conversion of the selves into self as self.[3] In Foucault's preliminary and ancient cartography of the self-to-self relation, this distance gained or accumulated amounts to (or circumscribes) nothing other than the social and constitutive self in its fluid fullness: where the other and its something come together to form a self-contained self; a self wherein finally 'one "belongs to [one]self",' says Foucault, where 'one is "his own master"; one is answerable only to oneself, one is *sui juris*; one exercises over oneself an *authority* that nothing limits or threatens; one holds the *potestas sui*.'[4] Indeed, this technology of the self is but a discursive human geography, a kind of permeable civil fortress of self-hoodedness that not only emphasizes *control* in the sense of establishing a peculiar masterliness of sorts that *can* defy limits or threats without, at the same time incubating in its wake the hegelian predisposition of the master/slave dialectic, but also emits of itself a specific *ethics* of control; the (ethical) control of the perpetual self-creating/self-inventing self.

3. Michel Foucault, *The Care of the Self: The History of Sexuality, Volume Three*, trans. by Robert Hurley, Vintage Books, New York 1988.

4. *Ibid*, p65, my emphasis.

We have before us, then, a *beheaded* rational mastery of self, a multiple personality *order*, controlling and controlled at the fleeting threshold of pleasured self-uses – a metamorphosis, a *conversio ad se*, a kind of flight of fancy Foucault names 'ecstatic' – sans a teleological 'desire' or transcendental 'ought to be'. And yet, its transitory momentum belies an oddly stable, though distinctly imaginative, mapping of the self, which, in this read, becomes both infinitely changeable and rigidly concrete, circumscribing an impossible arena of both self-possession (as in a juridical model of possession) and nomadic self-rule. For this is an ecstatic flight, a pleasured flight, which requires an entire preparation linking body with soul without referent to the old Western Masters of Desire or Lack or Lacuna, Castration or Law.[5] One's time becomes 'full time'; indeed, becomes focused, disciplined, dirty/gritty time, with the Oracle at Delphi – 'know thyself' – looming large. Indeed, in this multiple/singularity of self, unified (if this be the word) by the peculiar seductive acts of the 'being used', there is no space at all for the what will later be described (by Nietzsche) as 'toxic time', that is, the wasted, mediocre time, of the modern self-reflexive Being-as-Time.

5. Michel Foucault, 'Preface', in Gilles Deleuze and Félix Guattari's, *Anti-Oedipus: Capitalism and Schizophrenia*, trans. by Robert Hurley, Mark Seem, and Helen R. Lane, Athlone Press, London 1984.

The desiring subject is dead.

And in its wake, the pleasure/using 'other' of self-related-self emerges, one whose very relations invent/create an ethics of pleasure, in the fullest sense of the word pleasure: raw, pain, transformation, melancholia, mediation, *et al.*

Foucault thus writes:

> It was against the background of this cultivation of the self, of its themes and practices, that reflection on the ethics of pleasure developed in the first centuries of our era. As for the definition of the work that must be carried out on oneself, it too undergoes, in the cultivation of the self, a certain modification: through the exercises of abstinence and control that constitute the required *askesis*, the place allotted to self-knowledge becomes more important. The tasks of testing oneself, examining oneself, monitoring oneself in a series of clearly defined exercises, makes the question of truth – the truth concerning what one is, what one does, and what one is capable of doing – *central to the formation of the ethical subject*. Lastly, the end result of this elaboration is still and always, defined by the rule of the individual over himself. But this rule broadens into an experience in which the relation to self takes the form not only of a domination but also of an enjoyment without desire and without disturbance.[6]

6. *Care of The Self*, pp67-68.

This 'rule', which broadens into an experience, forms an 'other/self' (as the multiple-other-selves-of-the-that-which-lies-around-us), whose cohesiveness, in its metamorphosing seduction, presences an ethics of self-creation. An ethics, as Foucault says, 'which would not be their expression in the sphere of ideology; rather, [...] would constitute an original response to them, in the form of a new stylistics of existence.'[7]

7. *Care of the Self*, p71.

So it is that this fleeting relation of pleasure and its uses, this metamorphosis of self to self, is captured by Foucault with the term 'stylistics of existence', an ecstatic flight of invention – and seduction – which is no less than the ethico-political art of carving out one's life, should one be willing to journey onto the surface of the risk. Its metonymic rhythms, its poetic beat-beatings – repetitive, lyrical and distinct – have no *apriori* moral agency, though its cohesive synthetics emit nothing short of an ethical demand, an ethical demand made 'real' by virtue of its having been coagulated into a multiple something, whatever this something – or for that matter, its multiplicity – may be. A politics of 'making real' at the level of otherness, if ever there was one.

All this may be very interesting for our ancient boys and girls adhering (or otherwise) to the dream spaces of an Artemedorius or a Lucilius or a Seneca; but what does it have to do with us? The 'us' of a Judeo-Christian-Hindu-Moslem worldly world? The 'us' of a capitalist and racist and sexist and homophobic and heterophobic and genderphobic world? For, as Nietzsche intones in his *The Gay Science*, and quite rightly, too:

> #152. *The greatest change*. – The illumination and the colour of all things have changed. We no longer understand altogether how the ancients experienced what was most familiar and frequent – for example, the day and waking. [...] Every wrong had a different effect on men's feelings; for one feared divine retribution and not merely a civil punishment and

dishonour. What was joy in ages when one believed in devils and tempters? What was passion when one saw demons lying in wait nearby? What was philosophy when doubt was experienced as a sin of the most dangerous kind – as sacrilege against eternal love, as mistrust of all that was good, high, pure, and merciful? ...[8]

8. F. Nietzsche, *The Gay Science; with a prelude in rhymes and an appendix of songs*, trans. Walter Kaufmann, Vintage, New York 1974, pp196-7.

9. '#158. *An Inconvenient Trait*,' in *ibid*, p198.

#158. *An inconvenient trait.* – To find everything profound – that is an inconvenient trait. It makes one strain one's eyes all the time, and in the end one finds more than one might have wished.[9]

Let us be very careful then. Let us just steal a small leaf from Foucault's 'book', nodding to the infinite quagmire of change and attempting, in so doing, to avoid the profound. One step backward, then, two steps forward: let us link Foucault's notion of the ecstatic flight with the contemporary armour of fetishistic play to create what could be called, conceptually or otherwise, in our postmodern times 'ecstatic fetish'.

As we have seen, with this (seductive) sense of the ecstatic, a peculiar relation is formed based on the *impossibility* of a homogeneous other (or the impossibility of a homogeneous and singular negation). This has meant, also, the impossibility of a self-reflexive self-certainty, disrupting the convenience of 'either/or' polarities. For the 'other' negation that an ecstatic self-to-self relation exposes, is a 'quasi-negation' – a something else or something other – that plays with, circumscribes, and dances across the surface of each and every limit. We find then, a kind of otherness/identity, say for example, in being gay, that has little to do with being 'anti-' its supposed polar opposite (in this case, the so-called straight). Instead it elucidates a concept of self-as-other; i.e., a self no longer singular, unified and whole, but eliding multiplicities, self-as-selves-in-the-plural, based on the erupting surface between and amongst 'internal' and 'external' polarities.

To be clear, and to have some fun (why not?), let's now move to this queer little thing called 'fetish', and the ethics of multiplicity it may (or may not) speak to – resurrected and now laid out across a no longer inconspicuous use of the phrase 'the relation of the self-to-the-self'. For it can certainly be said that fetish/ fetishism, whilst including, initiating or cementing codes of behaviour and dress sense, does so in a way that neither privileges nor ignores this multiple sense of 'otherness' and with it, this multiple sense of negation. By saying this, I want to disengage the concept/reality of fetish from being thought of as the signifier of Death or of a failed Mourning or of a melancholia-writ-large-and-inescapable – as one finds in contemporary remarks on the subject. I do not wish to say that fetish is not at all connected to death or to grieving or to a weirdly cathected fashion sense – it is just to say it is not connected like *that*.

If one follows Foucault's general indications on the impossibility of homogeneous otherness and the like, we get a different read of the terrain: Fetish becomes a far more delicate, though like silk, rather durable, construction. Fetish is a far more raw (and explicit) bleed, though like blood, changes colour the moment its presence surfaces to air. Fetish is a far more complicated joke –

some say a 'compacted story', rather funny and alive, though precisely at the same time: desperate and clinging, painful, stillborn, and even gut-wrenching. Laugh till she cried. (And then cried for more? Yes, why not.)

For fetish, if it is anything at all, in at least being all these contradictory and mutating 'doubles', is precisely and only – the multiple singularity of: itself.

It has a kind of ripped and shared hermaphrodism (and I do not use this word lightly) which is not a metaphor 'standing in' for anything else. Neither is it an 'empty' container waiting to be filled by some endless struggle between this thing called (for example) heterosexual desire, this thing called homosexual desire, and this thing called bisexual desire mutated into one pair of rubber stockings, one certain 1960s hairstyle, one opened and smiling or tortured mouth. The fetishization of these creatures: male, female, transgendered beings, homo/lesbo/bisexed erotics, hairstyles and hose, cannot quite be reduced, however microscopic, to some kind of impenetrable mass, stuck together and 'understood' only in terms of their opposition, contradiction or annihilation.

For its synthesis, its moment, is not a 'something' that *can* be flung open and brought to public light, public scrutiny or even public 'liberation'. *It is far too vampiric for all that.* The meaning of the fetish both disappears *and* hovers at the very instant it seems most near to hand. There are neither truths nor secrets in a fetish; no discovery, no bringing to the surface its authentic point of departure; indeed, no 'authentic' point at all. This does not mean that it is meaningless; or that it describes no limit or can be seen as an infinite regression.

Rather, it is to say that fetish *is* the surface *and* the departure *and* the arrival; its whole point is that it is a squished up line at the very moment of its being a dot (and/or vice versa: an elongated dot cleverly doubled as a line); a process and an end-point, endlessly processional and finitely punctuated; the very threshold of a compacted story, a narrative that could never become 'meta'; never become 'spectacle' as such. Its presence, like all presents, is simply impossible (here, there, and gone at the exact same instant); a virtual 'to be', a mastery of the coming of masterliness. A radical mastery: a perfectly imperfect autonomous mastering, as de Sade would say, one without submission to a fixed and totalized Other. It is rather a *virtual* mastery, a radically impure mastery – desanitized over and again on the slippery slope between and amongst the relation of self to self.

An obsessional, virtual, metonymic surface. An unreal (but, on the other hand, no less real), floating, magical, pleasure seeking surface, shot through with the absurdity of the cruel, of the dead, of the wronged. Isn't life funny!? Isn't life grand?! A cyberspace of present tense passion, of perpetual movement going nowhere in particular, but going there with speed and agility and attentiveness to detail, nonetheless. *Not* a *becoming* of self, *not* an immanence as such; not a telos unfolding either to the known or unknown truth of self-awareness self; not a Law because, by definition, Law (and therewith, truth). Simply a coming without the 'be'; a coming without the identity relation of the 'to be'; a coming to the surface of the present tense presence; superficiality in all its glory, re-making and repres*ent*-ing the radical plurality of self without recourse to the always already signed, sealed, and delivered self-given self.

For fetish is simply, if it is anything at all, history with a Pop, the singularly self-identified-self, blown to smithereens, undone and redone in the *sacred* image of mutated selves, cyberselves; variegated selves of the re-thought-out selves, bent and re-designed in the instant coming of its come, by self-immolation self-exhibitionism, self-abuse, all fitted neatly into corset and collage. A mutilated series of selves (any selves), a repetitive series of selves, well-rehearsed some might say (ritualised, most would say) through the mirrored multiplicity of space in between (and amongst) the snap-crackle-pop of leather, latex and lace self forming selves.

Translation: No more 'inside' vs. the 'outside' of individual body selves. No more self-reflexive self. Fetish as a kind of marker, horizon, even a kind of 'skin' for the politically, emotionally liberal-impaired self; nothing more and nothing other than the infinite metamorphoses of the self into selves (or vice versa); the transformative mutations whose strange but somehow familiar (though utterly unchartered) pluralities meld into oddly coherent, albeit risky, wholes – holographic wholes – making metamorphosis, and with it, fetish, the very stuff of identity itself. An identity which is no more or less than the excessive ecstatic flights of seduction in all its varying 'other' possibilities.

In the fetish world: a world that is not community, not geared toward a 'something', but rather, a heterogeneous sense of coded regulations and conduct, we have then a peculiar imaginary of variegated impossibilities, an oozing excessivity of the self no longer outside the very processes of change, and therewith, no longer reduced to a singular, opaque and unblemished purity. Could it not be said, without overstating the case that we have, then, the possibility of routing out, if nothing else, a damning fascist logic of the fixed whole-truth-and-nothing-but-the-truth-so-help-us-god morality. And in its place? A fleeting, mutinous, fetishized, politics of existence, a peculiar form of ethics: social and multiple, mannered and refined, continuous in its rupturing of the aesthetic form (though aesthetic nonetheless); a kind of political-[aesthetic]-ethics whose integrity is graspable only at its multiple 'other' crossing.

Ecstatic fetish: it is not a profound Thought worthy of grounding any vision. It is a small, fleeting, ethical demand at the point of inventing the double joke of a multiple self: at the neither/nor threshold of a fetish gone to light; at the neither/nor pleasure of the come. Foucault, in his 'Introduction to the Non-Fascist Life', put it like this, and it is on this note I would like to conclude:

> ... Withdraw allegiance from the old categories of the Negative ..., which Western thought has so long held sacred as a form of power and an access to reality. Prefer what is positive and multiple: difference over uniformity,

flows over unities, mobile arrangements over systems. Believe that what is productive is not sedentary but nomadic ... [For what is needed is not to remain bound by subjectivity and its inherent self-reflexivity – any more than what was 'needed' was to be bound by an 'objective' truth] What is needed is to 'de-individualize' by means of multiplication and displacement, [ie, by means of] diverse combinations. The group must not be the organic bond uniting hierarchized individuals, but a constant generator of de-individualization ...[10]

10. M. Foucault, 'Preface,' in *Anti-Oedipus: Capitalism and Schizophrenia*, pxiii.

One small aspect of contemporary resistance to domination and insistence on change, not to mention fun: is this not precisely what a constant tango with ecstatic fetish, in our day and age, invents?

FROM SOCRATES TO FOUCAULT:
THE PROBLEM OF THE PHILOSOPHICAL LIFE

James Miller

Thanks to my New School colleagues Richard Bernstein, Richard Gaskins, and Richard Shusterman for their comments on earlier drafts of this paper.

In the winter of 1984, Michel Foucault devoted his last series of lectures at the Collège de France to the topic of *parrhesia*, or truth-telling in classical antiquity. Contemplating possible antecedents for the unusual character of his own approach to the truth, Foucault examined in turn the life of Socrates, and the far more colourful life of Diogenes the Cynic, legendary for living in a tub, masturbating in the marketplace, carrying a lit lamp in broad daylight, and telling anybody who was curious that 'I am looking for a man.'

Anecdotes like this once played a central role in philosophy and its cultural transmission. To be a philosopher had entailed living one's life in a certain way, and embodying in practice a certain style of thought – no matter how scandalous the implications. Still, as Foucault well knew, the lore surrounding Greek sages like Diogenes has, in our own day, rarely been taken seriously. The arguments found in Plato's dialogues are routinely parsed in philosophy departments, while questions about how Socrates lived and died are more often left in the shadows. As Karl Jaspers once put it, 'If philosophy is "doctrine", [then] Socrates is not a philosopher.'[1]

1. Karl Jaspers, *Socrates, Buddha, Confucius, Jesus*, trans. Ralph Manheim, New York 1962, p7.

For his part, Foucault emphatically deplored what he called our own modern 'negligence' of the problem of the philosophical life. This problem, he speculated, had gone into eclipse for two different reasons: first, because religious institutions had absorbed, or (in his words) 'confiscated' the 'theme of the practice of the true life'; and second, 'because the relationship to truth can now be made valid and manifest only in the form of scientific knowledge.'

Foucault, in passing, then suggested the potential fruitfulness of further research on this topic. 'It seems to me,' he remarked, 'that it would be interesting to write a history starting from the problem of the philosophical life, a problem ... envisaged as a choice which can be detected both through the events and decisions of a biography, and through [the elaboration of] the same problem in the interior of a system [of thought], and the place which has been given in this system to the problem of the philosophical life.'[2]

2. Michel Foucault, Collège de France lecture, 14 March 1984.

Ever since encountering these lectures, I have been intrigued by the prospect of undertaking a history of the sort that Foucault described. In my own view, a history of the problem of the philosophical life that started with Socrates and Diogenes might also include, for example, Zeno; Chrysippus; Seneca; Plutarch; St. Anthony; St. Augustine; Erasmus; Montaigne; Rousseau; Kierkegaard; Emerson; Nietzsche; Bataille, perhaps Wittgenstein; I would say Heidegger; and certainly Foucault himself.

These names, to me, suggest a coherent tradition within the larger history of western thought. It is, broadly speaking, a tradition inspired by the famous maxim inscribed on the façade of the temple of Apollo at Delphi: 'Know Thyself.' Preoccupied by this deceptively simple admonition, and often developing their ideas in conversation with one another, the philosophers working through this tradition comprise a family of figures similar to – though not identical with – those writers recently grouped together by Stanley Cavell as exemplars of what he calls 'moral perfectionism'.[3]

I would like to sketch out, in a series of more or less fragmentary reflections, some of the puzzles that I have encountered in trying to think about, and write about, various facets of this occluded, often disparaged current of philosophy. How might one approach the family of figures I have just enumerated? What must one know about the facts of a philosopher's life to do justice to what is truly 'philosophical' about that life? And why is the problem of the philosophical life so rarely taken seriously – not least by professional philosophers?

Despite a recent surge of interest among Anglo-American philosophers in questions of identity and selfhood (I am thinking, for example, of Martha Nussbaum's *The Therapy of Desire*, and also of Charles Taylor's recent magnum opus, *Sources of the Self*), it seems fair to say that most philosophers today have a 'resistance' – Cavell's word – to the very notion of the philosophical life. This should come as no surprise. After all, philosophy since Kant has been largely an academic calling. As it is normally taught today, it is a discipline that revolves around the analysis and justification of concepts and arguments, a practice in which students are routinely taught, among other things, that the truth of a proposition should be evaluated independently of anything we may know about the person holding that proposition. This is a curriculum that imparts crucial skills. But it does not pretend to present a model of how to live.

Writing a century before Foucault and Cavell, and anticipating their point of view on these matters, Nietzsche put it this way: 'The only critique of a philosophy that is possible and that proves anything, namely trying to see whether one can live in accordance with it, has never been taught at universities: all that has ever been taught is a critique of words by means of other words.'[4]

To start, it will be useful to recall briefly that first and most daunting of models for the philosophical life – namely Socrates. In Plato's *Apology*, Socrates famously asserts his ignorance while steadfastly defending his own reasoned convictions about how to live and die rightly. Scorning the dictates of the conventional wisdom on these topics, Socrates explains how he has tried to act in harmony with his inner *daimon* and the injunction he received from the oracle at Delphi: 'to live the life of a philosopher, to examine myself and others.'[5]

As Plato recounts his speech before the Athenian jury, Socrates takes some

3. See Stanley Cavell, *Conditions Handsome and Unhandsome*, Chicago, 1989, pp1-5. In his own work, Foucault emphasized the importance of caring for the self, rather than simply knowing the self: a distinction of some importance for the stress he would lay on spiritual exercises in antiquity.

4. Friedrich Nietzsche, 'Schophenhauer as Educator', in *Untimely Meditations*, trans. R.J. Hollingdale, Cambridge 1983, p187.

5. Plato, *Apology*, 28e.

pride in the consistency of his beliefs and actions. 'Throughout my life,' he declares, 'in any public activity I may have engaged in, I am the same man as I am in private life.' Conveying his views 'not in words but in action,' his defiant attitude towards the jury demonstrates that 'death is something I couldn't care less about, but that my whole concern is not to do anything unjust.'[6]

6. *Ibid.*, 32d-33a.

In short, to appreciate Socrates as a philosopher, we are invited – by Plato, certainly – to judge his *integrity*; and this requires understanding how his personal character harmonizes, or fails to harmonize, with his declared convictions.[7]

7. I owe this point, and much else besides, to Robert Solomon. See Robert C. Solomon, 'Nietzsche *Ad Hominem*: Perspectivism, Personality and *Ressentiment*,' to appear in Bernard Magnus, (ed), *Nietzsche* Cambridge University Press, forthcoming.

The English word 'integrity' is derived from the Latin word *integritas*; like its classical cognate, it has a range of connotations: from wholeness and completeness to soundness and freedom from defect. In English, integrity in certain contexts has a slightly archaic, even moralizing ring: the man or woman of integrity is said to be sincere, chaste, pure; perhaps even innocent, in the sense of freedom from sin. But in other contexts, integrity has a more concrete bearing, as when we speak of a sound physical structure – an intact bridge, say – as having integrity.

One thing seems to me clear. Whether or not it is used in a moralizing context, the concept of integrity, when applied to a human being, presupposes a certain capacity in that being for resoluteness and constancy, a certain power to organize and *integrate* one's impulses and impressions, habits and beliefs into a characteristic form of life, a form that, because it endures over time, allows us to speak of a coherent soul, or self.

Among the ancients – in writers from Plato to Seneca – the ability to produce a sound form of life was traced to the power always to will the same things, and always to oppose the same things; and this power was thought to grow out of the goodness of a will governed by reason. Integrity was a matter of just order in the soul.

Within virtually all of the classical schools, maintenance of a just order in the soul required adherence to a reasoned pattern of conduct. Integrity could be achieved, if at all, only through a break with the ingrained beliefs and habits that routinely regulate everyday life, followed by a potentially endless process of self-examination and personal reformation. In almost every school, this process entailed a rigorous exercise of thought, and also a more or less formalized regimen of spiritual, and sometimes corporeal exercises. The conviction animating all of these exercises was that a life of contemplative introspection, thoughtful dialogue, and proper subordination of the body to the soul might afford an earnest student some special measure of wisdom, or happiness, or peace of mind.

Now the value of such exercises has by no means been uncontested, least of all in our own day. Foucault of course challenged Plato's notion of a well-ordered philosophical life, referring acidly in *Discipline and Punish* to 'the soul, prison of the body'. And Richard Rorty, to cite still another prominent sceptic, has expressed equally strong doubts about the ability of *anyone* to achieve a state of perfect integrity. The philosopher, in Rorty's sarcastic words, would then have to exemplify 'an ideal human being: one who perfectly unites wisdom and kindness, insight and decency'. Like a lot of professional philosophers, and like a lot of ordinary people, Rorty has trouble taking this vision of the ideal philosopher seriously: 'All of us,' he writes derisively, 'hope to find such a guru – someone who will be everything our parents were not.'[8]

Such quips and ridicule, as Rorty doubtless knows, scarcely do justice to a figure like Socrates, who – at least if we credit the idea of an 'historical' Socrates – sincerely professed his ignorance, and refused (unlike Plato) to formulate a universal code of conduct. Nor does Rorty's sarcasm, or Foucault's inversion of Orphic formulas, discredit a living exemplar of philosophical scepticism like Montaigne. Indeed, for a wide variety of figures preoccupied with the living of a philosophical life after Plato, what I have called 'integrity' can not be simply conflated with the acquisition of knowledge of an immutable good, or attainment of an unblemished moral purity, or subordination of the body to an immortal soul, certainly not in Plato's terms. By the modern period, the teleological model of integrity elaborated by such Christian thinkers as Augustine had been supplemented by a quite different standard for the living of a coherent philosophical life, a standard that Nietzsche, for one, described in frankly aesthetic terms.

'One thing is needful,' Nietzsche writes in a famous passage in *The Gay Science*: to "give style" to one's character – a great and rare art! It is practised by those who survey all the strengths and weaknesses of their nature and then fit them into an artistic plan until every one of them appears as art and reason and even weaknesses delight the eye … In the end, when the work is finished, it becomes evident how the constraint of a single taste governed and formed everything large and small. Whether this taste was good or bad is less important than one might suppose, if only it was a single taste!'[9]

Let us suppose for a moment that we are, in fact, interested in recognizing – and appraising – a quality like integrity, or singleness of taste, call it what you will, in the life of a philosopher. What features of a philosopher's life should a biographer regard as pertinent? For that matter, what features of his or her life should a *philosopher* regard as pertinent?

Consider one of the sentences that opens one of the most famous of classical philosophical biographies, the life of Zeno by Diogenes Laertius: 'They say he was fond of eating green figs and of basking in the sun.'[10]

At first glance, these seem to be idle details, of no philosophical consequence. Quite apart from the dubious evidentiary value of the vague reference to what 'they say', what is one to make – if anything – of Zeno's fondness for green figs and basking in the sun? Of what possible relevance can this be to understanding his professed convictions?

Several pages later in his life of Zeno, Diogenes Laertius implicitly answers these questions. 'The food he used required no fire to dress, and the cloak he wore was thin,' he writes. 'Hence it was said of him:

8. Richard Rorty, 'Taking Philosophy Seriously', a review of Victor Farias, *Heidegger and Nazism*, in *The New Republic*, April 11, 1988, p33.

9. Nietzsche, *The Gay Science*, no290. Alexander Nehamas makes this aphorism a centerpiece of his masterful book – which has inspired a great deal of my own thinking – *Nietzsche: Life as Literature* Cambridge, Mass. 1985

10. Diogenes Laertius, *Lives of Eminent Philosophers*, trans. R.D. Hicks, Cambridge, Mass. 1925, Vol.II, p111.

The cold of winter and the ceaseless rain
Came powerless against him: weak the dart
of the fierce summer sun or racking pain
To bend that iron frame. He stands apart
Unspoiled by public feast and jollity:
Patient, unwearied night and day doth he
Cling to his studies of philosophy. '[11]

11. *Ibid.*, Vol.II, p139.

This, in my view, is not a pointless piece of antique doggerel. By documenting the popular image of the philosopher, Diogenes Laertius rather allows us to understand Zeno's fondness for green figs and basking in the sun as consistent with, and partially constitutive of, the ethos of contemplative self-sufficiency that he preached in what survive of his books.

It is perhaps worth making explicit what my view entails. In principle, *anything* about a philosopher's life may prove relevant to appraising his or her integrity. It all depends on how one interprets the evidence.

In his *Essays*, Montaigne points out a problem raised by the possible relevance of *anything*, from the most sublime of treatises to the most trivial of character traits, to living – and judging – a properly philosophical life. It is not that Montaigne has any difficulty in believing that a fondness for green figs might be of deep philosophical significance, certainly for anyone preoccupied, like himself, in honouring the Delphic precept, to 'Know Thyself '. On the contrary. 'Each particle,' writes Montaigne, 'each occupation of a man betrays him and reveals him just as well as any other.'[12]

12. Montaigne, *Essays*, trans. Donald M. Frame, Stanford, 1958, I, 1, p220.

The problem is what surveying this open-ended variety of evidence quickly reveals: namely, the apparent inconsistency of our beliefs and behaviour much of the time. Most of us divide our lives into different, often isolated compartments. If we examine honestly all of a human being's different aspects, we seem bound to find *in*coherence and contradiction. 'There is some justification for basing a judgment of a man on the most ordinary acts of his life,' remarks Montaigne, 'but in view of the natural instability of our conduct and opinions, it has often seemed to me that even good authors are wrong to insist on fashioning a consistent and solid fabric out of us.'[13]

13. *Ibid.*, II, i, p239.

One might suppose that Montaigne would therefore be sympathetic to Rorty's rejection of the very ideal of a philosophical life. Indeed Montaigne concedes that 'in all antiquity it is hard to pick out a dozen men who set their lives to a certain and constant course.'

Still, Montaigne in his *Essays* does not simply reject the classical ideal. Instead, he effectively *reinvents* it, showing us (in his words) 'a new figure: an unpremeditated and accidental philosopher!'[14]

14. *Ibid.*, II, xii, p409.

Affirming the human being's 'infinite capacity to produce innumerable forms', and consequently abandoning any assumption that the soul is, or ought to be, embarked on a logical pilgrimage toward one common and unchanging goal (call it the good, or call it God), Montaigne through his essays explores another possibility. Following his whim with unhesitant courage, he details the superficially chaotic contents of his inner experience, assaying his apparently amorphous individuality with studied sincerity – and so, paradoxically, precisely by writing his *Essays*, reveals the integrity of a unique and unmistakeable character, recognizable (in his own words) by 'a certain constancy of opinions'. Self-consciously emulating such pagan precursors as Socrates and Seneca, Montaigne strives mightily to bring together life and work: 'In other cases,' as he remarks, 'one may commend or blame the work apart from the workman; not so here; he who touches the one, touches the other.' At the same time, by frankly scrutinizing *all* aspects of himself, no matter how trivial, transient or – in the eyes of most ordinary philsophers – unseemly (by the end, for example, we know all about the author's struggle with sexual impotence), Montaigne demonstrates how (in Nietzsche's words) 'the constraint of a single taste' may integrate a large number of disparate elements, offering us a unified portrait of the 'freest and most vigorous of spirits' (as Nietzsche once described Montaigne).[15]

15. Ibid., III, vi, p692; II, i, p240; II, xii, p428; III, v, p677. For Montaigne's rejection of classical entelechy, see also Hugo Friedrich, *Montaigne*, trans. Dawn Eng, Berkeley, 1991, p218.

Still, the revelation, through uninhibited self-examination, of a 'constancy of opinions' or singleness of taste is no simple matter, whether we are interested in expressing what is uniquely 'free and vigorous' about our own selves, or rather interested in recognizing what is unique in the opinions and tastes of someone else. In appraising how a life and work may hang together, we must, as Montaigne puts it, 'refuse to judge men simply by their outward actions; we must probe the inside and discover what springs set men in motion.' Since we must nevertheless take our bearings at the start largely from outward actions and those character traits an 'accidental philosopher' like Montaigne (or for that matter Foucault) may display, willy-nilly, in his writing, we are confronted, as Montaigne stresses, with 'an arduous and hazardous undertaking.'[16]

16. Montaigne, *Essays*, II, i, p244.

In attempting to compose my own modern version of a philosophical life, *The Passion of Michel Foucault*, I took as my model for this 'arduous and hazardous undertaking' the work of Jean Starobinski, the great Genevan literary critic. In one of his characteristically incisive essays, Starobinski counsels a kind of 'free-floating attentiveness' to the matter at hand. Though he is speaking explicitly about how to read and interpret a text in order to appraise its possible psychological significance, his words can stand as well for the probing of *all* outwardly expressive acts, in search of their inner springs. Starobinski writes.

There must be an initial phase, a phase of [primarily passive] experience. In vigilant neutrality the gaze goes out to meet the reality presented to it without undue haste to identify definitive structures, for the danger is great that it would simply impose its own. As far as possible, one refrains from interpreting and simply takes in data for interpretation ... Little by little certain themes, certain similarities, will stand out. Attention is drawn to what [in a piece of writing, for example] the work passes over in silence, as well as the qualities of its intonation, its rhythms, its verbal energy and organization. Structures, connections, and 'networks' ... begin to take shape as if of their own accord, as the work develops a complex presence whose organic structure must be identified.[17]

17. Jean Starobinski, 'Psychoanalysis and Literary Understanding', in *The Living Eye*, trans. Arthur Goldhammer, Cambridge, Mass. 1989, p143.

From Starobinski's point of view, it makes no sense to speak of a hidden, latent integrity that the analyst brings to light. 'Rather than latent it is better to say *implicit*,' writes Starobinski: 'what is present *in* the work, not *behind* it, but which we were unable to decipher at first glance.'

Starobinski calls his procedure 'stylistics'. Through a subtle application of this procedure, he thinks that we may come to appreciate how 'the work, sustained by the individual who produces it, is itself an act of desire, a revealed intention.' Life and work will then no longer appear as incommensurable realities. Regarding the lifework as one irreducible whole, we will discern 'an expansive, continuous melody', as Starobinski puts it, 'that is at once life and work, destiny and expression.'[18]

18. *Ibid.*, pp143, 145.

It is at this juncture that Michel Foucault parted ways with the approach taken by Starobinski, whose work he both knew and otherwise admired.[19] The great danger of Starobinski's approach – as Starobinski himself freely acknowledged – was the unwarranted imputation of wholeness, or structural integrity, to a lifework. In search of coherence, we are all too likely to find just what we are looking for. The historian of a philosophical life unavoidably runs the risk of producing a one-sided or, worse, factitious account of coherence.

19. Apart from several passing references to Starobinski, Foucault devoted appreciative longer essays to the psychoanalytically-influenced work of J.-P. Richard on Mallarmé, and of Jean Laplanche on Holderlin.

It is true, I suppose, that most of us exhibit some minimal degree of coherence most of the time, in so far as human beings raised within a culture perforce become predictable creatures of habit, rational, obedient, dutiful even to the point of dullness.

But a wise, or unusually happy, or thoughtfully stylized type of coherence – the sorts of coherence at issue in the philosophical life ostensibly exemplified by Socrates, or that more plaintively described in the books of Nietzsche – surely appears in the lifework of only the rarest of men or women, if it appears in the lifework of anyone. As Foucault once expressed his own scepticism on this score, 'the simultaneous unravelling of poetic and psychological structures will never succeed in reducing the distance which separates them.'[20]

20. Michel Foucault, 'The Father's "No",' in *Language, Counter-Memory, Practice*, trans. Donald F. Bouchard, Ithaca, NY 1977, p85.

In this context, Starobinski's metaphor – of life and work harmonizing in a single melody – will not seem apt. Better to speak of dissonance, and to expect contradictions and unresolved tensions. As Nietzsche once remarked of Rousseau's avowed failure to realize a perfect sense of integrity, '[his] life ran along beside [his] knowledge like a wayward bass which refuses to harmonise with the melody.'[21]

21. Friedrich Nietzsche, *Daybreak*, trans. R.J. Hollingdale, Cambridge 1982, p192.

A philosophical biography that evoked some air of dissonance would best honour Foucault's own insistence on the irreducible distance between life and work; a gap (say, between the structure of one's philosophy and one's psychology) that may represent, among other things, the failure of a philosopher to shape a distinctive body of work; or his even more likely failure to embody a thoughtfully integrated character; or, most common of all, his all but inevitable failure to style a harmonious whole out of *both* life and work, for want of the requisite constancy and singleness of taste, or resoluteness of purpose.

It is telling, I think, that Foucault at the end of his life, despite his doubts about our ability ever to integrate fully life and work, nevertheless entertained the frankly utopian hope that, in a different society, perhaps organized under different rules of conduct, *all* of us might be able, despite the difficulties, to exemplify what I have been calling 'a philosophical life'. 'Couldn't everyone's life become a work of art,' wondered Foucault: 'Why should the lamp or the house be an art object, but not our life?'[22]

To a hard-boiled pragmatist like Richard Rorty, it is tempting to write remarks like this off as symptomatic of an absurd, because impossible, wish to live (in Rorty's words) 'a life of self-creation ... as complete and autonomous as Plato thought a life of contemplation might be.'[23]

But let us again grant what Rorty (in this respect like Montaigne and Rousseau and Nietzsche and Foucault) asserts, namely, that any life, of course, is *always* bound to seem incomplete at death, that any philosophical or poetic effort to transform 'the blind impress' of chance events into a coherent thing of virtue, or wisdom, or beauty, is *always*, finally, in some sense, bound to be a failure.

Is the game worth the candle?

Since I have neither the time nor the wisdom even to begin to answer that question – which I suspect is what really lies behind the resistance of many professional philosophers, as well as many ordinary people, to the vision of what I have been calling the philosophical life – I will instead close by citing a passage from America's greatest preacher of this life, one who cherished the democratic vistas he felt that Everyman's quest for self-creation might yet help to open up. This passage by Ralph Waldo Emerson I think speaks not only to Foucault's own unfinished quest for a life of philosophical integrity; but also to Richard Rorty's suspicion that a yearning for expressive wholeness boils down to a puerile wish to place one's self in the care of a perfect parent (even if that 'parent' turns out only to be one's own nagging sense of one's own better self).

'Patience and patience, we shall win at last,' Emerson writes bravely; although the impatient assertiveness of his language here betrays the fact that this particular sermon on the philosophical life amounts to a kind of prayer:

We must be very suspicious of the deceptions of the element of time. It takes a good deal of time to eat or to sleep, or to earn a hundred dollars, and a very little time to entertain a hope and an insight which becomes the light of our life. We dress our garden, eat our dinners, discuss the household with our wives, and these things make no impression, are forgotten next week; but in the solitude to which every man is always returning, he has a sanity

22. Michel Foucault, 'On the Genealogy of Ethics: An Overview of a Work in Progress,' in *The Foucault Reader*, Paul Rabinow (ed), New York 1984, p350.

23. Richard Rorty, *Contingency, Irony and Solidarity*, Cambridge 1989, p43.

and revelations, which in his passage into new worlds he will carry with him. Never mind the ridicule, never mind the defeat: up again, old heart! – it seems to say, – there is victory yet for all justice; and the true romance which the world exists to realize, will be the transformation of genius into practical power.[24]

24. Emerson, 'Experience', from Ralph Waldo Emerson, *Essays and Lectures*, New York 1983, p492. The insight that there is an aspect of prayer to this essay about loss, I owe to Stanley Cavell: see Cavell, *This New Yet Unapproachable America* Albuquerque, 1989, pp112-14.

FOUCAULT ON RACE AND COLONIALISM

Robert J.C. Young

Foucault had a lot to say about power, but he was curiously circumspect about the ways in which it has operated in the arenas of race and colonialism. His virtual silence on these issues is striking. In fact Foucault's work appears to be so scrupulously Eurocentric that you begin to wonder whether there isn't a deliberate strategy involved: consider, after all, the context of the Paris of Sartre, Fanon, Althusser, the traumatic defeat of the French at Dien Bien Phu in 1954, the Algerian War of Independence and the National Liberation Movements of the 1950s and 1960s. Foucault's few explicit writings in these areas are sometimes curious: take his comments on the revolution in Iran, where he discusses the Iranian Revolution in terms of what he considers to be its expression of 'an absolutely collective will' which he contrasts to the more mediated forms of European revolutions.[1] This distinction is constructed according to very European, indeed Orientalist, categories: the fantasy of Iran as subject of a collective will, as pure being, screens the historical relation of the revolution to its colonial adversaries.

Yet the lasting paradox is that despite the absence of explicit discussions of colonialism, Foucault's work has been a central theoretical reference point for postcolonial analysis. It provided the theoretical basis for what has effectively become the founding disciplinary text for contemporary postcolonial theory, Edward Said's *Orientalism* (1978).[2] What enabled *Orientalism* to be so outstandingly successful, and establish a whole new field of academic inquiry? The key factor was undoubtedly the way in which the idea of Orientalism as a *discourse* allowed the creation of a general theoretical paradigm through which the cultural forms of colonial and imperial ideologies could be analysed. While Marxist accounts had emphasized the primacy of the economic in the development of colonialism and imperialism, the diversity of economic conditions, the historical and geographical differences between colonies (how to compare, for example, the United States with India?) meant that there was no general schema through which the particularity of the cultural effects of colonialism and imperialism could be analysed.

Foucault's 'discourse' describes the particular kind of language which specialized knowledge has to conform to in order to be regarded as true (for example, medical discourse, the discourse of theoretical nuclear physics, of computers, literary criticism, love ...). According to Foucault, discourse always involves a form of violence in the way it imposes its linguistic order on the world: knowledge has to conform to its paradigms in order to be recognized as legitimate. Following Foucault, Said argued that Orientalism was less a body of objective scholarly knowledge than a discursive construction, whose conceptual

1. Michel Foucault, *Politics Philosophy Culture: Interviews and Other Writings*, Lawrence D. Kritzman (ed.), Routledge, New York 1988, p215.

2. Edward W. Said, *Orientalism: Western Representations of the Orient*, Routledge and Kegan Paul, London 1978.

structure determined the way in which the West understood the East. Though accepted in the West as true, Said's point was that Orientalism was a form of ideological fantasy, with no necessary relation to the actual cultures that it supposedly described and understood: the very Orient was itself an Orientalist fiction. At the same time Orientalism, as Said defines it, was a relationship of power, of cultural domination, the cultural equivalent of the colonialism which it accompanied. As Foucault puts it, 'it is in discourse that power and knowledge are joined together'.[3]

3. Michel Foucault, *The History of Sexuality Volume One: An Introduction*, trans. Robert Hurley, Allen Lane, London 1978, p100.

Said's Foucaldian emphasis on the way in which Orientalism developed as a partisan discursive construction has necessarily come to be balanced by the pursuit of what Orientalism excluded. Interestingly enough, it has been Foucault again who has provided the theoretical model for this 'archaeology of silence'. In terms of the social production of the subject, his early work *Madness and Civilization* (1961) has functioned as a founding study of the way in which European society has determined its forms of exclusion and the differences which limit it. Foucault himself described *Madness and Civilization* as a history of difference, of the expulsion of alterity:

> The history of madness would be the history of the Other – of that which, for a given culture, is at once interior and foreign, therefore to be excluded (so as to exorcise the interior danger) but by being shut away (in order to reduce its otherness).[4]

4. Michel Foucault, *The Order of Things: An Archaeology of the Human Sciences*, trans. anonymous, Tavistock Publications, London 1970, pxxiv.

In a similar way, Said's Orientalism constitutes a system of apparent knowledge about the Orient but one in which 'the Other' which makes up that Orient is never allowed, or invited to speak: the Oriental other is rather confined to fantasy. The discursive representation of Orientalism has been balanced by attention to the reality which that representation missed or excluded and has inspired a whole movement dedicated to retrieving the history of the silenced subaltern: both in terms of the objective history of subaltern or dominated, marginalized groups, 'counter-histories', and in terms of the subjective experience of the effects of colonialism and domination. Foucault's own formulation of history as a writing of singularity, where the event as event is only constituted through its repetition in thought as a 'phantasm', was itself clearly designed to facilitate the inscription of histories that had never yet been subjected to such hegemonic re-iteration.[5]

5. For further discussion of Foucault's theory of history, see my 'Foucault's Phantasms' in *White Mythologies: Writing History and the West*, Routledge, London 1990, pp69-87.

In the wake of *Orientalism*'s widespread influence, many commentators have criticized Said for employing too determining and univocal a notion of discourse. This is largely the result of his reliance on Foucault's initial account in *The Order of Discourse* (1971), which stresses its restrictive and homogenizing qualities.[6] Later critics such as Homi Bhabha have emphasized the rather different description of *The History of Sexuality* (1976), where Foucault writes:

6. Michel Foucault, 'The Order of Discourse', trans. Ian McLeod, in *Untying the Text: A Post-Structuralist Reader*, Robert Young (ed.), Routledge and Kegan Paul, London 1981, pp51-76.

> we must conceive discourse as a series of discontinuous segments whose tactical function is neither uniform nor stable. To be more precise, we must

not imagine a world of discourse divided between accepted discourse and excluded discourse, or between the dominant discourse and the dominated one; but as a multiplicity of discursive elements that can come into play in various strategies.[7]

7. Homi Bhabha, 'Difference, Discrimination, and the Discourse of Colonialism', in *The Politics of Theory*, Francis Barker *et al* (eds), University of Essex, Colchester 1983, pp199-200; Foucault, *The History of Sexuality*, p100.

According to Foucault here, the whole attempt to represent 'other voices' that have been silenced and excluded by discourse represents nothing less than a conceptual error. Just as power and resistance are necessarily imbricated within each other, so discourse also enacts its own effects of destabilization.

We must make allowance for the complex and unstable process whereby discourse can be both an instrument and an effect of power, but also a hindrance, a stumbling-block, a point of resistance and a starting point for an opposing strategy. Discourse transmits and produces power; it reinforces it, but also undermines and exposes it, renders it fragile and makes it possible to thwart it. In like manner, silence and secrecy are a shelter for power, anchoring its prohibitions; but they also loosen its holds and provide for relatively obscure areas of tolerance.[8]

8. *Ibid.* p101.

This more flexible, heterogeneous account of discourse suggests that Foucault himself had became wary of the inclusion/exclusion dialectic of *Madness and Civilization* that Derrida had challenged.[9] By the time of *The History of Sexuality* Foucault denies the very existence of a dominance/subversion paradigm:

There is not, on the one side, a discourse of power, and opposite it, another discourse that runs counter to it. Discourses are tactical elements or blocks operating in a field of force relations; there can exist different and even contradictory discourses within the same strategy; they can, on the contrary, circulate without changing their form from one strategy to another, opposing strategy.

9. Jacques Derrida, 'Cogito and the History of Madness', in *Writing and Difference*, trans. Alan Bass, Routledge and Kegan Paul, London 1978, pp31-63. Foucault's reply, appended to the second edition (1972) of his *Histoire de la folie*, is translated as 'My Body, This Paper, This Fire', in *Oxford Literary Review* 4:1, 1979.

For Foucault, therefore, power is neither intentional nor fully realized; it is rather 'a multiple and mobile field of force relations, wherein far-reaching, but never completely stable, effects of domination are produced'.[10] Despite this substantial revision, the earlier binary model continues to overshadow analyses of colonialism.

10. Michel Foucault, *op.cit.*, pp101-2.

Whether early or late, so much of Foucault seems to be applicable to the colonial arena – his emphasis on forms of authority and exclusion, for example, or his analysis of the operations of the technologies of power, of the apparatuses of surveillance. Foucault's own concepts have themselves become productive forms of conceptual power and authority. Even his images are extraordinarily suggestive: take, for example, the description with which *Madness and Civilization* begins, the Ship of Fools that carried from port to port its cargo of insane people who had been expelled from their native town. Later drunken boats would become the form of the enforced migration of surplus populations to North America, to Australia, or the wandering ships of Jewish refugees that travelled the Mediterranean when the British authorities in Palestine decided to accede to Palestinian demands for an end to Jewish immigration. Similarly, so many of Foucault's concepts involve suggestive spatial and geographical metaphors: position, displacement, interstice, site, field, territory, geopolitics – concepts that have been developed by anthropologists such as Johannes Fabian or historians such as John Noyes in his recent book *Colonial Space*.[11] Despite this, Foucault's own domains of reference remain resolutely fixed within the western world, and effectively within France.[12] This leads Gayatri C. Spivak to comment:

> Sometimes it seems as if the very brilliance of Foucault's analysis of the centuries of European imperialism produces a miniature version of that heterogeneous phenomenon: management of space – but by doctors; development of administrations – but in asylums; considerations of the periphery – but in terms of the insane, prisoners and children. The clinic, the asylum, the prison, the university – all seem to be screen allegories that foreclose a reading of the broader narratives of imperialism.[13]

Again and again the paradox of Foucault's work is that his analyses seem particularly appropriate to the colonial arena, and yet colonialism itself does not figure. What would be the psychic imperative impelling such foreclosure? Or was it a more considered strategy?

One clue comes at the end of *The Order of Things*, in the section entitled 'Psychoanalysis and Ethnology', where Foucault considers the development of ethnology at the turn of the nineteenth century. Given that ethnology means 'the science of human races, their characteristics, and their relations to one another', it is here, if anywhere, that you might expect Foucault to discuss questions of race and colonialism, of the increasing emphasis that was being placed at the close of the eighteenth century on the character of non-European peoples and their imagined intrinsic difference from Europeans.

Foucault, however, no doubt thinking of Kant's *Anthropology from a Pragmatic Point of View* (1800) which he translated in 1964, considers ethnology only as a synonym for anthropology, that is the science of man and the comparative analytic study of cultures. In producing a general model of how cultures organize and define themselves, ethnology for Foucault is not about the particular differences of other cultures, but about how such differences conform to an underlying theoretical pattern formulated according to the protocols of European thought. This means that

> ethnology ... avoids the representations that men in any civilization may give of themselves, of their life, of their needs, of the significations laid down in the language; and it sees emerging behind those representations the norms by which men perform the functions of life ... the rules through which they experience and maintain their needs, the systems against the background of

11. Johannes Fabian, *Language and Colonial Power: The Appropriation of Swahili in the Former Belgian Congo 1880-1938*, Cambridge University Press, Cambridge 1986, p78; *Time and The Work of Anthropology: Critical Essays 1971-1991*, Harwood, Chur 1991, p198; John Noyes, *Colonial Space: Spatiality in the Discourse of German South West Africa 1884-1915*, Harwood, Chur 1992, p52.

12. Cf. Michel Foucault, *Power/Knowledge: Selected Interviews & Other Writings 1972-1977*, Colin Gordon (ed), Pantheon Books, New York 1980, p67.

13. Gayatri Chakravorty Spivak, 'Can the Subaltern Speak? Speculations on Widow Sacrifice', in *Marxism and the Interpretation of Culture*, Cary Nelson and Lawrence Grossberg (eds), Macmillan, London 1988, p291.

which all signification is given to them.[14]

14. Michel Foucault, *The Order of Things*, p378. Further references will be cited in the text.

Ethnology corresponds at the social level to psychoanalysis at the individual level; it produces what Foucault calls the 'historical *a priori* of all the sciences of man', that is, that which makes objective knowledge of man possible. The special privilege of ethnology and psychoanalysis is therefore that they are 'sciences of the unconscious' – not because they analyse something that is below consciousness, but rather 'because they are directed towards that which, outside man, makes it possible to know, with a positive knowledge, that which is given to or eludes his consciousness' (378).

Foucault, in fact, ends his *Archaeology of the Human Sciences* by naming ethnology and psychoanalysis as the foundations of the human sciences in general. He argues that ethnology should describe itself in his terms – not as the study of societies without history, but as the study of 'the unconscious processes that characterize the system of a given culture': a 'pure theory of language ... would provide the ethnology and the psychoanalysis thus conceived with their formal model' (379, 381). Foucault's remarks seem here in effect to involve a programmatic statement for the linguistic structuralism of Lévi-Strauss and Lacan. Despite his frank confession of its dependence on a power relation of European sovereignty, his apparent endorsement of an ethnology which would analyse not the forms of knowledge developed by other societies for themselves but how they conformed to a general theoretical model of how societies function, developed out of western structural linguistics, seems today startlingly ethnocentric.

Few people have a good word to say about structuralism these days, and students of theory have been taught to dismiss it casually as hopelessly flawed. But the paradoxical argument that in language things can be both the same and different could be said to have constituted structuralism's basic methodological premise which enabled it to compare unlike things, as Fredric Jameson has argued, through the form of homology.[15] At a theoretical level, structuralism was developed as part of the post-war process of cultural decolonization, disputing the cultural hierarchy of racialism, and turning the critical ethnography that had been developed for the analysis of non-western cultures onto the culture of the West itself. This is the practice that Foucault emphasizes in *The Order of Things*. His interest in ethnography turns out to be the way in which it provides a means for producing a critical analysis of European society, a 'counter-science' to take the place of the Marxism which Foucault had by this time rejected: 'In attempting to uncover the deepest strata of western culture, I am restoring to our silent and apparently immobile soil its rifts, its instability, its flaws ...' (xxiv). Instead of making a moral argument against Eurocentrism, as we tend to do, Foucault is thus rather concerned to analyse the predicates which make it possible. Setting aside the question of its morality, it was no mean conceptual feat to organize the entire surface of the globe according to a particular system of knowledge. Foucault himself described his analysis in *The Order of Things* in terms of this incorporation of the

15. Fredric Jameson, *Postmodernism, or the Cultural Logic of Late Capitalism*, Verso, London 1991, pp185-6.

other into the same, of the history of the order imposed on things by European culture. *The Order of Things* could be seen as an analysis not of Eurocentrism as such, but of its philosophical and conceptual archaeology. Before we can undo eurocentrism, before we can undermine its continuing power, we have to understand how it was done.

At the same time, Foucault himself begins the book by pointing to the relativism of much European understanding in the human sciences – 'whence all the chimeras of the new humanisms, all the facile solutions of an "anthropology" understood as a universal reflection on man' (xxiii). In the concluding discussion of ethnology, he begins by pointing out that its very existence is only possible on the basis

> of an absolutely singular historical event which involves not only our historicity but also that of all men who can constitute the object of an ethnology ... ethnology has its roots, in fact, in a possibility that properly belongs to the history of our culture, even more to its fundamental relation with the whole of history, and enables it to link itself to other cultures in a mode of pure theory (376-7).

Ethnology is contingent on the terms according to which western reason was invented. This highlights the fragility of the project of the human sciences as such and exposes their constitution as knowledge through a form of power:

> There is a certain position of the western *ratio* that was constituted in its history and provides a foundation for the relation it can have with all other societies ... Obviously, this does not mean that the colonizing situation is indispensable to ethnology ... but ... ethnology can assume its proper dimensions only within the historical sovereignty – always restrained, but always present – of European thought and the relation that can bring it face to face with all cultures as well as with itself (377).

Ethnology, Foucault suggests, does not depend on the power relation of colonialism, but it does require 'the historical sovereignty ... of European thought'. Here we may recall the implicit racialism of Kant's *Anthropology*, which is predicated on the assumption of an historicized, developmental racial typology. Foucault characteristically emphasizes the historical contingency of reason's claim to universalism, even if he also recognizes its conceptual power. At the same time as emphasizing the impermanence of 'man', Foucault also suggests the way in which his invention has, since the nineteenth century, necessarily brought along his shadow, an 'element of darkness', with it:

> the Other that is not only a brother but a twin, born, not of man, nor in man, but beside him and at the same time, in an identical newness, in an unavoidable duality. This obscure space so readily interpreted as an abyssal region in man's nature, or as a uniquely impregnable fortress in his history,

is linked to him in an entirely different way; it is both exterior to him and indispensable to him: in one sense, the shadow cast by man as he emerged in the field of knowledge; in another, the blind stain by which it is possible to know him.(326)

Though this passage seems to be moving towards an analysis of the fabrication of the racial other, the penumbra of racism through which 'man' has been defined never gets a mention.

It was only in his later work that Foucault was to turn to the question of racism as such, in the very different context of his analysis of what he called 'bio-politics', the regulation of the individuated bodies of the social body through disciplinary techniques. The final, sixth volume of *The History of Sexuality* was originally to have been entitled 'Populations and Races', and this finale suggests the importance that Foucault attached to racialism within the general field of what he called 'biopower' within his history of sexuality. Biopower has not been among those concepts that have been most widely developed by Foucault's commentators; but then there has been a distinct silence on the question of race in Foucault. It is notable that in *The History of Sexuality* following the chapter on Method in which power is first defined, biopower describes one of the two great regulating techniques of the politics of sex. According to Foucault, its power involves the forms of control carried out in the name of the race, for the welfare of the species, for the survival of the population. Racism, for Foucault, is not a phenomenon in western society that can be safely compartmentalized as an aberration but constitutes an expansive part of the general production of sexuality. He describes it as operating in two phases: first of all, in the form of eugenics, it is directed towards the survival of class supremacy, and then it is deployed with respect to the control, ordering and supervision of the exploited classes. Foucault's analysis of the dynamics of this double function is both unusual and significant in its emphasis on the links between racism, sexuality and class. He concludes that 'sexuality is originally, historically bourgeois ... in its successive shifts and transpositions, it induces specific class effects'.[16] By inference, the same must be true of racialism.

The key ideological term that held class, sexuality and race together was that of blood. Foucault points to the significance of the way in which blood functions in a traditional society, based on systems of filiation and dynastic alliance, as 'an important element in the mechanisms of power, its manifestations, and its rituals'. In a society of blood, says Foucault,

16. Michel Foucault, *The History of Sexuality*, p127. Further references will be cited in the text.

power spoke *through* blood: the honour of war, the fear of famine, the triumph of death, the sovereign with his sword, executioners, and torturers; *blood was a reality with a symbolic function* (147).

This means of caste distinction was appropriated by the bourgeoisie when it laid claim to the vitality of its own body: 'the bourgeoisie's "blood" was its sex' (124). By the twentieth century, Foucault argues, this society of sanguinity has given way to one of sexuality, where the mechanisms of power are addressed to the body, to its health, to its progeny, to what causes it to proliferate or degenerate, to the vitality of the social body and the race. Modernity has comprised the substitution of sex for blood, not as a new organizing principle but rather because the new technologies and procedures of power 'were what caused our societies to go from *a symbolics of blood* to *an analytics of sexuality*' (148).

Although this is a late work of Foucault's, a consistent tendency to construct history through the substitution of one epistemic structure by another remains apparent. At the same time, he does not here suggest the precision of an epistemological break but allows for haunting symbolic overlappings in the transition from one regime to another. It is moreover, according to Foucault these overlappings of blood and sex that culminate in racism:

> Beginning in the second half of the nineteenth century, the thematics of blood was sometimes called on to lend its entire historical weight toward revitalizing the type of political power that was exercised through the devices of sexuality. Racism took shape at this point (racism in its modern, 'biologizing', statist form): it was then that a whole politics of settlement, family, marriage, education, social hierarchization, and property, accompanied by a long series of permanent interventions at the level of the body, conduct, and everyday life, received their colour and their justification from the mythical concern with protecting the purity of the blood and ensuring the triumph of the race.

Foucault is arguing that the technologies of power that disciplined the body through the dimension of sexuality, were repeated and reinforced through the thematics of blood which, in a racist dimension, meant that the social as well as the individual body became amenable to stringent control.

> Nazism was doubtless the most cunning and the most naive (and the former because of the latter) combination of the fantasies of blood and the paroxysms of a disciplinary power. A eugenic ordering of society, with all that implied in the way of extension and intensification of micro-powers, in the guise of an unrestricted state control, was accompanied by the oneiric exaltation of a superior blood.... (149-50)

For Foucault, the appearance of blood-consciousness in the second-half of the nineteenth century mediates the transition between the societies of sanguinity and of sexuality. It is not clear from his account whether racism was an effect of such mediation or its cause. The analysis is restricted to the ways in which racism, in its eugenicist form, encouraged and enabled the state to intervene and control the body through the techniques developed for the production of sexuality.

What is so effective is that Foucault does not analyse the link between racism and sexuality in terms of the individual desiring subject. Rather he shows how they were always linked at the level of the technology of the discipline. Foucault's dating of the appearance of blood in its most racist penumbra to the mid-nineteenth century is accurate: it is clearly central to Gobineau's *Essay on the Inequality of Races* of 1853-5, which cleverly fuses the idea of an aristocratic bloodline of an ancient family with the shared blood of the larger language 'family' of the Aryan.[17] Foucault's emphasis on the deployment of the mechanisms of power means that he says little about how racialism succeeded by strategies that always also carried a 'common sense' popular attraction, their appearance of reasonableness masking a deeper irrationality. So, for example, the appeal of the argument about maintaining racial purity through 'blood' was increased by the popular acceptance in the nineteenth century of the idea of *pangenesis*, that is that 'each part of the body contributed a fraction of itself to the sperm by way of the blood'. In the context of nineteenth-century scientific work on heredity – Galton, Darwin, Spencer – sperm came to be identified with blood. In 1872, in *Our Children*, the American sex expert, Dr Augustus Gardner, argued that sperm was 'the concentrated powers of man's perfected being.... Sperm is the purest extract of blood ... *totus homo semen est*'.[18] Semen becomes the essence of blood and of man, so that controlling the patriarchal dissemination of sperm becomes the literal means of preserving the purity of the blood.

Despite the fact that the volume on 'Populations and Races' was never to appear, it is possible to see that Foucault's account of power is particularly suited to the analysis of racism and racialism. Many commentators have complained about the lack of scope for traditional forms of political resistance in Foucault's theory of power. But in relation to the dynamic alliance of race with blood, his account of power as productive seems singularly appropriate:

> What gives power its hold, what makes it accepted, is quite simply the fact that it does not weigh like a force, which says no, but that it runs through, and produces, things, it induces pleasures, it forms knowledge, it produces discourses; it must be considered as a productive network which runs through the entire social body much more than as a negative instance whose function is repression.[19]

Racism and racialism must be one of the best – or the worst – examples of the silent and stealthy operation of this Foucaldian form of power/knowledge.

17. For further discussion of Gobineau, see my *Colonial Desire: Hybridity in Theory, Culture, and Race*, Routledge, London 1995, pp99-116.

18. See G.J. Barker-Benfield, 'The Spermatic Economy: A Nineteenth-Century View of Sexuality', in Michael Gordon, (ed.), *The American Family in Social-Historical Perspective*, 2nd ed., St Martin's Press, New York 1978, pp377-8.

19. Michel Foucault, *Power, Truth, Strategy*, Meaghan Morris and Paul Patton (eds), Feral Publications, Sydney 1979, pp35-6.

A NEW IMAGE OF THOUGHT

John Marks

1. See Michel
Foucault, *The
Archaeology of
Knowledge*, trans. by
A.M. Sheridan,
Tavistock, London
1972 and Michel
Foucault, *Discipline and
Punish: The Birth of the
Prison*, trans. by A.M.
Sheridan, Penguin,
Harmondsworth 1977.

2. See Gilles Deleuze
and Félix Guattari,
What is Philosophy?,
trans. Graham
Burchell and Hugh
Tomlinson, Verso,
London 1994, p5:
'That is, philosophy is
not a simple art of
forming, inventing or
fabricating concepts,
because concepts are
not necessarily forms,
discoveries, or
products. More
rigorously, philosophy
is the discipline that
involves *creating*
concepts.'

The importance of 'spatial' themes in the work of Michel Foucault cannot be denied. To take just two well-known examples, Foucault provides a detailed exposition of the concept of an 'archaeology' of knowledge. He also uses Bentham's plan for the Panopticon as the 'diagram' – a sort of potential architecture – of the emerging disciplinary society of the nineteenth century.[1] In order to analyse in any detail the importance of this form of thinking it is essential to place Foucault's work alongside that of his contemporary Gilles Deleuze, since Foucault and Deleuze enjoyed a prolonged mutual influence and exchange of ideas, beginning in the early 1960s. This influence is of a particular kind. It functions as an exchange of concepts which are taken up and developed without losing their initial force. Gilles Deleuze has recently emphasised that he considers his own task as a philosopher to be the production of concepts.[2] In keeping with Nietzsche's metaphor of the philosopher as an arrow, a concept is launched in the hope that another thinker will pick it up and relaunch it in turn. The mutual influence of Deleuze and Foucault provides an example of this use of concepts which repays detailed examination. In terms of 'space' and 'spatial thinking' Foucault, arguably under the influence of concepts taken from Deleuze, does not simply seek to reassert the privileges of space against the 'temporal' conception of a linear, evolutionary historical approach. (Notwithstanding the fact that Foucault occasionally appeared to be defending precisely such an opposition.) It is rather the case that, through his extensive use of spatial metaphors, he seeks to introduce a non-Euclidean concept of space into social theory which will help to break down the artificial opposition between space and time.

As well as placing Foucault's work alongside that of Deleuze, the general move towards a more complex conception of space in modern theoretical work should be acknowledged. Henri Lefebvre claims that the twentieth century sees a general paradigm shift away from the Euclidean concept of space. Although it is undeniably part of Lefebvre's critical agenda to reject Foucault's archaeological project as neglecting *social* space in favour of *mental* space, he provides an introduction to the place of space in philosophy and social theory which helps to contextualise the importance of spatial themes in contemporary philosophy and social theory. Lefebvre claims that the Euclidean conception of space was 'shattered' at the beginning of the twentieth century. This Euclidean or 'perspectivist' space had previously informed much of western thought and social practice, from daily discourse through art, philosophy and music: 'Euclidean and perspectivist space have disappeared as systems of reference, along with other former "commonplaces" such as the town, history, paternity, the tonal system in music, traditional morality and so forth.'[3] Pamela Major-Poetzl, in a relatively early study of Foucault's work, seeks to find analogies between Foucault's work and the way in which modern physics radically undermines the mechanical view of the physical world which was prevalent at the end of the nineteenth century. Major-Poetzl emphasises that Einstein's non-Euclidean geometry means that the separation of space and time is seen as artificial. It is now necessary to recognise a new category of 'space-time'. Space can no longer be regarded as a homogeneous void, but as a plurality of 'local geometries'.[4] The advantage of this new approach to space for Foucault and Deleuze is that it allows for a more nuanced consideration of time. When viewed in tandem, the work of Deleuze and Foucault moves in the direction of the concept of a 'space-time' dimension which is useful for philosophical work. This 'new' philosophical dimension contributes to the project of a 'new image of thought', one which attempts to go beyond models of thought based on representation and identity. It will be shown later that the concept of the *shape* in Deleuze's later work might be seen as a conceptual expression of the space-time dimension.

Before looking at the various ways in which Foucault and Deleuze have provided a set of suggestions towards a spatial method of thinking, it is necessary to address what at first sight appears to be a glaring contradiction between the two thinkers which would apparently preclude them reaching any agreement on the matter. This apparent contradiction centres on the interpretation of Bergson and his influence. On several occasions in the 1960s Foucault explicitly rejects what he sees as Bergson's unwarranted concentration on time in favour of space, and in turn seeks to reverse this preference. For example, in a widely-quoted interview on the 'geographical' themes in his work Foucault claims that the use of temporal metaphors to analyse transformations in discourse is inevitably linked to the model of individual consciousness. Space, on the other hand, enables him to look at these transformations in terms of power. He goes on to accuse Bergson of instituting this devaluation of space: 'A critique could be carried out of this devaluation of space that has prevailed for generations. Did it start with Bergson, or before? Space was treated as the dead, the fixed, the undialectical, the immobile. Time, on the contrary, was richness, fecundity, life, dialectic.'[5] Deleuze, on the other hand, published a book-length study of Bergson in 1966, in which he develops Bergson's critique of the overly spatialising tendency of the intellect, in order to create a form of thinking which takes account of the fact of becoming.[6] Deleuze goes on to employ this principle of being as becoming in the development of his own concepts of difference and repetition. He also returns, at length, to Bergson in his two works on cinema from the 1980s.[7] However, despite these apparent differences, it will be argued that Foucault and Deleuze in fact work along strikingly similar lines with regard to the idea of space, moving towards a concept of space-time.

Foucault tends to privilege spatial metaphors in much of his earlier work. As seen earlier, he claims that this spatial dimension offers him a way of analysing

3. Henri Lefebvre, *The Production of Space*, trans. by Donald Nicholson-Smith, Basil Blackwell, Oxford 1991, p25.

4. Pamela Major-Poetzl, *Michel Foucault's Archaeology of Western Culture: Toward a New Science of History*, Harvester, Brighton 1983, pp67-68.

5. Michel Foucault, 'Questions on Geography,' trans. by Colin Gordon, in *Power/Knowledge: Selected Interviews and Other Writings, 1972-77*, Colin Gordon (ed.), Harvester, Brighton 1980, p70. See also Michel Foucault, 'Of Other Spaces', translated by Jay Miskowiec, *Diacritics*, Spring, 1986, pp22-27. See also Michel Foucault, *The Birth of the Clinic*, trans. by A.M. Sheridan, Tavistock, London 1973, p170.

6. Gilles Deleuze, *Bergsonism*, trans. of *Le Bergsonisme* (1966) by Hugh Tomlinson and Barbara Habberjam, Zone Books, New York 1988.

7. Gilles Deleuze,
*Cinema 1: The
Movement-Image*, trans.
by Hugh Tomlinson
and Barbara
Habberjam, Athlone
Press, London 1986;
*Cinema 2: The Time-
Image*, trans. by Hugh
Tomlinson and
Barbara Habberjam,
Athlone Press,
London 1989.

8. Michel Foucault,
*The Archaeology of
Knowledge*, p17.

transformations in discourse without recourse to the model of individual consciousness. The final comments from the introduction to Foucault's *The Archaeology of Knowledge* develop this spatial metaphor with reference to Foucault's own work. He imagines a perplexed reader trying to track him down, lying in wait, having ventured into the labyrinth that Foucault has created for himself. He warns such a reader that he will never be where he is expected to be, but rather watching, laughing from another place.[8] In some ways, this remains Foucault's definitive statement on space. The courageous and inventive thinker needs to privilege space over time, at least when time means the revelation of a fixed identity, or the simple repetition of such a comforting identity. Rather than being 'fixed', 'undialectical', and 'immobile', Foucault seeks to emphasise the dynamic, fragmentary potential of space. However, as noted above, it is essential to understand that this undoubtedly spatial imagination does not represent an absolute rejection of time in favour of space. For example, in the opening pages of *The Archaeology of Knowledge* Foucault indirectly acknowledges the influences of the *Annales* school, and Fernand Braudel in particular. Braudel looks at temporal changes in new, arguably spatial terms. He suggests a layered system with three main varieties of historical time; a geographical time of slow cyclic regularities, a social time which relates to shifts in economic and social structures, and an 'individual' time of transitory everyday events. Braudel proposes an undeniably 'spatial' distinction between the small 'explosions' of *l'histoire événementielle* and the structure of the *longue durée*:

> In any case, it is in relation to these expanses of slow-moving history that the whole of history is to be rethought, as if on the basis of an infrastructure. All the stages, all the thousands of stages, all the thousand explosions of historical time can be understood on the basis of these depths. This semistillness. Everything gravitates around it.[9]

9. Fernand Braudel,
On History, trans. by
Sarah Matthews,
Weidenfeld and
Nicolson, London
1980, p33.

In his awareness of new historical thinking Foucault uses *The Archaeology of Knowledge* to indicate possibilities for a properly *material* approach to historical work on discourse. Braudel's interest in the 'layering' of different levels and rhythms of time – in other words, dealing with time as a series of strata – reflects this desire for an increasingly material history. In more abstract terms, Foucault's spatial metaphors are a strategy employed in order to escape into a labyrinth which helps him to undermine the concepts of identity and representation. Space is useful because there is always another space, another place, any space, several spaces. Some recent work which refers to Foucault's preoccupation with space has concentrated on the productive notion of *heterotopia*. For example, Edward Soja defines the figure of heterotopia as a heterogeneous and relational space, something akin to what 'Lefebvre would describe as *l'espace vécu*, actually lived and socially created spatiality, concrete and abstract at the same time, the habtius of social practices.'[10] This description is undoubtedly valid, but Foucault's concept of social space also contains a

10. Edward Soja,
*Postmodern Geographies:
The Reassertion of Space
in Critical Social Theory*,
Verso, London 1989,
p18.

broadly spatial approach to *thought*. Rather than being the product of the individual *cogito* – although Foucault does seem to allow for the possibility of creative individual thought – thought itself is rare and diffuse. Thought has a material dimension and can, for example, exist within institutions. Foucault, then, suggests a concept of *thought* as heterotopia. This concept is crucial to his own work, and is taken up in various ways by Gilles Deleuze. In *Difference and Repetition* Deleuze calls for a new, non-representational image of thought. Thought must escape from the images which imprison it and the philosopher, like Foucault, must become 'a larval subject of his own system'.[11] Thought, as writers such as Borges and Lewis Carroll show, is inextricably linked to chaos and flux, and the 'new image' of thought must be able to acknowledge the 'simultaneity and contemporaneity of all the divergent series'.[12] In summary then, as well as what might be called 'social' heterotopias Foucault also presents heterotopia as an image of thought, or rather of thought which seeks to escape the image of recognition.

Foucault's concept of heterotopia is dealt with at length in a conference paper originally delivered in 1967, entitled 'Of Other Spaces'.[13] Foucault preferred for a long time not to publish this paper, and a French version did not appear until 1984. It is in some ways easy to see why Foucault delayed publication. Rather than being a coherently argued piece, he presents here a sort of work-in-progress, a provocative set of ideas and suggestions for further research. In simple terms Foucault argues that the nineteenth century was preoccupied with the idea of history, and more precisely the menacing possibility of entropy. He suggests that we live now in another era, that of space; an era characterised by simultaneity, juxtaposition and dispersal. Throughout the paper, it is sometimes difficult to distinguish between abstract and concrete space, and theoretically, the paper refers to disparate sources. Foucault briefly appears to endorse the methods of structuralism, but also draws on Bachelard's work on social and scientific poetics. As Edward Soja has noted, Foucault proposes on one level a history of *external* spaces. That is to say, the real social spaces which surround us. These are heterotopias. Foucault suggests that such heterotopias – sites which juxtapose in a single real social 'place' several spaces – have existed throughout history. However, he also implies that contemporary spatiality, with its concentration on 'emplacement' – a figure characterised by relations between non-totalisable elements – is particularly and definitively heterotopic. Undoubtedly, the notion of heterotopia has proved useful for those considering real social spaces/places and the problems of identity, and Foucault himself obviously developed the notion of heterotopia in his work on the prison. The prison is a defined space or site which brings together heterogeneous discourses – punishment, reform, education – along with functions of surveillance and control, which are in turn juxtaposed with related but separate functions of control in hospital and schools. In 'Of Other Spaces' Foucault presents a series of 'real' heterotopias, splitting them into two types. There are heterotopias of crisis, spaces of transition or tension which are outside of society, such as the school in the nineteenth century and military

11. Gilles Deleuze, *Difference and Repetition*, trans. by Paul Patton, Athlone Press, London 1994, p119.

12. *Ibid.*, p124.

13. Michel Foucault 'Of Other Spaces'. This paper was originally delivered in 1967 and published as 'Des Espaces autres,' *Architecture-Mouvement-Continuité*, October, 1984, pp46-49.

service. Such a space is a sort of transitory site, a space which is quite literally set aside, in the development of the young person. According to Foucault, the dominant form of heterotopia in contemporary society is the heterotopia which refers to deviation. He refers as examples to prisons, psychiatric clinics and retirement homes.

However, in order to understand the Foucaldian/Deleuzian move towards space-time as a new image of thought attention must be directed to a series of more abstract heterotopic spatialities, namely the labyrinth, the mirror and the theatre. The structuralist notion of 'emplacement' finds its fullest expression in the form of the trope of dispersal in *The Archaeology of Knowledge*, published shortly after 'Of Other Spaces' originally appeared. Around this time, Foucault also develops the image of thought as a theatrical performance. Archaeology is designed to describe events in thought and, as with a theatrical performance, these events are dispersed and multiple, like the different scenes which punctuate the darkness of the stage, thus robbing thought of a comforting continuity and identity. In 'Of Other Spaces' Foucault introduces another image which seeks to interrogate identity when he talks of the 'mixed experience' which is somewhere between utopia and heterotopia. This experience is represented by the mirror. The mirror is a utopian space, since Foucault can see himself in an unreal, virtual space. However, the mirror is also a heterotopian space, in that it represents another space which reminds him of his own 'absence'.[14] The mirror, therefore, functions as a slightly different sort of heterotopia to the social heterotopias that Foucault also sets out in his paper. It creates a non-totalised relation between real and unreal space. As such, it functions as a presentation of thought, in much the same way as the labyrinth in Foucault's neglected study of Raymond Roussel.[15] He is actually sketching out a project for a spatial consideration of thought. In the same way, in *Difference and Repetition*, Gilles Deleuze notes the inevitable links between structuralism and a new kind of theatre which problematises identity. This is a theatre of problems rather than solutions:

> [...] a theatre of multiplicities opposed in every respect to the theatre of representation, which leaves intact neither the identity of the thing represented, nor author, nor spectator, nor character, nor representation which, through the vicissitudes of the play, can become the object of a production of knowledge or final recognition. Instead, a theatre of problems and always open questions [...].[16]

It is now necessary to look in more detail at the relationship between Foucault's work and that of Deleuze. As mentioned above, it is important to note that two thinkers whose work has been so intimately linked should take as their starting point on the question of space superficially opposed positions. To summarise briefly, Deleuze claims as one of his inspirations the work of Bergson, who rejected what he saw as the *spatialisation* of metaphysical thought. A 'spatial' view of memory sees it as a series of points spread out across a

14. *Ibid.*, p24 (47).

15. See Michel Foucault, *Death and the Labyrinth: The World of Raymond Roussel*, trans. by Charles Ruas, Athlone Press, London 1987.

16. Gilles Deleuze, *Difference and Repetition*, p192.

continuum, whereas Bergson sees memory as a fullness in which all moments co-exist with varying degrees of relaxation or contraction. Spatialised metaphysical thought also ignores the potential of *becoming* in being. Foucault, on the other hand, complains that space has been neglected as an analytical tool, asking whether this disqualification of space began with Bergson. However, these starting points are only superficially different. Both Foucault and Deleuze are concerned with the simultaneity and heterogeneity of elements within a system, together with a form of description which will both avoid the recognition of universals and allow for the indication of that which is new in thought. Both use spatial metaphors to achieve this end, and both work towards a new concept of 'space-time'. It should of course be noted that even Bergson's rejection of a certain spatial tendency in thought leads him in many ways to a rather different 'spatial' consideration of memory.

It was suggested above that, rather than thinking of Deleuze and Foucault as primarily spatial thinkers, it is perhaps better to consider them as involved in the creation of *shapes*. Shapes in this sense might be considered as undetermined and dynamic forms of space, or perhaps even sketches of space-time. Deleuze's recent work on cinema represents one of the most interesting attempts to investigate the production of thought in terms of spaces and shapes.[17] For Deleuze, cinema is not exactly a form of philosophy, but it is capable of producing its own concepts, and is in this way another material impetus to thought. One of the major points to emerge from Deleuze's two books on cinema, *The Movement-Image* and *The Time Image*, is the post-war move away from the 'sensory-motor situations' of the old realism, whereby characters reacted in a largely rational manner to the events and situations in which they found themselves. The viewer was encouraged to participate in this sensory-motor image by identification with the characters. The move away from a cinema dominated by the movement-image calls for a new spatial flexibility in film. Deleuze describes one component of this new set of spaces as the 'any-space-whatever' (*espace quelconque*). This is a space which has lost its homogeneity. It is a virtual space, 'grasped as pure locus of the possible', whose parts can be linked in an infinite number of ways. In short, it is a heterotopic, a heterogeneous space.[18] The any-space-whatever is characteristic of post-war neo-realism. In the preface to the English edition of *The Time-Image*, Deleuze describes these spaces, in which characters no longer react but rather record and observe.

> The fact is that, in Europe, the post-war period has greatly increased the situations which we no longer know how to react to, in spaces which we no longer know how to describe. These are 'any spaces whatever', deserted but inhabited, disused warehouses, waste ground, cities in the course of demolition or reconstruction. And in these any-spaces-whatever a new race of characters was stirring, a kind of mutant: they saw rather than acted, they were seers.[19]

17. See Marie-Claire Ropars-Wuilleumier, 'The Cinema, Reader of Gilles Deleuze,' in Constantin V. Boundas and Dorothea Olkowski, (eds), *Gilles Deleuze and the Theatre of Philosophy*, Routledge, London 1994, pp255-261. Ropars-Wuilleumier sees the main figure of Deleuze's analysis of time as 'the crystal where time scintillates,' which posits a theory of 'space-time' (p260).

18. Gilles Deleuze, *Cinema 1*, p109.

19. Gilles Deleuze, *Cinema 2*, 'Preface to the English Edition,' pxi.

Deleuze is interested in these spaces because they are symptomatic of cinema's experiments with new relationships between time and space. Returning to Edward Soja's *Postmodern Geographies*, he points out that Foucault uses structuralism in order to think of time as a series of juxtaposed and simultaneous elements, what Soja calls a 'synchronic "configuration" '.[20] In the same way, Deleuze sees post-war cinema's experiments with new spaces as experiments with time and thought in new configurations of simultaneity. In this cinema, particularly in the Italian neo-realism of Rosselini and Ozu's later films, time is no longer subordinated to movement. We are now presented with ' "a little time in the pure state" '. The new time image is 'a coexistence of distinct durations, or of levels of duration; a single event can belong to several levels: the sheets of past co-exist in a non-chronological order.'[21] That is to say, an image of space-time. Deleuze illustrates the notion of 'shape' in relation to thought in *Cinema 2: The Time-Image*. The chapter entitled 'The powers of the false' introduces the concept of 'crystalline narration'. This is opposed to an earlier, relatively 'truthful' type of narration in which characters react to specific situations, or act in such a way as to disclose the situation; the narration of 'sensory-motor schemata' discussed above. The type of space that film adopts when dealing with sensory-motor situations is 'hodological' or Euclidean, 'which is defined by a field of forces, oppositions and tensions between these forces, resolutions of these tensions according to the distribution of goals, obstacles, means, detours.'[22] The space of crystalline narration, on the other hand, is non-Euclidean. The loss of sensory-motor connections has various consequences for film. Bresson uses Riemanian spaces in which the connection of parts is a variable principle, whereas the films of Ozu and Antonioni suggest 'empty or amorphous' spaces. In general terms, these new filmic spaces are actually ways of presenting time directly. Film can now approach the problem of non-chronological time. In this way, crystalline narration is conscious of the indiscernibility of the true and the false. Freed from the constraints of chronological time it can describe the multiplicity of time. The concept of the 'shape', therefore, might be seen as the spatial presentation of time as becoming; a new image of space-time. Truth, instead of what is recognised and identified as such, is now created through shapes:

> Only the creative artist takes the power of the false to a degree which is realized, not in form, but in transformation. There is no longer either truth or appearance. There is no longer either invariable form or variable point of view on to a form. There is a point of view which belongs so much to the thing that the thing is constantly being transformed in a becoming identical to point of view. Metamorphosis of the true. What the artist is, is *creator of truth*, because truth is not to be achieved, formed, or reproduced; it has to be created. There is no other truth than the creation of the New: creativity, emergence, what Melville called 'shape' in contrast to 'form'. Art is the continual production of *shapes*, reliefs and projections.[23]

20. Edward Soja, *Postmodern Geographies*, p18.

21. Gilles Deleuze, *Cinema 2*, 'Preface to the English Edition', p.xii

22. Deleuze, *Cinema 2*, pp127-128.

23. Deleuze, *Cinema 2*, pp146-147.

In a recent article for *Screen* Laura U. Marks helps to underline the way in which Deleuze's work develops themes from Foucault in arguing convincingly that Deleuze's use of Bergson's work on image, memory and duration furnishes film theory with an 'archaeological' approach.[24] Marks shows how 'experimental diasporan cinema' such as Atom Egoyan's recent *Calendar* (1993) allows the viewer to 'dig between the strata' of public images and private memories, and holds the viewer 'in a series of evocative contemplations, where exploration is spatial more than temporal.'[25] As Marks points out, this capacity of film to provide a spatial consideration of time is crucial for Deleuze. It represents the possibility for film, in terms of its potential to explore consciousness, to replicate philosophy's revolutionary move away from an image of thought according to which time is subordinated to movement. In short, Deleuze sees a general tendency in French cinema which strives towards this idea of 'time as simultaneism and simultaneity'.[26]

Deleuze acknowledges the usefulness of Foucault's concept of archaeology in the chapter entitled 'The components of the the image' in *Cinema 2: The Time-Image*. Here, Deleuze examines the move from silent film to the 'talkie', and considers the way in which modern cinema has reacted to the consequences of this shift. Much of the chapter relies to a large part upon the general distinction that Deleuze draws between the visible and the articulable in Foucault's work.[27] In his work on cinema, Deleuze considers this distinction to be characteristic of modern film. The element of sound in film becomes separated from the image, allowing film to explore the archaeological dimensions of time. The image can now bring the viewer into contact with neglected layers of time. These 'lacunary layers' are in fact the 'any-space-whatevers' which are characteristic of modern cinema.[28] The vocation of film is potentially archaeological since, like Foucault's *The Archaeology of Knowledge*, it liberates history from the concept of the grand narrative of great individuals and important events. Foucault's concept of archaeology is a methodological consideration of the theme of epistemic shifts and ruptures which was outlined in *The Order of Things*,[29] and modern cinema appears to have adopted this approach to history:

> [...] everywhere a struggle marking the itinerary of a world which emerges from one historical moment to enter into another, the difficult birth of a new world, under the double forceps of words and things, speech-act and stratified space. It is a conception of history which simultaneously calls up the comic and the dramatic, the extraordinary and the everyday: new types of speech-act and new structurations of space. An 'archaeological' conception almost in Michel Foucault's sense.[30]

Deleuze reads this archaeological approach into the method of Godard, and in this way shows how it is linked to his own interest in a form of empiricism. Empiricism in this sense would entail an emphasis on juxtaposition and immanence rather than a discursive or ideological approach to philosophy

24. Laura U. Marks, 'A Deleuzian Politics of Hybrid Cinema,' *Screen*, Autumn, 1994, pp244-264.

25. *Ibid.*, p251-252.

26. Gilles Deleuze, *Cinema 1*, p46.

27. For a detailed discussion of this distinction see Gilles Deleuze, *Foucault*, trans. and edited by Seán Hand, University of Minnesota Press, Minneapolis 1988, particularly pp47-69.

28. Gilles Deleuze, *Cinema 2*, pp243-244.

29. Michel Foucault, *The Order of Things: An Archaeology of the Human Sciences*, anonymous translation, Tavistock, London 1970.

30. Gilles Deleuze, *Cinema 2*, p248.

31. See Gilles
Deleuze, *Pourparlers,
1972-1990*, Minuit,
Paris 1990, pp55-66.

and social theory. In an interview on Godard's documentary series *Six fois deux*, Deleuze outlines what he considers to be Godard's non-dialectical method.[31] In place of the verb *est* Godard employs the conjunction *et*. He is in this way concerned with multiplicity and diversity rather than questions of existence or attribution. To illustrate this diversity Deleuze uses the example of factory gates, which become different depending upon whether one is entering or leaving through them, or prevented by unemployment from doing either. Similarly, Godard seeks to prise apart the complicity of words and things. It would be wrong to assume that Deleuze proposes this 'empirical' approach as a straightforward method of ideological critique. It is rather a method for the proliferation of meaning by opening up the gap between words and things.

To summarise the import of Deleuze's work on cinema for an understanding of Foucault's spatial themes, it can be seen that both use space to describe or present the arguably temporal process of becoming. Foucault locates the 'becoming' of his own thought in the elusive non-place between the mirror and the spectator. In a similar way, post-war cinema, as read by Deleuze, locates contemporary cinematic thought in the any-space-whatever which gives access to 'a little time in its pure state'. Thought is diffuse and rare, and as such it exists in the gaps between words and things and between strata. Similarly, the space-time complexes that Foucault and Deleuze describe function as shapes which suggest what is genuinely new in the domain of thought.

Finally, it is necessary to look briefly at Deleuze's assessment of Foucault's work on forms of social theory in the 1970s. Together, Foucault and Deleuze propose a thoroughly material approach to thought, and this is, of course, the reason that Foucault finds spatial images and metaphors so useful in his social histories. For one thing, spatial descriptions avoid the problems of positing universals. For Deleuze likewise, thought is the product, not of recognition, but of an encounter. Thought is the result of a shock, in that something in the world forces us to think. It is the creation of a problem, rather than the recognition of a solution. We think only rarely, and Deleuze presents thought as a sort of crisis or collapse. In opposition to the Kantian model of the ordered courtroom, thought must engender its own crisis in order to think anything new. In this way, Deleuze introduces a set of spatial metaphors which emphasise the dynamic element of Foucault's initial experiments with the shape of thought. Spatial figures also provide a way of escaping from the model of ideology and repression. Deleuze speaks of the fold, the crack and the line of flight as impersonal spaces of fracture and resistance in contemporary power structures. The lines of power, knowledge and force which Deleuze sees as forming the architecture or social apparatus ('dispositif') of power are lines of becoming.[32]

32. See Gilles
Deleuze, 'What is a
dispositif?' in *Michel
Foucault Philosopher*,
trans. from French
and German by
Timothy J.
Armstrong, Harvester
Wheatsheaf, London
1992, pp159-168.

33. Gilles Deleuze,
Foucault. See note 27.

Deleuze provides a detailed discussion of spatial themes in his book on Foucault.[33] In particular, he takes up the question of the distinction between the visible and the articulable. According to Deleuze's assessment, this distinction is introduced in the form of the discursive/non-discursive duality in *The Archaeology of Knowledge*, but is given a more subtle expression in *Discipline and Punish.* Here, it is as if Foucault breaks down the relatively unwieldy discursive and non-discursive formations and reconstitutes his spatial images of power in a segmentary, serial form. In *Discipline and Punish*, Foucault proposes a form of power which is no longer located in a privileged place, such as the State, and which 'takes whatever is still pyramidal in the Marxist image and replaces it with a strict immanence where centres of power and disciplinary techniques form multiple segments.'[34] The other development that interests Deleuze in *Discipline and Punish* is the notion of the 'diagram'. The prison as a building and as an institution is a non-discursive formation which functions according to formalised discursive functions such as punishment, care and training. However, Deleuze suggests that the diagram – the example here being the generalised network of Panopticism – proposes a more open-ended cartography of power. The abstract diagram of Panopticism 'is always concerned with unformed and unorganized matter and unformalized, unfinalized functions, the two variables being indissolubly linked.'[35] Every society has a diagram which is a method for creating a social 'space-time'. It is in a constantly fluid state, and yet on one level expresses the image of thought that prevails in a given society. The Greek city, for example, enjoys a complementarity with Euclidean geometry in its organisation of space, time and power, and with the Greek conception of philosophy as the confrontation of opinions amongst a society of friends.[36] This Euclidean image of thought serves as the axiomatic system of the Greek city. According to Deleuze, classical philosophy took on the unfortunate role of justifying an image of thought which depended upon universals such as the Church and the State. Similarly, both Deleuze and Foucault argue that the contemporary human sciences such as psychoanalysis perform an equally unfortunate role in attempting to provide axioms for modern apparatuses of power.

In conclusion, it can be seen that the 'informal' diagram, as Deleuze calls it, is also linked to the absent place that has been shown to haunt Foucault's work. Drawing on his work on Bergson, Deleuze shows that the informal diagram is a virtual multiplicity which can fully express the divergence and differentiation of the visible and the articulable only when it is realised in concrete terms:

> Between the visible and the articulable a gap or disjunction opens up, but this disjunction of forms is the place – or 'non-place', as Foucault puts it – where the informal diagram is swallowed up and becomes embodied instead in two different directions that are necessarily divergent and irreducible. The concrete assemblages are therefore opened by a crack that determines how the abstract machine performs.[37]

The diagram is different from the structure, in that it refers to a system in disequilibrium rather than a closed system of equivalence and exchange. Both Deleuze and Foucault seek to create such 'open' systems for their own images of thought which they employ critically and descriptively. This image is best thought of as that of the problem or the problematisation. Deleuze deals with

34. Gilles Deleuze, *Foucault*, p27.

35. *Ibid*, p34.

36. See Gilles Deleuze and Félix Guattari, *What is Philosophy?*, p99, p145.

37. Gilles Deleuze, *Foucault*, p38.

the importance of the problem in his study of Bergson, and in particular Bergson's concept of intuition. Bergson considers intuition to be a willed act of self-consciousness. Intuition is precisely the attempt to overturn the dominant image of thought, in that it is designed to resist the tendency of the intellect towards artificial closure. That is to say, its tendency to spatialise and to quantify. In its 'problematising' function, intuition would open the intellect to the heterogeneous nature of reality. Far too often, the intellect imposes an artificial closure upon 'badly analysed composites'.[38] Following Bergson, Deleuze rejects the idea that the question of truth is concerned only with solutions. Such 'solutions' are too reductive, reflecting the dominant bureaucratic concerns of social organisation. Problems and their ready-made solutions reduce the question of truth to the level of school homework. Although the problematising method that Deleuze develops from Bergson is in one way explicitly anti-spatial its function is to introduce a new, differentiated *shape* or image of thought. Likewise, Foucault considers 'problematisation' as a method of historical analysis. The historian of thought must understand that a particular set of difficulties will elicit several responses at any one time. The task for the historian of thought would therefore be 'to rediscover at the root of these diverse solutions the general form of problematization that has made them possible'.[39] Thought must be seen in terms of non-totalisable problematisations rather than solutions. A problematisation is an open or, as Deleuze would have it, an 'a-centred' system. In his desire to write something different, to use thought as a means of escaping the poverty of identity, Foucault has left a set of concepts which aspire to an ethic of problematisation.

38. Gilles Deleuze, *Bergsonism*, p28.

39. Michel Foucault, 'Polemics, Politics, and Problematizations: An Interview', in Paul Rabinow (ed), *The Foucault Reader*, Penguin, Harmondsworth 1984, p389.

AFTER GRIEF?
WHAT KINDS OF INHUMAN SELVES?

Wendy Wheeler

I THE INHUMAN

In his Introduction to the collection of essays and lectures gathered together in the volume entitled *The Inhuman*, Jean-François Lyotard asks 'what if human beings, in humanism's sense, were in the process of, constrained into, becoming inhuman (that's the first part)? And (the second part), what if what is "proper" to humankind were to be inhabited by the inhuman?'.[1] What Lyotard has in mind are two senses of inhuman. Firstly, he means the inhuman-ness of techno-scientific complexification and the ways in which its 'metaphysical' language is used to legitimate political and/or socio-economic choices. Lyotard calls this metaphysical logic 'development'. Secondly, he means something raw and savage, something excessive in relation to what we usually and carelessly think of as human, but which actually – in its resistances to the 'human' and in the pain, terror and joy by which it is in the main constrained to *be* 'human' – constitutes precisely the human-ness of human beings. Elsewhere, Lyotard has referred to this as the sublime.[2]

> We should ... remember that if the name of human can and must oscillate between native indetermination and instituted or self-instituting reason, it is the same for the name of inhuman. All education is inhuman because it does not happen without constraint and terror; I mean the least controlled, the least pedagogical terror, the one Freud calls castration and which makes him say, in relation to the 'good way' of bringing up children, that in any case it will be bad (close in this to Kantian melancholy). And conversely, everything in the instituted which, in the event, can cut deep with distress and indetermination is so threatening that the reasonable mind cannot fail to fear in it, and rightly, an inhuman power of deregulation.[3]

In this article, I want to bring together two kinds of arguments about the contemporary – one concerning postmodern nostalgia (a form of melancholia) and the other concerning the sublime. I will also draw briefly upon the later work of Michel Foucault on practices of the self, and upon a recent paper by James Miller which considers the latter,[4] in order to discuss the relinquishment of humanism's narcissisms and to ask what kinds of inhuman, but principled, selves might now be imagined.

1. J-F. Lyotard, *The Inhuman*, trans. G. Bennington and R. Bowlby, Polity Press, Cambridge 1991, p2.

2. See, for example, J-F. Lyotard, 'Answering the Question: What is Postmodernism?', trans. R. Durand, in Lyotard, *The Postmodern Condition: A Report on Knowledge*, trans. G. Bennington and B. Massumi, Manchester University Press, Manchester 1984; and J-F. Lyotard, 'The Sublime and the Avant-Garde' in *The Inhuman, op.cit.*

3. J-F. Lyotard, *The Inhuman*, p5.

4. J. Miller, 'From Socrates to Foucault: The Problem of the Philosophical Life', in this collection.

II GREEN DREAMS AND NARCISSI: THE SYMPTOMATOLOGY OF CONTEMPORARY ELEGY

The substance of my argument revolves around an understanding of the subject of Enlightenment Modernity as haunted by specific kinds of unresolved narcissisms. Drawing upon the work of Eric Santner, my contention will be that, if we are to think ourselves 'beyond' modernity, and yet still remain socially and politically continent beings, these narcissisms must be relinquished.[5] The question which arises from this proposition concerning the need to work through unresolved narcissisms (and hence, as a corollary, to develop appropriate techniques for a different but necessary sense of self) is how such 'invented selves', with a necessary narcissism but of a different sort (one characterized by the experience of disintegration but seeking integration on a basis other than that of Romanticism and a universalised idea of unity), can at the same time be imagined as selves possessing a necessary social and political integrity.[6] A central problem in beginning to try to answer this question is that of identifying a language (and hence a practice) in which the resolution of narcissistic fantasies can be thought. I will be suggesting that the contemporary insistence of nostalgic forms can be understood as a symptomatology – of modernity coming to grief – which does direct us towards such a language.

Postmodernism is a rather overdone term. Lyotard notes, however, that it has been used, albeit 'badly rather than well',[7] to designate something of the inhuman transformations of which he writes. But this task – one which is essentially elegiac – of relinquishing the narcissisms of Romanticism, and of thinking about (in humanism's and Romanticism's sense) inhuman selves – seems to me to constitute the task and obligation of what might as well be called the ethos appropriate to, for want of a better designation, the postmodern. The argument which follows is essentially directed towards attempting to think through, albeit in an initially limited way, a politics (in the broadest sense) of what is now usually referred to as the postmodern.

In his careful and illuminating work on elegy, Peter Sacks has written compellingly of the twentieth century's difficulty with the use of traditional elegiac forms.[8] In particular, and with detailed reference to the poems of Yeats, Pound and Auden, Sacks notices modern disenchantment with the elegy's traditional need both to demonstrate reverence for the father and the law, and also to offer consoling figures of 'continuity and regenerative power'.[9] In the post-war poetry of Geoffrey Hill, Sacks finds consolation linked to the most bleak images of judgement. In 'Requiem for the Plantagenet Kings' (1955) and 'Two Formal Elegies' (subtitled 'For the Jews in Europe') (1955-6), Sacks notes Hill's 'refusal to console without first stressing decimation and the bleak harshness of judgement',[10] and notes also the invocation of the terrible God of the Old Testament, of ancient sacrifice, and of a martyrdom which is barely Christian. The presence of this fearsome God, Sacks suggests, stands as a figure for the ' "fierce heart" brought to judgement'.[11] This harsh and

5. E.L. Santner, *Stranded Objects: Mourning, Memory, and Film in Postwar Germany*, Cornell University Press, 1990.

6. Fredric Jameson's 1984 essay, 'Postmodernism or, the Cultural Logic of Late Capitalism', in *Postmodernism or the Cultural Logic of Late Capitalism*, Verso, London 1991 charts the disintegrations of contemporary subjectivity. His closing demand for a new 'aesthetics of cognitive mapping' seems directed towards the task of imagining forms of integrity for social and political selves.

7. J-F. Lyotard, *The Inhuman*, p5.

8. Peter M. Sacks, *The English Elegy: Studies in the Genre from Spenser to Yeats*, Johns Hopkins University Press, London 1987.

9. *Ibid.*, p301.

10. *Ibid.*, p309.

11. *Ibid.*, p310.

demanding God stands in sharp distinction to the loving God of Christian doctrine. In the more recent 'Veni Coronaberis' (1978), harshness is tempered by the traditional elegiac images of spring and rebirth –

> The crocus armies from the dead
> rise up, the realm of love renews
> the battle it was born to lose
> though for a time the snows have fled

– but, in spite of this, love does not conquer all, not for ever after. Sacks says that this poem 'performs the mourner's submissive recognition of the inevitable defeat, almost from birth, of "love". As we have seen so often, an admission of that defeat is crucial to the establishment of any consolation'.[12]

I want to suggest that the emergence of the term postmodernism in British cultural debate over the past fifteen years or so can be linked – especially in its close deployment with the 'deconstructive' languages of contemporary theory – to deep undercurrents of thought presently at work in almost all aspects of British cultural life. Further, I want to suggest that these undercurrents are engaged in what Eric Santner calls 'rhetoric of grief'.[13] These nostalgic languages – of loss, fragmentation and dismemberment, or of pastiched and collaged reassemblings of English green dreams – confront what Santner, again, has called the 'no longer possibles' of a certain kind of (humanist, Romantic) subject and a certain kind of (narcissistic, melancholic) space for 'love'. They enact the failure of the Symbolic Law of a Father increasingly seen in his sublime aspect as the 'leering', dangerous and unstable, 'father-*jouissance*' in whose fictions faith may no longer be placed. In what follows, I will discuss grief in its double aspect – as mourning and as melancholia – in order to argue that this melancholy, narcissistic subjectivity, and its infantile aim of laying hold of, rather than submitting to, the sublime, must be relinquished so that the mourningful invention of new symbolic worlds and selves can be imagined.

One of the most persistent contours traced in the cultural and political life of the past decade and a half in Britain – the period of New Right government from 1979 to the present – has been what I would like to call, borrowing a little from Graham Swift, the 'green dream of England'. This nostalgic dream is well caught – albeit with a great degree of self-conscious irony – in Swift's 1992 novel *Ever After* (*EA*).[14] In a passage towards the end of the novel, the narrator and central protagonist, Bill Unwin, is meditating upon the identity of his unknown father – a train driver on Brunel's Great Western Railway where Bill, as a child, used to go train-spotting:

> But as I grew up in those far off days, I saw myself as a child of the future. I was enamoured – little thinking that the object of my passion was doomed, too, soon to become an anachronism – of that roaring, hurtling, up-to-the-minute thing, the steam engine. And, hardly appreciating that my wish was the oldest wish in the book, I wanted to be, as every little boy was

12. *Ibid.*, p311.

13. E.L. Santner, *op. cit.*

14. G. Swift, *Ever After*, Pan Books, London 1992.

supposed to want to be – ha! – an engine driver ... Between Aldermaston Wharf and Midgham, where the Reading-Newbury line clipped the side of the hill and entered a short cutting – a favourite spot for these enthralled vigils, so limply known as 'train-spotting' – I could look out on a vista which might have formed the model for one of those contrived scenes in a children's encyclopaedia, depicting the theme of 'Old and New'. River, canal and railway line were all in view ... I must have seen it once – many times – that living palimpsest. And no doubt I should have been struck by some prescient, elegiac pang at the sight of those great expresses steaming only to their own oblivion, and taking with them a whole lost age. O West Country world! O creamy, bucket-and-spade summers! O thatched cottages and smugglers' coves! O nestling market towns! O green dreams! O Mendips! O Quantocks! O England! (*EA* p199).

In the passage which follows, Unwin makes the Freudian subtext (the phallic symbols of every boy's train-driver fantasies, and the unconscious wish for recognition and identification[15]) quite explicit:

15. S. Freud, 'Three Essays on the Theory of Sexuality' (1905), *On Sexuality*, Penguin, Harmondsworth 1977, p121.

And the great thing, of course, as the mighty engines sped by, was to catch a blurred and exalting glimpse of those heroes of the rails. To leap up in a frenzy of adulatory, emulatory waving, hoping for the magic return wave. And one of those knights of steam, though I never knew it, one of those lords of the footplate ... was – my father ... he is mounted, appropriately enough for my sureptitious begetter, on a giant phallic symbol. I see him careering round the countryside, siring bastard after bastard. Sometimes I think he is grinning at me, leering at me – oh yes, he is waving all right – as he rushes unrecognizably by (*EA* p200).

The nostalgic contours of Southern England, and the 'elegiac pang' for the father not simply lost but neither known nor knowable, are reflected in *Ever After*'s other story – the tale within the tale – which is of the mid-nineteenth-century loss of faith experienced by Bill's distant maternal relative, and surveyor for the Great Western Railway, Matthew Pearce. Here, a theme which is constant throughout Swift's work – that of the weak, troubled, or troubling father – is explicitly linked to the crisis which modernity articulates. This is not merely Nietzsche's 'death of the divine Father' but is, more broadly, the crisis of the 'paternal fiction' in general.

If the paternal fiction is that fiction – enunciated in Lacanian psychoanalytic theory as the castrating '*Nom/non du père*' – whereby the sign (and the possibility of symbolic worlds and selves) is the consolation offered for the loss of the narcissistic oedipal relation, in what ways can we understand its collapse to be signified by a symptomatology of nostalgia? As Jean Starobinski's essay on the topic makes clear, the structure of nostalgia is melancholic.[16] What I want to suggest is that the contemporary – the postmodern – can be understood in terms of the tasks of transforming a pathological melancholia into a healthy mourning.

16. J. Starobinski, 'The Idea of Nostalgia', *Diogenes*, 54, 1966.

In the psychoanalytic account, the ending of narcissism, and the loss which that establishes, is the ground upon which subjectivity becomes possible. Under the Name of the Father, and according to his symbolic law, loss is made good – or made good enough – by the substitutions of the sign. In this way, the whole panoply of order, hierarchy and difference is organized as a consolation for loss. As in the movement of elegy, the grieving infant is offered the compensations enacted in displacements and replacements. In elegy, this is the replacement of one poetic voice by another. In the elegiacs of psychoanalysis, the compensation is the supposed identity of the subject of the enunciation with the subject of the enounced – the identity of the subject of the voice as identity, difference and placing, in other words. Every shattering of narcissism, every experience of the loss of a loved object, must recapitulate these processes of symbolization and symbolic re-building. Loss imposes itself as an obligation (to life rather than death) and as a task. The name we give to the task is, of course, mourning.

The language which psychoanalysis provides for bereavement consists in Freud's division of the experience of grave loss into two modalities: mourning and melancholia.[17] Mourning is a state of sickness which is so 'normal' that no-one ever comments upon it. The processes of mourning involve the recapitulation of all earlier experience of loss, and the reconstitution, or invention, of a self shattered by the loss of an object in which profound investments have been made. The experience of mourning consists in the lengthy process whereby 'each single one of the memories and expectations in which the libido is bound to the object is brought up and hypercathected, and detachment of the libido is accomplished in respect of it'.[18] Freud calls this process 'reality-testing'. Melanie Klein's account of mourning processes makes even clearer the extent to which this process consists not only in the rebuilding of an outer reality, but in the dialectical rebuilding of an inner, psychical, reality also.[19] Klein's account paints a more vivid picture of the fragmented (psychotically violent) psychical condition which the mourner must recapitulate and renegotiate in order to recover.

Melancholia, on the other hand, is a pathological condition. Any experience of grave loss recapitulates the 'original' ending of primary narcissism. The successful mourner is one who – upon the basis of an earlier successful negotiation of fundamental loss – is able to negotiate the later loss. The melancholic is one who has never properly negotiated the ending of narcissistic fantasies, and whose narcissisms are thus unresolved. The melancholic has never satisfactorily negotiated the fact that 'you and I have edges'.[20] He remains caught in the compulsions of the narcissistic fantasy that the self-completing object can be had, and that the Real (the 'reality' of the 'whole and the one' in Lyotard) can be seized hold of. In other words, the melancholic remains caught in the compulsion to repeat the trauma of loss in order to master it (a thing he has never properly done). He remains under the thrall of the promise of *jouissance*. Unable to acknowledge the fact of loss, he is compelled to repetition and to the return to and of the traumatic event in

17. S. Freud, 'Mourning and Melancholia' (1917[1915]), *On Metapsychology*, Penguin, Harmondsworth 1984.

18. *Ibid.*, p253.

19. M. Klein, 'Mourning and Its Relation to Manic-Depressive States' (1940), in J. Mitchell, (ed.), *The Selected Melanie Klein*, Penguin, Harmondsworth 1986.

20. Santner, *Stranded Objects*, p19.

dreams, fantasies, and other substitute forms. Whilst, in part, such repetitions are an attempt at mastery of trauma, their 'other' side may lie in the desire to repeat the condition of *jouissance* which is *not being*. As Freud's discussion in 'Beyond the Pleasure Principle' makes clear, the melancholia of unresolved traumas remains under the sway of the death drive.[21]

21. S. Freud, 'Beyond the Pleasure Principle' (1920), *op.cit.*

Since he has never fully negotiated the fact of difference, the melancholic experiences the loss of the other as the loss of himself. His condition is characterized by disavowal. He both knows he has lost something and also disavows the fact. Under the compulsions of repetition and the death drive, this often – at worst – leads sufferers of melancholia to suicide. At best, the unresolved narcissism of melancholia may lead to what Eric Santner calls the 'elegiac loop' of disavowal.[22] Typically, this also leads to the development of what Santner calls 'fetish narratives'. These either claim that 'nothing was really lost', or else stage the site of loss elsewhere:

22. Santner, *Stranded Objects*, p29.

Narrative fetishism ... is the way an inability or refusal to mourn emplots traumatic events; it is a strategy of undoing, in fantasy, the need for mourning by simulating a condition of intactness, typically by situating the site and origin of loss elsewhere. Narrative fetishism releases one from the burden of having to reconstitute one's self-identity under 'posttraumatic' conditions; in narrative fetishism, the 'post' is indefinitely postponed.[23]

23. E.L. Santner, 'History Beyond the Pleasure Principle: Some Thoughts on the Representation of Trauma', in S. Friedlander, (ed.), *Probing the Limits of Representation: Nazism and the 'Final Solution'*, Harvard University Press, Cambridge, Massachusetts 1992, p144.

The above quotation is taken from Santner's essay on the German refusal to mourn the Holocaust, but he places this within a broader conception of the postmodern more generally. Certainly, the melancholic inability to negotiate, or to bear shared witness to, loss (and the development of narratives of disavowal and displacement), can be seen as having political consequences – as Santner's discussion of contemporary German historical and aesthetic debates, in the essay referred to above, indicates.

But, as a symptomatology of the contemporary, nostalgia is not necessarily simply melancholic through and through. As is the case with all symptoms, it contains the seeds of its own cure – albeit in distorted or troped form. The regret over loss (castration) which nostalgia speaks may also bespeak a 'future-oriented remembering' in *both* senses of the word 're-member'.[24] As Susannah Radstone, in an article particularly concerned with feminist working-through of regret, points out, it is possible to find – in feminine elegiac forms – a 'remembering [which] works through nostalgia's fantasies of plenitude (remembrance as defence against *dismemberment*) but is sustained by nostalgia's desire that things might be different'.[25] Contemporary nostalgia thus marks a sort of half-way house between melancholia and mourning. It can appear as a dangerous form of disavowal, but it can also turn its face to the future.

24. S. Radstone, 'Remembering Medea: The Uses of Nostalgia', *Critical Quarterly*, Autumn 1993, p59.

25. *Ibid.*, 'Remembering Medea', p60.

On one hand, we can understand the melancholic's fantasies of sublime plenitude in terms of the unresolved narcissism which, refusing castration, seeks to maintain the condition of undifferentiation associated with unspeakable joy in the mother's body and desire. But the register of plenitudinous *jouissance* should alert us also to the aesthetic mode in which such awesome plenitude is expressed. Although Terry Eagleton's reading of Burke places the sublime to the Father's account,[26] this 'Father' must be understood to be the dangerous *'père-jouissance'*: 'behind the father who is the bearer of the law, and as such reduced to the "Name of the Father" (i.e. the dead father), there is the horrible castrating figure that Lacan has called the 'father-*jouissance*', the father who wouldn't die and who comes to haunt the Law (and actually endows it with its effectiveness)'.[27] It is this 'leering' father-*jouissance* which haunts *Ever After* and which Bill Unwin, in learning to mourn, must also learn to lay to some form of rest.

26. T. Eagleton, *The Ideology of the Aesthetic*, Blackwell, Oxford 1990, p55.

From the 'Now' in Swift's first novel, *The Sweet Shop Owner* (1980), to the 'Here and Now' in *Waterland* (1983), and beyond to the various haunting paternal fictions of *Ever After*, Swift's work is marked by the emergence of sublime and uncanny figurations within the supposedly safe and loving spaces of the domestic and familiar. His 'dream of England', drawing on a long and by no means always conservative Romantic tradition of such dreaming, is one in which the urge is to make an *unheimlich* 'home' bearable. But whilst the leering father may finally endow the law with its effectiveness, his uncanniness makes him a deathly 'disturber of love'.[28] The effectivity of a Symbolic Law based upon a certain kind of space for narcissistic love, but one from which the good (i.e. dead) Father is absent or withdrawn, is thus called into question. The withdrawal of the loving Father, and the appearance of figurations of uncanny *père-jouissance* which haunt modern subjectivity from within, can, however, be historically placed. They co-incide with European Enlightenment and with the formulation of a Romantic aesthetic.

27. M. Dolar, ' "I Shall Be with You on Your Wedding-Night": Lacan and the Uncanny', *October*, Fall 1991, p10.

28. Dolar, 'Wedding-Night', p10; Freud, 'The Uncanny' (1919), *Art and Literature*, Penguin, Harmondsworth 1985, p353.

Swift's novels are, from his first to his latest, engaged in a sustained struggle with the problems of Romanticisms of all kinds. This 'problem' can be cast in terms in which the Romantic aesthetic, and all the varied romanticisms which flow from it, can be seen as an historical response to a certain narcissistic structure of subjectivity. The Romantic emphasis on the momentary overcoming of difference – a fleeting intimation of unity within diversity, and the final promise of 'absolute knowledge' in the whole and the one – is an essentially narcissistic formulation. Swift's problematizing of Romanticism, and his turn to the more open-ended form of allegory, mirrors similar contemporary theoretical responses made elsewhere. I want, thus, to expand upon the idea of the sublime, and its relation to narcissism and to mourning, by looking at two theoretical uses of the category of the sublime. These are those offered by Jean-François Lyotard, and the Lacanian theorists Slavoj Žižek and Mladen Dolar.

III THE SUBLIME AND UNCANNY SUBJECT OF MODERNITY

It seems clear, from, for example, Lyotard's writings on the sublime, Slavoj Žižek's writings on the same in terms of the Lacanian idea of the Real, and from Mladen Dolar's writing on the uncanny, that a common thread can be

29. See, for example, Lyotard on the sublime in 'Answering the Question' and also *The Inhuman*, op.cit.; S. Žižek, *The Sublime Object of Ideology*, Verso, London 1989; Dolar, 'Wedding-Night'.

30. See also, R. Wolin, 'Modernism vs. Postmodernism', *Telos*, Winter 1984-5.

31. Dolar, 'Wedding-Night', p7.

identified in some contemporary critical thought.[29] Briefly, this thread is one which conceives modern subjectivity as haunted by something which – with the advent of Enlightenment modernity – becomes unplaceable and, strictly speaking, unrepresentable with the demise of a world integrated within the schema of the sacred.[30] For Lyotard and Žižek, it is named by the category of the sublime. For Dolar, it appears in the modality of the uncanny:

It seems that Freud speaks about a 'universal' of human experience when he speaks of the uncanny, yet his own examples tacitly point to its location in a specific historical conjuncture, to the particular historical rupture brought about by the Enlightenment. There is *a specific dimension of the uncanny that emerges with modernity.*[31]

As Dolar's discussion makes clear, what becomes unplaceable is, in obvious and simple terms, the fact of a *meaningless* death and the unplaceability of the death drive which now emerges in uncanny ways. As Foucault, amongst others, notices, it is Baudelaire's consciousness of the fact that modern selves are all 'celebrating some funeral – mutes in love, political mutes, bourgeois mutes' which makes him such an acute observer of modernity.[32] For Baudelaire, *the painter of modern life* (Constantin Guys) is one who is able to show the defiant mock heroism and self-ironizing melancholy of the dandy, and the dark funereal frock coat, as the *necessary* attitude and fashion of the time.[33]

32. M. Foucault, 'What is Enlightenment?', P. Rabinow (ed), *The Foucault Reader*, Penguin, Harmondsworth 1984, p40.

33. C. Baudelaire, 'The Painter of Modern Life' in C. Baudelaire, *The Painter of Modern Life and Other Essays*, trans. and ed. J. Mayne, Phaidon, London 1964.

Both Žižek and Dolar make use of the Lacanian tripartite schema of Symbolic, Imaginary and Real in order to argue that what becomes unplaceable (sublime in Žižek's discussion, uncanny in Dolar's) and unsymbolizable in modernity is the fantasy of the self-completing object:

What I am interested in is not the uncanny as such, but the uncanny that is closely linked with the advent of modernity and which constantly haunts it from the inside. To put it simply, in premodern societies the dimension of the uncanny was largely covered (and veiled) by the area of the sacred and untouchable. It was assigned to a religiously and socially sanctioned place in the symbolic from which the structure of power, sovereignty, and a hierarchy of values emanated. With the triumph of the Enlightenment, this privileged and excluded place (the exclusion that founded society) was no more. That is to say that the uncanny became unplaceable: it became uncanny in the strict sense.[34]

34. Dolar, 'Wedding-Night', p7.

In the psychoanalytic account, the self-completing object is the *objet petit a* retrospectively associated with the mother and with the state of primary narcissism in which no distinction between self and other is yet possible. This condition of completion and wholeness is ruptured by the mimetic specular image (in whatever form it is granted). With that recognition, there is already a split: 'I cannot recognize myself and at the same time be one with myself. With the recognition I have already lost what one could call 'self-being', the immediate coincidence with myself in my being and *jouissance* ... The Mirror double immediately introduces the dimension of castration'.[35] The desire constituted within this split is the desire of the other, the desire of the *objet petit a*. But this little object is, in fact, always lost to the Real (the traumatic and unsymbolizable *fact* of loss). One *cannot have it*. It is this lack (which the Symbolic Order promises to make good – an endlessly deferred and awful gift) which founds the subject. To lay hold of the Real – to possess the object in all its appalling and sublime plenitude – would be to lack the lack which founds the subject, and to be *not* a subject:

> the Lacanian account of anxiety differs sharply from other theories: it is not produced by a lack or a loss or an incertitude; it is not the anxiety of losing something (the firm support, one's bearings, etc). On the contrary, it is the anxiety of gaining something too much, of a too-close presence of the object. What one loses with anxiety is precisely the loss – the loss that made it possible to deal with a coherent reality. 'Anxiety is the lack of the support of the lack,' says Lacan: the lack lacks, and this brings about the uncanny.[36]

In the face of seemingly meaningless death, modern man searches for the secret which only the dead seem to possess; the 'little letter' which, as in A.S. Byatt's *Possession*, for example, lies buried in the grave but which 'tells' everything and thus 'closes' the Romance.[37] But the secret the dead possess is terrible *jouissance*. To *attain* one's heart's desire (the Romantic fantasy) would be to move beyond Eros and the pleasure principle. As we know, what lies beyond the pleasure principle is ghastly repetition and death. To say 'I hope you attain your heart's desire' can only be the most dreadful of curses.

In essence, what we are being asked to consider in discussions such as Dolar's is, firstly, the idea that symbolic formulations within sacred systems make 'lack' good in the form of a transcendant parent figure (or ideal Subject) which will, eventually – 'after' or 'with' death – fill in the void which human life on earth experiences, and, secondly, that modernity exposes the Real as the sublime 'lack of the lack'. The psychoanalytic account of the subject, as offered by Lacan, is of one fundamentally caught between narcissism and its impossibility. To be a subject is to be divided and lacking – and yet always to seek the little object of desire supposed to restore wholeness and 'intactness'; supposed, in other words, to complete the narcissistic circle. When this difficulty of subjectivity could be symbolized (in the forms of the sacred) as attainable (albeit by death), the promise of plentitudinous self-presence (narcissistic self-completion) seemed to hold good. What Lacanian psychoanalysis dolefully theorizes is the impossibility of such narcissistic makings good. The problem which psychoanalytic theories of the subject seem to propose is that of asking how on earth something good can be made from something really quite bad?

This elegiac question, of finding something good from something bad, is in

35. *Ibid.*, p12.

36. *Ibid.*, p13.

37. A.S. Byatt, *Possession: A Romance*, Chatto & Windus, London 1990.

fact addressed within psychoanalytic theory, but in a slightly different register – that of an account of the psychical processes of grief. Significantly, this account is one which offers a theorization of something like a technique of self-mastery. At least it describes a manner of understanding the re-invention of a shattered self in the form of a mastering of narcissistic fantasies of dependence upon and completion by the other. The successful mourner must struggle again and again with the harsh fact of an irreducible difference, and with renunciation, until she has both made it her own and also made from its substitutive symbolizations, in a sense, a consoled self. Before I return to Freudian melancholy, however, I want to look briefly at Lyotard's account of the significance of the idea of the sublime, since this adds some political force to arguments about the dangers of narcissism.

Lyotard's discussion of the postmodern in 'Answering the Question: What is Postmodernism?' also leads his readers to a contemplation of narcissism. The modern can only take place, says Lyotard, with the discovery of the unreality of reality. Realism is a response to this. Realism tries to cover over the unreality of reality with an insistence upon 'unity, simplicity, communicability'.[38] Aesthetic – perhaps particularly literary – realism remains, on the whole, under the dominance of Romanticism which offers an aesthetic of unity (and the apprehension of Truth) in the momentary transcendance of the symbol divulged by the genius to the man of taste. Romanticism, as has often been said, offers a secularized version of the overcoming of the dualism articulated by Descartes. The form of the beautiful provides, momentarily, an overcoming of alienation.

For Lyotard, the sublime is a form of barbarity (its formless unpresentability is precisely what discloses its sublimity) which prevents the 'unity from diversity' which marks a Romantic aesthetic. Since Romantic aesthetics (and social, political and psychological Romanticisms) are directed towards an apprehension of 'the whole and the one', the sublime – for Lyotard – must be preserved as the necessary irritant which prevents the possibility of the narcissistic fantasy of 'completion'. This latter is the fantasy that reality (the noumenal in-itself as a positivity; the *objet a* and the Real in Lacan) can really be seized hold of. For Lyotard, this fantasy always leads to terror:

> The nineteenth and twentieth centuries have given us as much terror as we can take. We have paid a high enough price for the nostalgia of the whole and the one, for the reconciliation of the concept and the sensible, of the transparent and communicable experience. Under the general demand for slackening and for appeasement, we can hear the mutterings of the desire for a return to terror, for the realization of the fantasy to seize reality. The answer is let us wage a war on totality; let us be witnesses to the unpresentable; let us activate the differences and save the honour of the name.[39]

38. Lyotard, Answering the Question', p75.

39. *Ibid.*, pp81-2.

IV NOSTALGIA AND CONTEMPORARY GRIEF

Bearing in mind that I have suggested that psychoanalysis does provide a language in which the ending of narcissism can be understood, and that, as Santner points out, this language includes the idea of social witness as essential to the reconstitution of the grieving self,[40] ('mourning without solidarity is the beginning of madness'[41]) I now want to turn to one of the most insistent symptomatologies of the contemporary: nostalgia. In current debates, nostalgia is almost always identified as something socially regressive and politically reactionary. What I want to argue is that, as a particularly insistent symptomatology of the present, nostalgia needs to be thought about in a little more detail because, as a symptom of a collective melancholy which is also potentially 'future-oriented', it can be understood as directing us towards possible modes of resolving contemporary dis-ease.

> 40. Santner, *Stranded Objects*, p40.
>
> 41. *Ibid.*, p26.

The history of the term is instructive. In an article published in 1966, Jean Starobinski shows that the idea of nostalgia emerged as the medicalization of a condition long recognized as a form of melancholia.[42] *Heimweh*, or home-sickness, was recognized as a condition very similar to love-melancholy. Both these conditions were recognized as (what would come to be thought of as) pathological states in which the loss of a primal love object remained unresolved. In love-melancholy it was the loved object as lover, in nostalgia (homesickness) it was the loss of the original *Heim*.

> 42. Starobinski, 'The Idea of Nostalgia'.

The term nostalgia (from the Greek *Nostos* – meaning the return, usually or most often to one's original dwelling place, and *Algos* – meaning pain, sickness or sorrow) was coined by Johannes Hofer in 1688 in order to describe the symptoms exhibited by young Swiss mercenaries away from home for the first time. In particular, Hofer noted that the young soldiers' distress was especially due to separation from their mothers, from their good breakfast soups, and from 'the thick milk from their own valley'.[43] As Starobinski points out, 'The modern psychiatrist should be thankful to Johannes Hofer for underlining straight off the role of this deprivation: the loss of childhood, of "oral satisfactions", of motherly coaxing'.[44] In sum, what Hofer identifies as nostalgia is the melancholia which results from unresolved narcissisms.

> 43. *Ibid.*, p87.
>
> 44. *Ibid.*

Once it becomes possible to understand that the symptomatology of contemporary nostalgia is a symptomatology of grief, it becomes equally possible to understand that postmodern nostalgia might most usefully be thought about in terms of the formulation of a language of mourning. The structure of nostalgia is melancholic, and this provides a clue to its contemporary significance. In fact, and as I have argued elsewhere,[45] because contemporary nostalgias are so overdetermined by the extensive and collective image-repertoire provided by mass forms of communication, postmodern nostalgia takes particularly collective psycho-social forms. It indicates a shared symptomatology which points towards a possible *future* community of interest and towards possible social and political formulations. As Starobinski points out, the longed-for *Heim* is no longer the village home of the seventeenth and

> 45. W. Wheeler, 'Nostalgia Isn't Nasty: The Postmodernizing of Parliamentary Democracy', *Altered States: Postmodernism, Politics, Culture*, Lawrence & Wishart, London 1994.

46. Starobinski, 'The Idea of Nostalgia', pp102-3.

47. *Ibid.*, p103,

eighteenth centuries. With modernity the nostalgic affect assumes new names: 'anaclitic depression ... maternal deprivation' and 'regression'.[46] In Starobinski's words, with modernity 'the village is interiorized'.[47] Contemporary nostalgia is a symptomatology which is both more starkly psychical ('interiorized') and, via a mass image-repertoire, collective.

I suggested earlier that Melanie Klein's account of the processes of grief gives a clear indication of the extent to which mourning tasks involve symbolic rebuilding. My question involves asking what forms such rebuilding might take for subjects in the process of abandoning the narcissisms of Romantic humanism or, in Lyotard's terminology, in the process of becoming inhuman.

V AFTER LOVE

48. J. Kristeva, *Tales of Love*, Columbia University Press, New York 1987.

In *Tales of Love*, Julia Kristeva traces a history of western narcissism from the convergence of Greco-Roman and Judeo-Christian thought in the 1st century A.D., through Plotinus to medieval scholasticism, and on through Romanticism to the present. She concludes that this narcissian subjectivity reaches its limits in modernity.[48] Gradually deprived of the various religious and secular symbolic structures which have been its supports, narcissistic subjectivity finds its last 'space for love' in psychoanalysis and, specifically, in the transference. After the withdrawal of theology 'in the face of a philosophy that grounds *being* on knowledge rather than on affection ... The receptive mind of a disappointed Goethian Jew, living in Central Europe between the two wars, continues to be the only one to come forward as capable of fitting out – with considerable risk and uncertainty – a new space for love'.[49]

49. *Ibid.*, p61.

Very briefly, Kristeva's argument is that the crisis of contempory experience consists in the failure of symbolizations which would allow narcissian modern subjectivity to find a proper space for love. Only psychoanalysis, as the site of transference love, any longer provides such an *unheimlich* 'home'. These are the 'stakes' and the 'crisis' of psychoanalysis. Concerning contemporary subjects, Kristeva asks of psychoanalysts,

> Are we concerned with rebuilding their own proper space, a 'home' for contemporary Narcissi: repair the father, soothe the mother, allow them to build a solid introspective inside, master of its losses and wanderings, assuming that such a goal is attainable? Or does not the abundance of sufferers who find their fulfilment, their relaxation, and their satisfaction only in intoxication (from drugs to sacred music, which do away with individuality and sex for the sake of infinity) indicate that a psychic era has come to an end? I see psychoanalysis rather as the instrument of a departure from that enclosure, not as its warden. Does the old psychic space, the machinery of projections and identifications that relied more or less on neuroses for reinforcement, no longer hold together? Well, it may be because another mode of being, of unbeing, is attempting to take its place.[50]

50. *Ibid.*, pp379-80

So what is the new mode of inhuman 'unbeing' to be? For Kristeva, 'Freud, the post-Romanticist, was the first to turn love into a cure: he did this, not to allow one to grasp a truth, but to provoke a rebirth'.[51] And for Kristeva this rebirth lies in 'imagination as an antidote for the crisis'.[52] Santner writes in a similar vein on contemporary theoretical and creative practices when he suggests that the relinquishment of a certain form of narcissism is a prerequisite for the imagination and invention of new 'postmodern post-holocaust' selves. His focus, as with Kristeva, is the moment at which love breaks down, but he places this within the Freudian account of mourning. In doing so, he offers, perhaps, a more specific account of the ways in which psychoanalysis might be thought of as providing 'an instrument of departure' from a psychic era that has come to an end. In other words, in the reflections upon mourning, psychoanalysis offers some account of the ways in which the narcissistic subjectivity it theorizes might be transformed – or cured of a certain kind of love. The contemporary analytical task, it transpires, is precisely the elegiac work of rebirth that the task of mourning inscribes. Both Freud's and Melanie Klein's work on mourning suggests that the task of mourning consists in a recapitulation of the ending of primary narcissism and thus in the work of rebuilding or, perhaps more accurately, inventing symbolic worlds and selves. This is, as Kristeva argues, an imaginative task in the proper psychoanalytic sense. She says, 'Speaking, writing? Is that not again building "one's own", be it polyvalent? While waiting for social institutions to integrate such extra-terrestrials, those survivors of primary narcissism, it is still in the imagination and symbolic realizations that their faltering identity will best find a way to construct itself as necessarily false – imaginary'.[53]

The psychoanalytic – specifically the post-Lacanian – account of the subject offers, then, the story of a self at the limits. This self is no longer supported by the fictions of the symbolic structures which should hold it in place. These are, themselves, increasingly invaded by a sublimity of the sort figured in *Ever After* as an unknowable and libidinally incontinent father. But rather than seeking (as in socially and politically conservative formulations) to bring the Father (and the subject) back to his place, perhaps – as with Swift's Unwin ('The world will not shatter because of a single – misconception' (*EA* p204) – we should submit to the sublime, to Geoffrey Hill's terrible Father of Judgement as the harshest figure of negativity, and to the failure of narcissistic 'loves' of all kinds. In this way we might, collectively, begin to mourn.

But this psychoanalytic prescription to grieve remains vague. It was, perhaps, always hard enough to mourn, even in a world where the wearing of weeds, the period of mourning, the meaning of loss, were all more or less solidly encoded. The final question I want to ask is this: what theorists can we find, beyond disintegration, who offer either any model for mourning now, or any outline of the inhuman selves postmodern mourners might become? It is here, in the final part of my argument, that I want to turn to an alternative account of the invention of worlds and selves.

51. *Ibid.*, p381.
52. *Ibid.*.

53. *Ibid.*, p380.

VI THREADS THAT BIND

Michel Foucault's late work on technologies of the self is, of course, centrally concerned with the contingency of the selves we have happened to be. Recent psychoanalytic and Foucauldian accounts of modernity to some extent converge around the matter of endings and beginnings of certain kinds of selves. Kristeva sees psychoanalysis as providing the 'instruments of departure' for a psychic era that has come to an end. I have described these 'instruments' in terms of the psychoanalytic language of melancholia – which fails to depart – and mourning – which succeeds in departing. In his description of what he terms the contemporary ethos of a 'limit-attitude',[54] Foucault describes the instruments of departure as genealogical in design and archaeological in method. In other words, in discovering the contingencies of what we have counted as knowledge, and of what we have been, we may learn to exercise some freedom in regard to the contingencies of what we might be willing to count as truth, in regard to the means by which a relation to truth is established, and in regard to what we might become.

What every successful mourner discovers, nonetheless, is that however historically contingent the re-invented self, there can be no contingency between the symbolic forms invented and the life that is lived. In other words, for successful mourning to take place, there must be threads which bind. Not only must there be the poetic coherence between the painfully altered 'living' and the elegiacly transformed 'dead', but there must also be a personal poetic; a coherence between what is thought and said on the one hand, and what is done on the other. This is not, and cannot be, an injunction to continue investments in something which can no longer be had. It is an injunction to find something good – and thus consoling – in the fact of shattering, loss and transformation itself. The 'sign' which substitutes for the 'thing' must, in other words, have sufficient integrity to bear the dead weight it carries. Without wishing to enter into the notable difficulties of Freud's use of the term, it is worth pointing out that the process of sublimation is one in which such elegiac reparations, inasmuch as they must convert libidinal energy from one aim to another, must necessarily forge adequate connections.[55] Celeste Schenck has argued that specificly feminine elegiac forms evince a strong will towards connectedness rather than simply towards substitution.[56] This raises interesting questions – which I shall not pursue here – about whether we would want to think the 'binding institutions'[57] of a different symbolic ordering as being, precisely, 'paternal'. One thing is certain, however: forms of symbolization – worlds and selves – in which there are no such binding threads cannot console.

In the years immediately preceding his death, and perhaps with an exceptional stoicism in which he was able to transform his own recognition of the mourner's task by bringing it to bear on the theoretical questions raised by his work on techniques of the self, Foucault increasingly focussed on the matter of ethical coherence and the means by which, historically, such a relation to

54. M. Foucault, 'What is Enlightenment?', in P. Rabinow (ed), *The Foucault Reader*, Penguin, Harmondsworth 1984, p45.

55. For a comprehensive overview of sublimation as the term appears in Freud's work, see J. Laplanche and J-B Pontalis, *The Language of Psycho-Analysis*, trans. D. Nicholson-Smith, Hogarth Press, London 1985, pp431-4.

56. C. Schenck, 'Feminism and Deconstruction: Reconstructing the Elegy', *Tulsa Studies in Women's Literature*, Spring 1986.

57. D. LaCapra, 'History and Psychoanalysis', *Critical Enquiry*, Winter, 1987.

truth had been established.

In a series of interviews – 'On the Genealogy of Ethics: An Overview of Work in Progress' – given in April 1983, just over a year before he died, Foucault described two walks – both meditative exercises in ascetic self-mastery, and examples of what he called practices of the self.[58] The first is a walking exercise recommended by the Stoic philosopher Epictetus. The second is a Christian walking exercise performed by a young, seventeenth-century seminarist. What Foucault is looking at here is the problematic of the self as this emerged in seventeenth-century European cultures, and the ways in which such a problematic gives rise to 'thought'. Specifically, he is interested in historical responses to this problematic. The Christian re-activation of Epictetan Stoicism was one such response; Cartesianism provided another. As we know, it was the Cartesian account which, as it were, won the day, but at a cost. That cost, says Foucault, was the breakdown of a certain relation – in which an ethics is grounded – between ascetic self-mastery and the truth.

Each walk involves a series of confrontations with the world. Speaking of the ways in which Christian doctrine, in the wake of the religious crises of the sixteenth century, was able to avail itself of – or to 'reactivate' – a number of ancient Stoic practices, Foucault says:

> Let me take as an example the walking exercise recommended by Epictetus. Each morning, while taking a walk in the city, one should try to determine with respect to each thing (a public official or an attractive woman), one's motives, whether one is impressed by or drawn to it, or whether one has sufficient self-mastery so as to be indifferent. In Christianity one has the same sort of exercises, but they serve to test one's dependence on God. I remember having found in a seventeenth-century text an exercise reminiscent of Epictetus, where a young seminarist, when he is walking, does certain exercises which show in what way each thing shows his dependence vis-a-vis God – which permit him to decipher the presence of divine providence. These two walks correspond to the extent that you have a case with Epictetus of a walk during which the individual assures himself of his own sovereignty over himself and shows that he is dependent on nothing. While in the Christian case the seminarist walks and before each thing he sees, says, 'Oh, how God's goodness is great! He who made this holds all things in his power, and me, in particular,' thus reminding himself that he is nothing.[59]

Foucault says that the two walks correspond inasmuch as neither employ techniques designed to uncover an inner truth of the self, but are attempts to 'determine what one can and cannot do with one's available freedom'.[60] The Christian exercise is no longer, here, concerned with 'discovering a truth hidden inside the self' – its principle is not confessional – but, rather, it invokes a relation between self and world. It is not a delving within, but is a building of the self from without as it were. But, even as the seminarist walks, an account of

58. Foucault, 'On the Genealogy of Ethics: An Overview of Work in Progress', Foucault Reader, op.cit.

59. Ibid., pp368-9.

60. Ibid., p368.

the self is emerging in which this ascetic work on self and truth will be displaced. Foucault says:

> In European culture up to the sixteenth century, the problem remains: What is the work which I must effect upon myself so as to be capable and worthy of acceding to the truth? To put it another way: truth always has a price; no access to truth without ascesis ... Descartes, I think, broke with this when he said, 'To accede to truth, it suffices that I be *any* subject which can see what is evident.' Evidence is substituted for ascesis at the point where the relationship to the self intersects the relationship to others and the world. The relationship to the self no longer needs to be ascetic to get into relation to the truth ... Thus, I can be immoral and know the truth.[61]

61. *Ibid.*, pp371-2.

Where the two walks do not correspond, however, is in the marked difference between the Stoic's prideful independence and the Christian's humble dependence. Where the Epictetan Stoic masters himself in a process characterized by indifference to an indifferent world, the Christian self is mastered in relation to a world which exists entirely in and through God's love. For the Christian, what the world reveals is his yearning for the divine love before which the self is known in all its aching humility. This relationship of love – in which I must love myself in order to be worthy of God's love – is something with which we are familiar from Plotinus, medieval scholasticism and Christian mysticism. The author of *The Cloud of Unknowing* (c.1349), for example, describes the transcendence of God as 'dwelling hid in the "dark cloud of unknowing" which can be pierced only by "the sharp dart of longing love" '.[62] Julian of Norwich, similarly, expressed her faith in 'the ultimate triumph of love'.[63]

62. J.R.H. Moorman, *A History of the Church in England*, A & C Black, London 1980, p128.

63. *Ibid.*, p129.

The trope in the two walks is something/nothing. Whilst the stoic gathers his mastery of sensations and desires together in a castrating gesture of cutting off from the world and from dependence upon it, and thus delineates a self, the Christian is full of a narcissistic yearning in which his self is only completed and made whole in the knowledge of his dependence upon a world entirely granted by divine goodness and love.

The seminarist's meditation, borrowing from Epictetus, suggests one particular response to an historical point at which the self emerges within a problematic in which, eventually, it is recognized as posing certain kinds of questions which must be answered. At the same moment, the Cartesian account of the self offers a different – and in many ways opposed – answer. For reasons arising out of the conditions in which the problem of the self was historically recognized as such in the seventeenth century, the Cartesian answer proved the most compelling. At the same time, however, it also produced all the problems – of dualism, of representation and truth, and of morality – which Enlightenment then attempted to answer. In a world in which theology no longer served, this answer was, perhaps, most evidently sought in aesthetic Romanticism and, beyond that, in Romanticisms of many dangerous and seductive kinds. The development of Romanticism – with its aesthetic model of a transcendent unity potentially graspable within diversity – clearly answers to an historical *structure* of the subject (that narcissistic structure described by Kristeva) from which Cartesianism had not escaped.

Whilst Cartesianism offered an historically compelling solution to the problematic of the self as it was posed for seventeenth-century European culture, the Cartesian subject still inherited this narcissistic structure of the Christian tradition which was, by the eighteenth century, displaced into, and indeed became part of the formulation of, aesthetics. Adorno's famous question about the possibility of poetry after Auschwitz probably marks the limit-point of this two-hundred-year-old Romantic self and, with it, the limit-point of its narcissistic fantasies of totalization (the yearning for what Lyotard has described as 'the whole and the one') more generally. We may say that, under the emblem of Auschwitz and everything it means, the era of the humanist subject and its particular rationalities reaches its limits.[64]

In an interview given a month before his death, Foucault described what he meant by 'thought'.[65] 'Thought' is the motion by which one detaches oneself from a certain habitual way of doing things – acting, reacting and so on – in order to establish this familiarity as an object and to reflect upon it as a problem. 'Thought' arises precisely when what has been familiar and habitual becomes difficult and strange. A problematic arises when something necessitates 'thought' in this sense. 'Thought' is very like mourning. A year earlier, Foucault had also suggested that the final anchoring-point of critical thought, the final place where one might reach a judgement concerning a thinker's ethos, could only be found in the degree of vigilance exercized by that thinker in relation to his or her own life. In other words, the final anchoring point of all critical 'thought' is to be found in the personal ethos – the 'demanding, prudent', meditative self-mastery – of the critic.

In an echo of the critical language of 'thinking', 'saying' and 'doing' used to describe the 'limit-attitude' in the 1984 'Enlightenment' essay, Foucault, here, draws a specifically ethical connection between 'thinking' and 'saying' on the one hand, and 'doing' on the other. Cut free from this ethical connection, mere theory can be turned in any direction:

> I do not conclude … that one may say just anything within the order of theory, but, on the contrary, that a demanding, prudent, 'experimental' attitude is necessary; at every moment, step by step, one must confront what one is thinking and saying with what one is doing, with what one is … The key to the personal poetic attitude of a philosopher is not to be sought in his ideas, as if it could be deduced from them, but rather in his philosophy-as-life, in his philosophical life, his ethos.[66]

The Stoic's exercise – in which there is self-pride, but not yearning love, and a self-mastering in the relation between one's thoughts and words on the one hand, and one's actions on the other – re-emerges and attains clear outlines in

64. See Foucault, 'Space, Knowledge and Power', *Foucault Reader*, p249.

65. Foucault, 'Polemics, Politics and Problematizations: An Interview', *Foucault Reader*, p388.

66. Foucault, 'Politics and Ethics: An Interview', *Foucault Reader*, p374.

Foucault's last works. It is, perhaps, a fitting elegy to suggest that Foucault's legacy may be not only to have provided the 'instruments' for mourning the selves we have been, but also to have provided a design, a method, and an ethical anchoring-point for 'thought' in inventing the selves we might become.

Finally, I want to turn to James Miller's discussion.[67] Miller asks, of Foucault, how can we understand his project? One answer is offered by Foucault's 1984 essay 'What is Enlightenment?'.[68] In this Foucault suggests that the ethos of the contemporary should be understood as a 'limit-attitude'[69] which would consist in discovering the ' "contemporary limits of the necessary," that is … what is not, or is no longer, indispensable for the constitution of ourselves as autonomous subjects'.[70] This involves a 'practical critique' of the 'singular' and 'contingent' constraints through which 'we' are – or have been – produced as subjects.[71] The practical critique takes the form of the genealogy of the present. As such it is (inevitably) potentially transgressive. But Miller's question is slightly different. Stemming from his work as a biographer of Foucault, Miller implicitly asks how we can think the contingencies and dissonances of a human life in terms of *one* life. In other words, how might we think some sense of unity (of this one particular life and thus of a continent group of lives) *without* humanism's narcissistic search for completion?

The answer Miller offers, and I take it as a useful model of the symbolically ordered life which is inhuman, takes the form of a discussion of the concept of the good life, by which Miller means the philosophical life. It is significant that the contemporary idea of the good life is the self-gratifying life. In its original Platonic formulation, the good life meant the integrated life. Miller's argument draws upon Nietzsche ('The only critique of a philosophy that is possible and that proves anything, namely trying to see whether one can live in accordance with it, has never been taught at universities: all that has ever been taught is a critique of words by means of other words'[72]), upon Nietzsche's attentiveness, in *The Gay Science*, to the rule of 'a single taste', whether morally 'good' or 'bad', which should govern the invented self, and upon Foucault's 'frankly utopian hope that, in a different society, perhaps organized under different rules of conduct, *all* of us might be able, despite the difficulties, to exemplify what I have been calling "a philosophical life" '.[73]

In other words, anything can be done with ideas and 'theory', but 'thought' – understood as the hypercathecting then decathecting task of mourning the loss of others, ideas, or selves – allows the mourner to discover a principle of freedom in relation to the world and self he or she can invent. 'Thought', however, demands integrity.

VII CONCLUSION

I have suggested that nostalgia is a form (but potentially future-oriented, and perhaps in a 'feminine' mode) of melancholia, and that – in recognizing this – we might be able to think about the processes whereby humans can relinquish Romantic narcissisms and be inhabited by the inhuman as a form of resistance

67. J. Miller, 'From Socrates to Foucault'.

68. Foucault, 'What is Enlightenment?'.

69. *Ibid.*, p45.

70. *Ibid.*, p43.

71. *Ibid.*, p45.

72. F. Nietzsche, 'Schopenhauer as Educator', in *Untimely Meditations*, trans. R.J. Hollingdale, Cambridge University Press, Cambridge 1983, p187.

73. Foucault, 'On the Genealogy of Ethics', p350.

to Lyotard's other inhuman. A certain narcissism is both inevitable and necessary. Taking the symbolic rebuilding of mourning tasks as a model, I have suggested that a form of necessary narcissism that is imaginable can be drawn from Foucault's discussions of the ethical invention of the self. Without the ethos of integrity, whereby access to truth is gained by some form of self-discipline – a mastery of the idea of non-mastery, an elegiac renunciation of the 'harshest' kind – self-invention can only remain caught in the elegiac loops of desire which imagine possession of the object as a possibility.

Writing on the contemporary elegies of Geoffrey Hill, Peter Sacks says,

> We saw in our study of revenge tragedies and of 'Lycidas' that the issues of justice and of judgement become prominent precisely when the inherited fictions and modes of consolation have grown weakest. And as 'Lycidas' revealed, only the bleakest scenarios of dismemberment, drowning, and divine revenge could reinstate a language of comfort. Hill's power draws on this situation. His elegies are sacrificial and expiatory in the extreme. By recognizing not only the connection between the horror of contemporary history and the violence of ancient theology but also the necessity of extreme chastisement for the gain of any solace, he has written some of the few consoling poems of our time.[74]

74. Sacks, *English Elegy*, p310.

Psychoanalysis describes 'healthy' mourning in terms of the final recognition of the impossibility of narcissistic desire and transcendent, all-fulfilling 'love'. The melancholic Hamlet-identified narrator of Graham Swift's *Ever After* begins (following the deaths of his wife, mother and father, and his own foiled suicide-attempt), 'I feel as though I have *moved on*, in some critical but indefinable way, from what I was before. I have left my former self, whatever that was, behind. I am changed ... I simply feel as though I have become some-one else'. (*EA* p3) *Ever After* is an elegy to the modern self which also, finally, confronts the problem of consolation, and of the adequacy of symbolic forms in which a new, postmodern self can be invented. The adequacy of the substitutive signs discovered at the novel's end is minimal – a highly ambiguous repetitive one-sentence narrative ('He took his life, he took his life' (*EA* p261)) which, hanging precariously between the deathly and erotic senses of the verb, hangs between melancholia and mourning also. Just as the necessary narcissism of the mourner must be one which tolerates castration and the 'no longer possibles' of enjoyment in the 'whole and the one', so the reader is similarly asked to bear with, and bear witness to, a difference which cannot ever, after all, be finally resolved.

Nostalgia points towards grief and towards the invention of new social selves. Understanding the tasks of the contemporary as essentially elegiac may help in thinking through the symbolic forms in which human selves can become inhabited by the inhuman whilst, at the same time, being capable of resisting the disintegrations of that other, absolutely unethical, inhumanity of which Lyotard writes.

SPEAKING UP IN A PUBLIC SPACE:
THE STRANGE CASE OF RACHEL WHITEREAD'S *HOUSE*

Nick Couldry

INTRODUCTION

Competing theories of social interaction have privileged either its textual aspects or its nature as practice (recent theories of 'media events' being a hybrid case). But how do we understand what happens when multiple textual and other practices *confront each other* in a public space that is also a site in media narratives? What gives rise, suddenly, to the 'sense of an event'? When media space and public space *overlap*, the answers must lie beyond media-centred theories – but where? These questions are not readily answered yet are fundamental to an account of the media's role in society. Recent practice in public art offers an important and insufficiently studied means of approaching these questions. This article seeks to open up this territory by examining the controversy that raged around *House*, a public sculpture displayed in London's East End, late in 1993.

Rachel Whiteread's *House* was in Bow: the concrete cast of a house's inside, left exposed when the last of a Victorian terrace was demolished to extend parkland. *House* was also an event or rather many events (private and public) focused, through the media, on the sculpture, its reception and ultimate demolition. I attempt to make sense of those events.[1]

I am *not* trying to expound *House*'s meaning, nor to judge its value as art. By 'making sense' I intend more the unravelling of the differnt processes which generated meanings in relation to *House*. A broad canvas is necessary, stretching beyond art discourse. Here Sharon Zukin's work is exemplary, especially her book-length study of the New York loft scene.[2] Zukin's insistence on grasping the loft scene as 'a space, a symbol and a site under contention by major social forces' remains an essential guide.[3] Her analysis however tends to reduce the intentions and messages of artists to underlying social patterns of appropriation. This closes off a possibility which I will leave open: that art itself is a strand in debates about those very social conditions.

Another broad context of this article is the continuing debate on the public sphere which has evolved from Habermas' original critique of liberal models to a notion of the public sphere as one *or more* spaces in which identities and values are developed in a process of 'discursive will formation'.[4] In its wake has come fascinating work on the 'new social movements', which have recently developed in the face of the 'information society'.[5] These movements while largely submerged in civil society are capable of 'temporary mobilisations' in the public sphere.[6] Their mode of action fuses 'public and private roles ... instrumental and expressive behaviour'.[7] Indeed, through 'the defining power of media

1. Many thanks to Dave Morley for his criticisms and advice throughout the writing of this article. Thanks also for their generous help with documentation to James Lingwood, Director of The Artangel Trust, and Councillor Ludlow and the Planning Department of Bow Neighbourhood.

2. Sharon Zukin, *Loft Living: Culture and Capital in Urban Change,* Johns Hopkins University Press, Baltimore 1982.

3. *Ibid.*, p174.

4. Jürgen Habermas, *The Structural Transformation of the Public Sphere: An Inquiry into a Category of Bourgeois Society*, Polity Press, Cambridge 1989 and 'Concluding Remarks' in Craig Colhoun (ed) *Habermas and the Public Sphere*, MIT Press, Cambridge, Mass. 1991; Sonya Benhabib: *Situating The Self: Gender, Community and Postmodernism in Contemporary Ethics*, Polity Press, Cambridge 1992, chapter 3.

Rachel Whiteread's House seen against the background of London's Docklands. (From a colour transparency by Sue Ormerod, reproduced by kind permission of Artangel).

5. Alberto Melucci,
*Nomads of the Present:
Social Movements and
Individual Needs in
Contemporary Society*,
Hutchinson Radius,
London 1989; Claus
Offe 'New Social
Movements:
Challenging the
Boundaries of
Institutional Politics' in
Social Research,
Volume 52, Number 4
1985, pp817-68;
Ulrich Beck, *Risk
Society: Towards a New
Modernity*, Sage,
London 1992.

6. Melucci, *op.cit.*,
pp79, 227-8.

7. Offe, *op.cit.*,
829-830.

8. Melucci, *op.cit.*,
pp227-8, Beck, *op.cit.*,
p198.

9. Dick Hebdige
'Redeeming Witness –
In The Tracks of the
Homeless Vehicle
Project', *Cultural
Studies*, Volume 7,
Number 2, 1993,
pp173-223 cf. Neil
Smith 'Homeless/
Global: Scaling Places'
in Jon Bird *et al.*, (eds),
*Mapping the Futures:
Local Cultures Global
Change*, Routledge,
London 1993.

10. Hebdige, *op.cit.*,
p186, my emphasis.

11. Jean Baudrillard,
*For a Critique of the
Political Economy of the
Sign*, Telos Press, New
York 1981, chapter 4.

12. Gilles Deleuze and
Felix Guattari, *A
Thousand Plateaus:
Capitalism and
Schizophrenia*, Athlone
Press, London 1988,
p4.

publicity', the media emerges as a central 'site' for this new 'sub-politics'.[8] This is useful background for understanding *House* (with its strange alchemy of public and private space, its structure as media event and latent political content).

There is however little specific precedent for investigating a work such as *House*. Dick Hebdige's recent pioneering study of Krzysztof Wodiczko's *Homeless Vehicle Project* is therefore this article's third and indispensable context.[9] Hebdige, through an impassioned analysis of how Wodiczko's work addresses its viewers, develops the important notion of 'witnessing' as a form of social awareness. A weakness is that Hebdige conceives 'witnessing' entirely within the frame of the act of reading the art work itself. In a typical passage, he comments: 'What makes it so difficult to dismiss this project out of hand is the challenge it issues *to all those who enter into dialogue with it* to improve upon Wodiczko's own "modest proposals" [to help the homeless]'.[10] The qualification is crucial. For it is precisely behind the cover of that qualification that we must investigate: who enters into dialogue, how, in what context and on whose terms?

A certain scepticism is necessary. Like Baudrillard we should question whether a work of art 'speaks to us' directly, let alone 'confronts reality'.[11] I aim to be less a 'witness' of what *House* 'revealed', still less an explicator of the work's 'inside', more an investigator of its outside(s), conceiving art, like the book in Deleuze and Guattari's formulation, to 'exist only through the outside and on the outside', the outside(s), that is, of public space and the public sphere themselves.[12]

I   *HOUSE* AND ITS RECEPTION

Background

Like most houses in Bow, 193 Grove Road, the site or rather frame of *House*, was terraced.

Bow is a 'neighbourhood' of Tower Hamlets (an administrative division of the Borough introduced in the 1980s). Tower Hamlets (due east of London's financial centre, The City and having as its southernmost region Docklands, where a new business centre famously failed in the 1980s) is one of London's poorest boroughs with high unemployment and severe housing problems. Bow is not one of the poorest neighbourhoods but shares many of Tower Hamlets' general characteristics: 57 per cent of its housing is council-provided, less than 1 per cent is detached or semi-detached and almost 60 per cent of its households do not have a car.[13]

Housing is a central political issue locally. Claims of 'bias' in favour of ethnic minorities on the council waiting list characterised the campaign of a British National Party candidate elected in Docklands in September 1993. Nor is the public evironment a neutral issue: the extension of the park which required 193 Grove Road's demolition conformed to a general council policy of improving the look of the area: 'old-style' lampposts, ornamental park gates, plaques marking the Bow Heritage Trail. Some councillors hoped a bold, new public sculpture would benefit the neighbourhood's image.

13. Figures based on the 1991 UK Government census.

What was the background to the artistic conception of *House*? The history of art in public spaces is complex but two points are crucial. First, during the twentieth century many ideas have influenced public art apart from its long-term antecedents in monuments and architecture: the search for art's wider public function; increasing dissatisfaction with the limitations of the painting frame and gallery space; and a critique through artistic intervention of conventions of public space and architecture.[14]

Secondly, a break in this history occurred in the late 1970s and early 1980s when new questions about how art interacts with its public became central. Many factors came together: feminist critiques of art institutions, Joseph Beuys' notion of 'social sculpture', the practice of art in community programmes, critiques of the implication of earlier public art with corporate interests. This new public art emphasised not just process, but the particular active process of making art with the public. It could envisage public art as a discursive space, 'a community meeting place' (Vito Acconci).[15] It often favoured public sculpture which avoided claims to permanence yet was politically engaged.[16]

14. See for example, Rosalind Krauss, 'Sculpture in the Expanded Field' in *The Originality of the Avant Garde and Other Modernist Myths*, MIT Press, Cambridge, Mass. 1985, and Michael Archer, in Nicholas De Oliveira *et al* (eds), *Installation Art*, Thames and Hudson, London 1994.

House was intended as temporary and to have relevance to issues of local significance. It belongs therefore to this new phase of public art.

15. Quoted in Michael North, 'The Public as Sculpture: From Heavenly City to Mass Ornament' in W.J.T. Mitchell, (ed), *Art and the Public Interest*, University of Chicago Press, Chicago 1992, p20.

The Sequence of Events

Early in 1993 Artangel (who commissioned *House*) agreed with Bow Neighbourhood a temporary lease of 193 Grove Road after researching widely for a suitable location for Rachel Whiteread's projected piece. Substantial audiences and media coverage for *House* were expected; the proposal was endorsed by prominent art bodies and sponsored by Beck's Beer.

16. See for example Krzysztof Wodiczko quoted in Hebdige *op.cit.*, p190.

Delays in starting the casting process meant the sculpture was not unveiled until 25 October (leaving less time than planned for viewing before the lease expired at the end of November). Sidney Gale, the house's occupant, was rehoused by the council over the summer. After the opening, there was an explosion of praise from the national broadsheets. Opposition to the sculpture (from local people and critics) was already newsworthy.[17] Soon people were reported as travelling long distances to see *House*.[18]

A crucial factor in this public and media interest was the context of the Turner Prize, given annually by the Tate Gallery to a young British artist for an outstanding exhibition in the last twelve months. The prize's alleged bias towards neoconceptual art had been controversial for years, but with Whiteread one of the four prize nominees, *House* became a principal focus of attention in the often hostile coverage of the prize. Interest was intensified by the K Foundation (a front for the former pop group, the KLF) who advertised an award of double the Turner Prize money for the 'worst' artist, to be nominated by the public from the Turner nominees.

17. *News At Ten*, 25 October, *Independent*, 26 October, *Evening Standard*, 28 October 1993.

18. Letter to *Independent*, 4 November 1993.

On Tuesday 23 November, the Turner Prizegiving was to be televised live on

Channel 4. The K Foundation had booked an advertising slot in the programme to announce the result of their counter-prize. Earlier that evening, a councillors' meeting to consider Artangel's request for extension of the lease (already publicly rejected by Eric Flounders, the chair of Bow Neighbourhood) was scheduled.

Within a few hours, Whiteread was awarded the Turner Prize and the K Foundation's Prize (in the form of almost £40,000 in cash nailed to a frame and chained to the Tate Gallery's railings) and the Bow Neighbourhood (on a split vote) rejected extension. Debate about *House* intensified. The neighbourhood received more than a hundred letters overwhelmingly supporting extension, the Bow Neighbourhood Forum voted similarly and the local Labour MP obtained House of Commons support to put down a motion calling for a local referendum on *House's* life. The next weekend the surrounding parkland was full of people viewing, arguing and being lobbied by different sides. Substantial petitions for and against *House's* removal were collected.

Delays in arranging demolition ensured that *House* survived beyond 30 November, the reprieve becoming official when benefactors, including Channel 4 and Beck's, paid to extend the lease until the New Year.

By the eventual demolition on 11 January 1994, Artangel claimed 100,000 visitors to the site. Demolition occurred in front of television cameras, Rachel Whiteread and Sidney Gale looking on. By then the press had already billed the episode as an example of 'the eternal struggle between art and authority', a dispute 'In the House of the Philistines' or 'one of the most enjoyable cultural squabbles for years'.[19]

19. Respectively, *Guardian Weekly*, 5 December, *Guardian*, 31 December and *Sunday Telegraph*, 5 December 1993.

Media Coverage

UK media attention was extensive: 20 reviews, 3 editorials, almost 50 news and comment items, 32 items in letters columns and more than ten cartoons and other humorous references. There was regular coverage in the *East London Advertiser* and at key points coverage in many regional newspapers across Britain. There was also considerable interest in weekly magazines, in addition to television and the international press coverage.

The storyline *House* emerged against the background of well-established storylines about modern art and the 'follies' of the Turner Prize in particular. In addition, *House* quickly became a convenient reference point for other issues: the standing of a controversial critic who opposed *House* (Brian Sewell), the adequacy of government arts funding and the value of business sponsorship.

Clear patterns emerge. There was universal and exceptional acclaim for *House* from the *arts* correspondents in the broadsheets. *House* was typically read as some kind of statement: for example 'a stark comment on social realities' or 'as commemorating a century of domestic life even as it insists on the impossibility of recovering the lost lives spent within it'.[20] As the controversy heightened, positions became increasingly rhetorical, with calls (more appropriate to debates on earlier *permanent* public art) for *House* to be

20. Respectively, *Time Out*, 27 October/3 November and *The Times*, 5 November 1993.

preserved.[21]

Hostility to *House* took three forms: (i) reviews by arts correspondents of some conservative tabloids; (ii) comment by *non-art* columnists in both those tabloids and also some broadsheets (in the latter case, conflicting with those papers' own arts correspondents); and (iii) indirectly, through news items about the sculpture which emphasised negative local reaction. *House* was criticised *not* for failing in its artistic aims but more fundamentally for not being art: it was 'junk', 'facile and fleeting', 'ultimately boring'.[22]

Positions taken on *House* itself and on the Turner Prize were generally matched. Writers hostile to *House* connected it with a wider malaise represented by a Turner Prize under the control of a new 'arts establishment' or 'arts elite', generally described as 'rich', always as unrepresentative of popular taste.[23] *House*'s supporters generally supported the Prize although some qualified their position.

Both sides of the debate sought to represent popular opinion on the sculpture, in news stories about reactions, vox pops and in references to popular support in the course of review and comment.[24]

Many arts figures contacted Bow calling for *House*'s reprieve. Within the media, *House* became a controversy in which 'it was important to know which side you're on'.[25]

Popular Reaction

Aside from media representations, what was the actual balance of popular opinion?

The majority of views recorded were expressed in the context of interest in whether *House*'s life should be extended. Sources available to me were as follows: letters to national and local newspapers (both for and against extension), the petition against extension (containing little explicit comment), vox pops and scattered references in media coverage, and unpublished letters written to Bow. In the last category, I saw 129 letters of which 3 opposed and the rest supported extension (32 were identifiably from arts professionals and 10 from pupils at a local school): unfortunately the letters written to Whiteread were unavailable to me. The views of those indifferent or hostile to the sculpture are likely to be underrepresented in these written records. Beyond that, lies the largely irrecoverable territory of the discussions on and off site. Any conclusions must therefore be tentative.

It is clear however that local opinion was split. Those lobbying for *House*'s removal claimed 90 per cent support in the immediate neighbourhood although their petition is consistent with a lower level of support. It was this position that Councillor Flounders sought to represent. But a significant local minority liked the sculpture or at least were interested in it. This was reflected in letters to the council and the press, in anecdotal references from the site and most strikingly in the political disagreements (among councillors and between the council and the local MP). There was also wide interest in *House* across London and Britain: many letters mention long journeys to visit it, others refer

21. Editorial in *Independent*, 3 November 1993.

22. Respectively, *Observer*, 28 November (Richard Ingrams), *The Times*, 20 November (Simon Jenkins), and *Mail on Sunday*, 28 November 1993.

23. *Sunday Telegraph*, 31 October and editorial, 7 November, *The Economist*, 20-26 November, *Financial Times*, 27 November (Anthony Thorncroft) and *Evening Standard*, 4 November 1993.

24. News items: e.g. *Independent on Sunday*, 24 October, *East London Advertiser*, 28 October and *Evening Standard*, 28 October 1993.

25. *Guardian*, 31 December 1993 (Arts Editor).

to frequent return visits.

Recorded views expressed against *House* fell into three categories. First, the view that the sculpture was 'rubbish', just 'concrete': a refusal to read the work in any way at all. Here there was partial overlap with media hostility in spite of a difference in language. Secondly, the view (normally combined with the first) of *House* as an unwelcome interference by (rich, successful) 'outsiders' in the affairs of 'locals'.[26] A related complaint was that the sculpture's funding would have been better spent on actual housing. Finally, a few connected with the arts world argued that *House* failed as public art as it ignored local issues, recalling old debates within public art.[27]

Recorded views in favour of *House* were more varied. Among 'public' reasons were: the economic benefit accruing from *House* in terms of tourism; *House* as civic asset giving pleasure to local people (many suggested landscaping the park to accommodate it); *House* as bringing international attention to the neighbourhood. There were more personal reasons: *House's* value as a statement (whether on housing policy or simply on 'how things were'); the issue of democracy (the right of people to see the sculpture and participate in the debate); and finally an anxiety to be among 'those who will have seen' *House*.[28]

Whatever the actual balance of opinion, *House* acquired national notoriety, as stock material for press cartoons and end-of-year quizzes.

Preliminary Comments

We should not dismiss these events as a media-enhanced version of an old battle: 'modern art' against an uncomprehending public. That would be too simple as can easily be shown.

Although *House* provoked a split in opinion, both sides shared one thing: they misrepresented each other. *Opponents* of *House* who accused it of being a sport 'for the gallery-going classes of Hampstead' (Flounders) or the Turner Prize of being a 'freak show' representing 'a clique of rich and silly people' (Sewell) completely ignored the considerable public interest in both, stretching beyond one locality or socio-economic group. *Supporters* of *House* frequently referred to their opponents as the tabloid press who prevented 'the people' appreciating *House* fully. Yet on the contrary, the largest circulation tabloids made nothing of the story and a number of writers in the broadsheets attacked *House*. Nor were all the opponents of *House* 'philistines' (as its supporters' rhetoric often suggested): many of its media opponents (often themselves articulate commentators on art or other matters) including the KLF supported a *different kind* of art, rather than rejecting art as such.

These misrepresentations were convenient for the claims of both sides that they (not their opponents) represented popular opinion. In *House* (a space where 'the people' actually gathered together and could be 'consulted') 'representing' what the people thought acquired a charged significance. But *what was it* on which people were being represented? Certainly not the issues which Whiteread sought to raise: there was little debate about housing during the controversy. Certainly not either the issue of what form public art should

26. See especially Flounders' published letters, (*Independent*, 4, 17, 25 November and *The Guardian*, 1 December 1993).

27. Letters in *Guardian*, 13 December and *East London Advertiser*, 4 November 1993.

28. Cf. Claus-Dieter Rath, 'The Invisible Network' in P. Drummond and R. Paterson (eds), *Television and its Audiences*, British Film Institute, London 1988.

take, which while raised implicitly by *House's* supporters was ignored by virtually all its opponents. Certainly not merely the value of *House* as individual work. Throughout there was at stake the issue: what is art ('Is it art?') and, underlying that, who is qualified to define what art is. *House* was not only an individual statement on public issues but also a token in a quite different, long-standing dispute about the capital (in Bourdieu's extended sense) at stake in the visual arts, a dispute dramatised in the heightened rhetoric of the Turner Prize ceremony.

This may explain the 'alliance' between (i) art correspondents of conservative newspapers and some non-art columnists (together representing an earlier arts establishment with a rival form of capital to that represented by *House*), (ii) local people hostile to *House* (who often lacked cultural capital) and (iii) the K Foundation (who claimed to despise capital).

We should not assume that popular opinion simply *reproduced* the polarisation in media coverage of *House*. As the letters to Bow in particular make clear, some people began hostile and became supporters of *House*, others remained sceptical but argued for an extension in the interests of debate, still others expressed limited interest in *House* itself but supported its permanent installation on economic grounds.

Popular reaction may have operated in part *beyond* the confines of the media debate.

II MODELS

In this section, I will consider various possible models for understanding *House* and reactions to it. I aim to show not only that each model is inadequate but also that the search for an all-encompassing model is misguided.

Art as Text

House was a non-verbal physical structure. Yet there is plenty of precedent for understanding its reception on a model developed primarily in the context of verbal communication (on conceiving the non-verbal as 'text'): from the implicit textualism of ideological theories of art (Janet Wolff)[29] to explicitly textual interpretations developed from semiotics (Barthes, Stuart Hall's encoding/decoding model of television, John Fiske's interpretation of the beach as text).[30] A theory of visual art based on Halliday's social semiotics has recently been developed by Michael O'Toole.[31]

There is initial plausibility in applying a textual model to *House*. Supportive critics *did* regard it as a communication whose content could be analysed. We might also analyse the Turner Prize process as a 'text' of which the K Foundation's counter-prize was an 'oppositional reading'.[32]

But any textual model must at least identify a 'communication' which is the 'text' to be interpreted. A fundamental difficulty with *House* is that the differences between its supporters and opponents were precisely not differences about *how* to interpret it, operating on the shared ground that it

29. Janet Wolff, *The Social Production of Art*, Macmillan, Basingstoke, 1981.

30. Roland Barthes, *Mythologies*, Paladin, London, 1972; Stuart Hall 'Encoding/ Decoding' in Stuart Hall *et al*, (eds), *Culture, Media, Language*, Routledge, London 1992; John Fiske, *Reading the Popular*, Unwin Hyman, London 1989, pp43ff.

31. Michael O'Toole, *The Language of Displayed Art*, Leicester University Press, Leicester 1994.

32. Cf Hall, *op.cit.*

was something-to-be-interpreted. Rather, opponents *refused* the act of interpretation and thereby *House's* status as text, rejecting in principle the textual claims of many of *House's* supporters: as Flounders wrote, '*House* is not a statement about housing under Thatcher or anything else. It is rubbish'. (Nor should we simply assume that *House's* supporters liked it only because they interpreted it in certain ways: they may have liked it partly because it was a space which enabled other discursive practices not directed at *House* e.g. memory.)

Any model of *House* which privileges its 'textuality' thereby neglects the extent to which its status as text was contested. The virtue which O'Toole claims for his theory of art (that 'it *starts* with the text of the art work itself') is precisely its limitation.[33] The same limitation is disguised in practice beneath unexamined claims of the statements art works make. I clarify below what role textuality should play in any account of *House*.

33. O'Toole, *op.cit.*, p170, my emphasis.

Distinction

Once we acknowledge that *House's* status as text was contested, we require some grasp of the social practices in which related meaning-claims were made, received – and rejected. The most developed such thesis is Pierre Bourdieu's class-based theory of taste which interprets individuals' artistic taste in terms of strategies to maximise their (symbolic and economic) capital, strategies which themselves reflect the 'habitus' or 'system of dispositions' shaped by common experiences of the classes to which those individuals belong.[34]

34. Pierre Bourdieu, *Distinction: a Social Critique of the Judgment of Taste*, Routledge, London 1984.

Without full empirical evidence (of class status, educational history etc.) we cannot determine whether Bourdieu's theory was exemplified by reactions to *House*. But is his theory a plausible starting-point for understanding *House*? In particular, are the two fundamental divisions that result from the theory helpful: (i) between the 'aesthetic code' (of the dominant, capital-holding class) and the 'non-aesthetic', purely functional attitude to art of the dominated, working class who lack capital and whose early experiences are shaped by 'necessity'; and (ii) (within the dominant class) between the aesthetic attitude of the dominant fraction (the bourgeoisie, with predominantly economic capital) requiring from art 'emblems of distinction' and that of the 'dominated' fraction (the intellectuals, with predominantly symbolic capital) requiring from art 'a symbolic challenging of social reality'.[35]

35. *Ibid.*, pp54-57 and 293.

36. See Pierre Bourdieu, 'Cultural Reproduction and Social Reproduction' in R. Brown (ed), *Knowledge, Education and Cultural Change*, Tavistock, London 1973, and Eileen Hooper-Greenhill, 'Counting Visitors or Visitors who Count?' in Robert Lumley (ed), *The Museum Time Machine: Putting Cultures on Display*, Comedia, London 1988.

House was ideally suited to demonstrate both divisions: (i) as a conversion of a functional object (a home) into a non-functional object situated in functional spaces (park and street); and (ii) as an art object which expended economic capital yet had no apparent economic worth and was viewable by anyone whatever their capital. *House* should have provided living proof of these divisions in open public space beyond the museum (whose audience is preselected to reflect those divisions).[36]

Media views of *House* can be seen partly in terms of a dispute about capital within the aesthetic field: Section I. Bourdieu's theory of distinction cannot however provide a total explanatory model of reactions, as becomes clear when we examine its underlying principles.

First, Bourdieu's account of capital-maximising strategies gets purchase *only* relative to 'fields' where specific types of capital are already agreed to be at stake.[37] What if there is no such agreement? Bourdieu's theory contains no criteria to resolve which field action belongs to. Nor therefore can it explain situations where the question 'Which field?' is itself contested by the agents. Yet some hostile reactions judged *House* not in terms of its aesthetic status but in terms of other forms of capital: for instance, the field of professional skills (implicit in local portrayals of Whiteread as a 'top' artist intervening in an 'ordinary' house in the locality).[38]

Second, Bourdieu's theory has as its building blocks clearly distinguishable class aesthetics: it cannot adequately explain why in the case of *House* there were divisions (angrily contested) within the local, predominantly working- and lower-middle-class population, let alone why individuals who began prejudiced against art changed their opinion. If letters by art professionals and children are excluded, 10 per cent of the unpublished letters on *House* claim such a change.

From which follows the third difficulty. Bourdieu depicts habitus as an 'objective intention ... which *always outruns* his [the agent's] conscious intentions' and in only one way: 'in a class society, *all* the products of a given agent ... speak *inseparably and simultaneously* of his class'.[39] By excluding individual reaction and adjustments, Bourdieu's theory is silent on how practices may be articulated together in a shared situation (the Foucauldian question of how discourses form the objects of which they speak). It omits therefore perhaps the most important aspect of *House*.

Some theory of distinction may still be useful here. Paul Dimaggio's rather different theory proposes that the arts (and media generally) provide society's shared material in terms of which various strategies of social differentiation can be pursued. It follows that groups with different educational and social histories may differ less in their orientation to cultural objects and more in their facility to range across the cultural terrain.[40] This theory is open to the possibility that social groups may be 'exposed' to each other through the mediation of art, especially art which becomes a media event. We need now to address *House's* status as a broadcast event.

Media Influence and Media Events

We can hardly make sense of *House* as event except within the dramaturgical structure it acquired through its media coverage (especially the coincidence of its display and the Turner Prize build-up).

The polarisation of media coverage turned on depicting *House* as a token for 'the state of modern art' around which rival definitions of aesthetic capital could compete. Depicting Whiteread as individual battling against uncomprehending authority was no less conventionally dramatised in the storyline of *House's* demolition. The principal sources for this presentation were standard: critics, organisers, and journalists with a general interest in art or national affairs. Other opinion was filtered through vox pops or confined to letters

37. Cf. Richard Jenkins, *Pierre Bourdieu*, Routledge, London 1992, p85.

38. See e.g. *East London Advertiser*, 29 July and 28 October 1993 and Flounders' letters cited in note 26.

39. Pierre Bourdieu, *Outline of a Theory of Practice*, Cambridge University Press, Cambridge 1977, pp79 and 87, my emphasis.

40. Paul Dimaggio, 'Classification in Art', *American Sociological Review*, Volume 52, Number 4, 1987, pp440-455.

pages. *Policing The Crisis* remains useful in explaining how production time pressures dictate reliance on standard story repertoire and a limited range of official sources, so that more complex patterns of non-official discourse are

41. Stuart Hall *et al*, *Policing the Crisis: 'Mugging', the State and Law and Order*, Macmillan, Basingstoke, 1978.

systematically ignored.[41] Less plausible is applying that book's wider thesis to argue that media coverage served the interests of a dominant group. What set of interests united the Government, Bow councillors, Beck's Beer, Artangel and the Tate Gallery?

The work of Dayan and Katz on 'media events', although concentrated on the live presentation of national ceremonials, establishes important principles here.[42] They explain how national media coverage of a flow of events may be 'performative' in J.L. Austin's sense, creating a media event in the act of performing it.[43] The event so 'performed' will have a narrative structure suitable for its media presentation: for example the 'Contest', fulfilled at various levels in *House*.[44] By 'retextualizing' social action, the media may reformulate it in a 'subjunctive', 'as-if' mode, so that its unfolding foregrounds different issues from those relevant to the actions comprising its 'raw material'.[45]

42. D. Dayan and E. Katz, *Media Events: The Live Broadcasting of History*, Harvard University Press, Cambridge, Massachusetts. 1992.

43. *Ibid.*, pp20, 114.

44. *Ibid.*, p38.

45. *Ibid.*, pp100-101.

Dayan and Katz's recognition of the transformative power of media events allows us to reintegrate the textual aspects of *House*. We do need not a formal textual model but we need to focus on textualizing as a process which is contingent, multiple and contestable. This entails relativizing the term 'text' to mean what is framed when a relative stability of context enables one or more structures of interpretation. An event such as *House* may contain many virtual texts sustained for different periods by different sources and for different readers.[46] The media have a privileged but not exclusive role in generating such virtual texts.

46. Cf. the discussion of the 'virtual power of metaphor', in Dick Hebdige, 'Training Some Thoughts on the Future', in Jon Bird *et al* (eds), *op.cit.*

de Certeau's Anti-model

Michel de Certeau, however, posed an important challenge to each of the preceding types of model by arguing that *within* whatever strategies or structures we identify (textual, practical, media-centred) there is always space in which other heterogeneous tactics subsist unacknowledged, unarticulated: practices 'the trajectories [of which] trace out the ruses of other interests and desires that are neither determined nor captured by the systems in which they develop'.[47] In particular, de Certeau draws attention to 'anti-texts' which found spaces by juxtaposing elements of existing texts: for example, the private, barely unacknowledged stories which people tell about places or which they enact by walking through them.[48] Because the tactics of 'the weak' are precisely those regularities which are not articulated within formal discourse, no discourse on his view is adequate to model the totality of strategies and tactics. In that sense his position is an anti-model.

47. Michel de Certeau, *The Practice of Everyday Life*, University of California Press, Berkeley, 1984 pxviii.

48. *Ibid*, pp106-7.

Is this a way of holding in suspense each of the different elements (textuality, practice, media effects) so far considered without arbitrating between them (a tempting 'solution')? Certainly many aspects of *House* can be seen as tactics: the graffiti, the discussions on site, the joke estate agent's board erected outside. de

Certeau's observations on the generation of anti-texts have an affinity with the process of reappropriation in recent visual art of which *House* is just one example.[49] Indeed in his observations on how private memory inheres in houses, he wrote what is virtually *House's* epitaph: 'It is striking here that the places people live in are like the presences of diverse absences. What can be seen designates what is no longer there: "you *see*, here there used to be ...", but it can no longer be seen'.[50]

We cannot assume however (as John Fiske in his adaptations of de Certeau appears to imply) that tactics as such automatically comprise resistance by 'the people' (in some positive sense) and are opposed to strategies (associated with power, in some pejorative sense).[51] Although we know very little of individual viewers' experiences on site, it seems plausible that 'tactics' (reminiscing, the recontextualizing involved in walking around the site) were practised as much by those with discursive power as by those without and that even the latter adopted strategies aimed at closing off the tactical space which *House* had become. We should concentrate less on the distinction between strategy and tactics in itself and more on how both strategic power and tactical freedom are distributed unevenly. I return to the issue(s) of power below.

Beyond Models

House was not only an object in art or media discourse, it was also a physical object in shared space. Many theorists recently have emphasised the centrality of spatial practice to understanding social phenomena.[52]

Consider the physical situation of *House*. When first displayed, numbers visiting it were limited: you could view it alone (as I did). If we remember Goffman's observations on the embarrassment of lacking a screen between oneself and other interactions in the same place, we can see that viewing *House* alone (in view of passing cars or pedestrians) may have involved the embarrassment of being looked at while looking, an embarrassment perhaps all the more acute for anyone self-conscious about not knowing how to look like someone who knew how to look at art![53]

Consider how the space around *House* changed as audiences increased and (as a televised site) it became charged with media significance. Now it was the focus of multiple social situations, chance interactions, became perhaps what Amos Rapoport has called a 'critical space' where spatial and other meanings are intensified.[54]

Rapoport's work has explored how buildings bear meaning, especially 'users' meaning' which may differ from constructors' or planners' meanings. *House* potentially bore users' meaning in a number of ways: as a quasi-domestic structure, as an alteration of the wider environment (street and park), as the focus of a public social space. Yet its meanings were certainly not clear: while lacking the normal external features of a house, its outside bore the traces of normally unseen inner space, it was an addition to public space that was in some senses private. Even its graffiti had meaning, suggesting a possible deterioration of the public environment, a fall in property values (as some

49. See e.g. Robert Hewison, *Future Tense: A New Art for the Nineties*, Methuen, London 1990; Neil Cummings, 'Reading Things: The Alibi of Use', in Neil Cummings (ed), *Reading Texts*, Chance Books, London 1993; Nick de Ville, 'The Noumenal and the Everyday', in *Refusing to Surface: Art and the Transformation of the Ordinary*, John Hansard Gallery, Southampton/Ikon Gallery, Birmingham 1993.

50. de Certeau, *op.cit.*, p108.

51. John Fiske, *Power Plays Power Works*, Routledge, London 1993.

52. See e.g. Torsten Hagerstrand, 'Space, Time and Human Conditions' in A. Karlqvist *et al* (eds), *Dynamic Allocation of Urban Space*, Saxon House, London 1975; Allan Pred, *Making Histories and Constructing Human Geographies: The Local Transformation of Practice, Power Relations and Consciousness*, Westview Press, Boulder 1990.

53. Erving Goffman, *Behavior in Public Places*, Free Press of Glencoe, New York 1963, pp125-6.

54. Amos Rapoport, *The Meaning of the Built Environment: A Nonverbal Communication Approach*, Sage, London 1992, pp191ff.

55. *Ibid. passim.*

living opposite feared).[55]

Consider also the wider spatial context: how the 'time-space lines' (Hagerstrand) of 'locals' (who saw *House* on their way to somewhere else) differed sharply from those of visitors (who came to view it and then returned to somewhere else). This had real practical significance: the traffic congestion as taxis and cars unloaded visitors at the site.

In all these ways, space mattered – continuously, variously (although the details are largely lost to us).

We need to connect these insights with the theories discussed earlier in this section. Paradoxically, I would argue, we can only do so if we recognise that no single model (however complex) can make the necessary connections. We can focus this issue by considering aspects of the spatial itself.

56. Doreen Massey, 'Politics and Space/ Time' in *New Left Review*, November/ December 1992, pp65-84.

57. *Ibid.*, p80.

Doreen Massey's comments are important here.[56] Avoiding any metaphorical characterisation of spatiality, she emphasises the spatial as literally 'the simultaneous coexistence of social interrelations and interactions at all spatial scales, from the most local to the most global'.[57] Here 'simultaneous coexistence' implies not the possibility of being understood together but rather the radical complexity of space-time, as the frame for events which cannot be reduced to a single coherent reading. Thus, although in *House* many actions, many texts, came together in one spatio-temporal frame, this 'coming together' bore no promise of a unified explanatory model.

58. Dayan and Katz, *op.cit.*, p20.

Grasping that complexity should not lead us to underestimate those processes (including media narrative and art discourse) by which the heterogeneous may appear to be focused in an event. This appearance is 'transformative' (in Dayan and Katz's term);[58] transforming one or more levels of social action into an event, but transformative within theory also, inducing in theory a sense of 'falling' (between levels, between and beyond models). My conclusion will explore these thoughts further.

III CONTEXTS

Before that I want to sketch briefly other contexts in which *House* (as work and event) can be understood. I intend to imply no hierarchy among these contexts or the virtual texts available within them.

Public and Private Space

House was not just a monument. It was an issue in the official ordering of public space, affecting traffic flows and long-term planning decisions. It was also a space through which the public moved, where people stayed to argue and reflect. A discursive space, broadcast nationally, whose physical preservation became a democratic issue as shown in people's concern that the sculpture should be reprieved so that others could have the chance to 'make up their minds' (there are 20 examples of this in the unpublished letters, cf. letters in *The Independent*, 20 November and 1 December 1993). A counter-example perhaps to theories that public space has been destroyed by the speed of communications.[59]

House was also at least two private spaces: the former home of Sidney Gale and the neighbourhood of those who lived close by. Sidney Gale's opposition to *House* was understandable yet, when it was demolished, he talked as if it actually *was* his home coming down, confirming indirectly the sculpture's symbolic power ('they're pulling down my bedroom now').[60]

House could stand in for other domestic spaces too: for home as the place where humans face death;[61] home as site of resistance against authority.[62] One woman (about to lose her home to make way for the M11 motorway) wrote to Bow that *House* was 'extremely relevant to the predicament facing a great many East Londoners'. Beyond that, *House* by dramatising the loss of a single home provoked many different perspectives of loss: the loss of an era (perhaps mythical?) of comfortable public housing, the loss of the East End 'as it was'. And while housing issues figured little in public discussion explicitly, they were present obliquely in the text painted on *House's* side: HOUSES FOR ALL BLACK AND WHITE.

Local/Global

We saw earlier how an opposition between 'locals' and (rich, privileged) 'outsiders' was common to much local hostility to *House*. Wider issues are at stake.

First, *House* (the transformation into art of a domestic space) might, however unfairly, be interpreted as a colonisation, connecting with old attacks on public art,[63] as well as the process of gentrification.[64] Gentrification crucially involves raising the economic value of properties and improving their immediate environment: hence the importance of preservation and 'aesthetic selection', a process whereby elites transform 'the vernacular' into 'a new landscape of power'.[65] *House's* construction was *not* of course a direct example of gentrification; instead it prolonged temporarily a house that was already condemned. Yet debates about *House* were certainly marked by that wider issue: e.g. Councillor Flounders claimed those supporting *House's* reprieve were mainly 'gentrifiers'.[66] As Zukin reminds us, artistic practice is rarely innocent of actual spatial claims.

Secondly, *House*, which required co-ordination of information, funding and skills from beyond the locality, was an operation in what Lefebvre analysed as the abstract space in which capital and information are circulated and what Castells has called the 'space of information flows'.[67] Yet as an object inserted in a specific locality, *House* was also part of a different process whereby local meaning was contested. It therefore illustrated Castells' thesis that increasingly intense disputes about the uses of local space (fought often at the expense of and in opposition to wider communicative connections) are the counterpart to the increasingly powerful flow of capital and information beyond and largely without reference to localities.[68]

It does not follow that local matters are of no interest to capital: on the

59. See Paul Virilio, *Speed and Politics*, Semiotext(e), New York 1986.

60. *Daily Mail*, 12 January 1994.

61. Cf. Martin Heidegger, 'Building Dwelling Thinking' in *Poetry, Language, Thought*, trans. A. Hofstadter, Harper and Row, New York 1975, p157.

62. Cf. bell hooks, *Yearning: Race, Gender and Cultural Politics*, Turnaround, London 1991, chapter 5.

63. See Malcolm Miles *et al, Art For Public Places: Critical Essays*, Winchester School of Art Press, Winchester 1989, p86.

64. See e.g. Neil Smith and Peter Williams, *Gentrification in the City*, Allen and Unwin, Winchester, Massachusetts. 1986.

65. Sharon Zukin, 'The City as Landscape of Power in Global Finance and Urban Living: London and New York as Global Financial Capitals' in L. Budd and S. Whimster, *Global Finance and Urban Living: A Study of Metropolitan Change*, Routledge, London 1992, especially pp198-9.

66. *Independent on Sunday*, 5 December 1993.

67. Henri Lefebvre, *The Social Production of Space*, Blackwell, Oxford 1991; Manuel Castells, *The Informational City: Information Technology, Economic Restructuring and The Urban-Regional Process*, Blackwell, Oxford 1989.

68. Castells, *op.cit.*, pp349-350.

69. David Harvey, *The Condition of Postmodernity*, Blackwell, Oxford 1989, pp295ff.

70. *East London Advertiser*, 2 December 1993.

71. See e.g. *Time Out*, 27 October 1993.

72. See S.C. Carpenter, *Winnington-Ingram: The Biography of Arthur Foley Winnington-Ingram, Bishop of London 1901-1939*, Hodder and Stoughton, London 1949, pp30 and 27 respectively.

73. See Stefan Muthesius, *The English Terraced House*, Yale University Press, New Haven 1982, p11.

74. Respectively, *The Times*, 27 November 1993 and *Frieze*, January/February 1994.

75. See Patrick Wright, *On Living in an Old Country*, Verso, London 1985, especially chapter 6.

76. Harvey, *op.cit.*, p292.

contrary, as Harvey has argued, 'local colour' (whether architecture or festivals) is economically advantageous on a larger scale by distinguishing metropolitan areas from each other as attractive sites for capital.[69] Accordingly arguments based exclusively on local use may conflict with arguments based on the possibility of attracting spending from outside the locality: Bow Neighbourhood (arguing for more parkland) and locals (arguing for *House* as tourist attraction) were on opposite sides of such a conflict.

The global/local issue was not just economic. *House* also seemed to connect Bow as ordinary locality to the international arts world which *House* represented. Many letters expressed satisfaction that *House* had, as one put it, 'put Bow on the international contemporary arts map'.[70] This local interest directed at the 'centre' was matched by the 'centre's' disdain for the merely local, epitomised in critics' formulaic references to the 'dog toilet' of a park which would, supposedly, replace *House*.[71] There are historical resonances here too. It was only four or five generations ago that a desperately poor East End attracted evangelists' zeal: the period (from the 1880s until the Second World War) of extensive church building and the 'Settlements' by Oxford University ministers and undergraduates. Then 'men fresh from the studies and sports of the Universities went and lived among the poor and made friends with them' and a prominent vicar aimed to remove the Eastenders' 'poverty of life' 'by contact with those who possessed the means of higher life'.[72] Here perhaps lies part of the submerged context for some Eastenders' resistance to *House*, at least in the canonized form in which some supporters presented it.

Memory

House dramatised the demise of an earlier era of class-homogeneous housing: the terraced house that in 1911 comprised around 87 per cent of English homes but by 1971 only 30 per cent.[73] In this respect (as well as in its construction) *House's* role of monument might seem obvious and effective (it was a commonplace of critics' comments). Was this commemorative association more widely shared? Whiteread and Artangel emphasised the importance of memory in reactions to *House* they received, yet this was true of only a small minority of the letters sent to Bow.[74] We should beware of reading back into the gaps in the evidence the effect we assume *House* should have had. Yet *House* as representation of home was surely connected with wider processes: the growing obsession with preservation and heritage;[75] and the increasing role of the house as refuge from public space, as 'private museum'.[76]

House was intended as temporary yet (unlike the recent 'Counter-monuments' of German sculptors commissioned to mark aspects of Nazism or the Holocaust) its temporariness was not intended to be dramatised.[77] Yet Bow's intervention transformed it from the merely-temporary into the potentially-permanent-but-to-be-destroyed: becoming precisely a *counter-monument*, a monument to forgetting, whose destruction played out the memory erasure that it had been aimed (mutely) to resist.

Gender

As a public monument under a woman's direction, *House* ran counter to important stereotypes: the gendering of the public/private distinction;[78] the historical exclusion of women from 'monumental' art and their confinement to 'domestic' art;[79] and the regulation of women's circulation in public space.[80] While suggesting another stereotype (woman as 'defender of the home'), *House* (a home filled in to become unliveable) negated Ruskin's classic image of home as 'place of Peace'. Indeed it embodied Ruskin's suspicion that 'so far as the anxieties of the outer life penetrate into it ... it [the house] ceases to be home; it is then only a part of that outer world which you have roofed over'.[81]

House also reversed the cultural pattern which Bourdieu analysed in detail in Morocco in the 1960s yet which may still have importance: the house as closed private space, hidden from public view except in the perspective of the (male) controller of the house (entering from the surrounding public space).[82] *House* exposed the form of a house's inside by displaying a structure that could no longer be entered.[83] Yet although Whiteread was the first woman to win the Turner Prize, gender issues received little explicit comment. Nor do the letters written to Bow show significantly more women than men among *House's* supporters, although strikingly no woman attacked it publicly. More eloquent perhaps (but to whom?) were the photos of Whiteread on site in overalls and hard hat, surrounded by the signs of stereotypically 'man's work'.

Such contexts and virtual texts could be multiplied further. We cannot be exhaustive. We know only a small percentage of reactions at the time and indifference can be expected to leave few traces. Even an ethnographic study conducted today would tell us little of how *House* may by now variously have been forgotten.

IV CONCLUSION

I began by questioning any easy notion that art 'speaks to us directly'. I have been equally sceptical about whether the aspects of *House* can be reduced to a single model. I seem to have answered scepticism by scepticism. Yet any scepticism must earn its keep, by suggesting a wider space of connection and enquiry. I must now turn to the reverse, positive side of the earlier sceptical arguments. In particular I must defend the assumption, implicit throughout, that cultural studies should attempt to map (even if not model) the complexity of singular events. I will have to deal with the many issues arising rather schematically.

1. So ingrained is the temptation to seek textual objects as a sure starting point for interpretation, that (deconstruction notwithstanding) it remains useful to emphasise that general cultural analysis begins not from this or that text but from textualizing as a process, a process which analysis finds at work in particular complex circumstances (I am ignoring here the special case of the

77. See James Young, 'The Counter-Monument: Memory Against Itself in Germany Today' in Mitchell, *op.cit.*

78. See e.g. Michelle Rosaldo, 'Woman, Culture and Society: A Theoretical Overview', in Michelle Rosaldo and Louise Lamphere (eds), *Woman, Culture and Society*, Stanford University Press, Stanford 1974.

79. Roszika Parker and Griselda Pollock, *Old Mistresses: Women, Art and Ideology*, Routledge, London 1981.

80. Elizabeth Wilson, *The Sphinx and the City: Urban Life, The Control of Disorder and Women*, Virago, London 1991.

81. John Ruskin, *Sesame and Lilies*, Longmans, Green & Co., London 1925, p66.

82. Pierre Bourdieu, 'The Berber House' in Mary Douglas (ed), *Rules and Meanings*, Penguin, Harmondsworth 1972.

83. On the logic of 'reversed buildings' see Bill Hillier and Julienne Hanson, *The Social Logic of Space*, Cambridge University Press, Cambridge 1984, chapter 5.

literary text). *House* was no exception. We should see textualizing as the open-ended process producing the spaces across which connections, differences, negations (in short discursive processes) operate. This process endlessly repeats itself across events and the (relatively) stable objects we call texts. Both events and texts may therefore focus collections of virtual texts.

2. How are virtual texts connected to social context? First, if textualizing is open-ended, the meaning of a text cannot be fixed by the social context where it was originally formed. As Paul Willis has argued, many messages are 'made messages', they are 'made' (at least partly) 'in reception'.[84] The temporary alliances (Willis calls them 'proto-communities') that enable these messages to pass are contingent and their members may be unknown to each other. *House* surely generated a 'proto-community'. Yet textualizing is performed by agents with determinate resources, that set some limits on their actions. Bourdieu's theoretical position rightly insists upon the effectiveness of those limits beyond conscious planning; its weakness is to ignore how practice is a continual adjustment of resources and habits to context and context is established at least in part by a reflexive process open to conscious correction.[85] Not least surely among the sources of context is the process of media significance whereby media production sustains a shared general framework of significance against which more specific frameworks develop. This is not to supplant the process of social distinction entirely but rather to acknowledge the force of those media processes whereby practices, tastes and texts generally kept apart are brought together arbitrarily and with arbitrary speed;[86] producing the slippage that is more than just decontextualization, the shared sense of 'falling', the 'gravity' of an event.

3. *House* was precisely such a slippage: a breach or discontinuity which brought together in public conflicting practices, thereby stimulating new discourse.[87] Slippage, I would suggest, occurs when agents within one practice have to adjust to other practices (which may be represented by texts). Thus in *House*, different practices in relation to art and public space (a local spatial practice and a global discursive practice) confronted and adjusted to each other.

In the gravity of an event, the 'as-if' is lived for real, and the event's participants are the 'witnesses' (recalling Hebdige's term) of a conflict and resolution without precedent, which *only then* are being textualized. Such a 'confrontation' may occur either through the constructed simultaneity of a media event or in the proximity of public space. In *House*, remarkably, these circumstances were combined. *House* was both a spatial and a media frame in which many heterogeneous elements (art discourse, local politics, national issues, private memories) intersected, within and beyond available media narratives.

4. Alongside every such event runs the power of definition – and its contestation. Access to such power may itself be part of the capital on which strategies of distinction focus.[88] Public space (the overlapping nexus of many private

84. Paul Willis, *Common Culture: Symbolic Work at Play in the Everyday Cultures of the Young*, Open University Press, Milton Keynes 1990 pp133-145.

85. On the importance of reflexive adjustment in social 'reproduction' see Anthony Giddens, *The Constitution of Society*, Polity Press, Cambridge 1984.

86. Cf. Joshua Meyrowitz, *No Sense of Place: The Impact of Electronic Media on Social Behavior*, Oxford University Press, New York 1985.

87. Cf. Victor Turner, *Dramas, Fields and Metaphors: Symbolic Action in Human Society*, Cornell University Press, Ithaca 1974, pp38, 135.

88. Cf. Guy Debord, *Society of the Spectacle*, Black & Red, Detroit 1983.

spaces and public appropriations)[89] is a rich site for contesting such power, especially when (as with *House*) it is integrated into media narratives. Here perhaps we come close to the 'systematic dimension' according to which the 'gesture' of public art 'is organised' in the media age.[90]

5. I have talked of media events, the sense of an event and of events in general. Yet the term 'event' itself may raise difficulties. Any event is a multi-dimensional intersection of discursive and non-discursive practices, each of them irreducible to each other. An event therefore will not be reducible to a single model. But if we cannot in principle satisfactorily model an event, should we conclude that events are mere chimaeras and unworthy of study? No, provided we maintain Donald Davidson's distinction between an event (as such) and an event under description.[91] Whether an event has occurred is, he argues, quite independent from how it may be described. It follows that an event may exist under an infinite number of descriptions (some inconsistent with each other and all incomplete) without that calling into question whether the event occurred. Moreover (and this is the other aspect of his argument), that events exist is an irreducible presupposition of our language of action and explanation.[92] The most circumspect account of the play of discourses must assume that this was spoken/written then and there (extradiscursive fact).

6. Indeed, far from being problematic, events may be central to cultural analysis precisely because as events (occurrences in *specific spatio-temporal locations*) they reveal how the discursive and the extradiscursive, text and practice, intersect.[93] Moreover, as just argued, the spatial aspects of *House* were crucial, not marginal, to its particular power as event. Recalling Doreen Massey's insight, we can see that the spatiality of events is the guarantee both of their radical complexity and their theoretical importance.

The attempt to understand what happens when art intervenes in public space can, then, help us understand those other textualizing processes (the media in general) which offer accounts of 'the world'.[94] We cannot, however, assume we know the space where art speaks, still less what, to whom and in the name of whom it speaks.

We are all, unavoidably, readers of events in public space, all potential 'witnesses at the scene'. All readings, as Hebdige stresses, are necessarily partial yet in the shared and radically uncertain terrain of public space and the public sphere, to rest on individual partiality is not enough. Lacking the (only ever imagined) privilege of an Archimedean point from which to picture the whole, we must seek such perspective as we can. Here we need scepticism as much, perhaps more, than our personal loyalties, if we hope to make sense of what happens when someone (always more than one) speaks up in a public place.

89. Cf. Vito Acconci, 'Public Space in a Private Time' in Mitchell, *op.cit.*

90. Adapting Baudrillard's comment on modern painting: Baudrillard, *op.cit.*, p107.

91. Donald Davidson, *Essays on Actions and Events*, Oxford University Press, Oxford 1980, p155.

92. *Ibid.*, pp164-5.

93. On the importance of studying events rather than texts, see Janet Staiger, *Interpreting Films: Studies in the Historical Reception of American Cinema*, Princeton University Press, Princeton 1992, p9.

94. Compare Willis, *op.cit.*, p140.

IS NOTHING SACRED?

Rumina Sethi

Vassilis Lambropoulos, *The Rise of Eurocentrism: Anatomy of Interpretation*, Princeton University Press, Princeton 1993, pp471; £19.95 cloth.

Marx has noted that the ideas of the ruling class are in every epoch the ruling ideas. These ideas comprise the 'ideal expression' of the ruling material relationships of that class. Marx's views on the interests of the dominant groups in society forms, generally, the basis of Antonio Gramsci's theory of hegemony which gives the most thoroughgoing understanding of how a ruling group exercises and sustains domination through consent and persuasion. In other words, the ideas of the ruling class are not directly imposed through coercion over subordinate groups but permeated in society through a consensus of subordinate will in order to appear legitimate and normal.

In his recent book, *The Rise of Eurocentrism*, Vassilis Lambropoulos treats the controversial subject of the western hegemonic tradition, especially its development since the Protestant Reformation. His argument centres on the politics of 'interpretive imperative' and thus he goes on to explain the various Hellenic-Hebraic dialectical formations and the Hebraization of culture in the twentieth century. Lambropoulos' work is significant in present-day discussions concerning exegesis, canonicity, interpretive authority, tradition, originality and textuality, as he argues with much scholarship how the hermeneutics of interpretation constitutes, to take one example, the dominant impression of an unblemished, idolized Hellas – or a neglected, marginalized Israel. All such intellectual formations, in his view, bear the distinctive imprints of their political, religious, and philosophical structures.

It is interesting that Lambropoulos' book and Edward Said's *Culture and Imperialism* were published almost around the same time: both consider culture as a vehicle for the imperialist venture rather than as an area of art and learning alone. Following Gramscian parameters by treating culture as an instrument of political control, *Culture and Imperialism* has the ambitious scope of defining the patterns of relationships between the western world and its overseas territories.[1] Spurred by American forays into imperialism, Said takes the reader through two hundred years of narrative history with a view to highlight the unconscious imperial attitudes that underline the narratives of those writers scarcely associated with the governance of 'others'. Connecting Conrad and Jane Austen, for instance, with this enterprise, Said holds them culpable of depicting native peoples as 'marginally visible' and 'people without History'. It is in the very omission of the salient fact of imperialism that much English literature from *Jane Eyre*, *Vanity Fair* and *Great Expectations* to Raymond

1. Edward W. Said, *Culture and Imperialism*, Chatto and Windus, London 1993.

Williams' *Culture and Society* assumes its character. For Said, Conrad may be deeply anti-imperialist, but he is also an author who believes with equal conviction that Africa or South America could never have had a history or culture independent of their western masters. Earlier, *Robinson Crusoe* introduced to English gentry the founder of a new world and Defoe's *Captain Singleton*, less explicitly but surely, related to the annexation of riches and lands abroad. Less directly, Fielding, Richardson, Smolett, and Sterne did the same. Indeed, the English cultural forms like the novel and the opera served as important cultural affiliations within England, yet, unconsciously perhaps, ignored the presence of an area outside 'felt vaguely and ineptly to be out there' instead of, as a body of humanistic ideas, preventing the acceleration of imperial powers.

Quite in the same way, Lambropoulos is inclined to link scholarship and power since the formation of any intellectual heritage is not simply a romantic exercise for disinterested seekers. Both Said and Lambropoulos are extremely useful in any discussion that brings the role of knowledge and power into the understanding of intellectual formations in the cultural sphere, and the consequent dialectical tensions between, say, Auerbach's Homeric-Biblical, Schiller's naive-sentimental, Hölderlin's Hellenic-Hesperian, Lukács' epic-novel or even Nietzsche's Apollonian-Dionysian archetypes. What makes Lambropoulos interesting is his willingness to consider both historical and legendary material in his interpretation of reality. In spite of existing polarities, he endorses Walcott's belief that the *Iliad* can still be read as a Caribbean epic without recourse to distinguishing between 'biblical narrative based on resentment and mythical narrative based on desire'. Within this debate, another Caribbean writer's ideas are worth mentioning: Wilson Harris advocates the need for fictions with the multidimensionality of seascape, skyscape, and riverscape. He uses ways of crossing boundaries through intuitive response and imagination. Blake's 'Tyger' from the perspective of Amerindian jaguar myths gives it a different place in the South American canon. These links can be forged, he believes, not by intellectualising, but by the workings of the imagination. But his thinking still leaves a concern about actual experiences which are invalidated by the crossing of boundaries. Any reasoning, then, can only be an interpretation, imaginative or otherwise. The subtitle of Auerbach's *Mimesis*, Lambropoulos reasons, should in fact read 'The Interpretation of the Representation of Reality in Western Literature' and not 'The Representation of Reality in Western Literature'. True to its claims, the purpose of Lambropoulos's book lies not in analysing dominant modes of representation, but in interpreting them. Of course, he agrees that 'to those who are happy to be explained, emancipated, assimilated into the civil rites of interpretation, anyone not sharing the aesthetic communion appears uncivilized and threatening'.

Lambropoulos does not chart a linear history or a chronological narrative of how reason and morality followed the spiritual, but through a series of digressions each beginning with a prominent twentieth-century aesthetic position (Martin Bernal, Horkheimer and Adorno, Levinas etc), examines in detail and with clarity the various ideals of autonomy. Auerbach can serve as illustration here since *Mimesis* exemplifies a strong Biblical view of literary history. All of Auerbach's selected texts are from within the canonical European tradition, and are furthermore arranged with the Bible in mind which in his view is the absolute Book. It follows that there exists no other literature before it. In fact, no other literature, in his view, can match the glorious achievements of the western masters. As Lambropoulos writes of Auerbach's Story of Literature: 'The notion of the tradition itself is not discussed, and its authority is recognized unquestionably. The unity, borders, jurisdiction, and goals of that authority are established. The driving implication is that the West has its own Bible, although a secular one, which is its literary canon'. Two things emerge from Auerbach's claims to historical truth: that there is only one literature worth reading, and that there is only one way of reading it, the Biblical way.

But then these are familiar characteristics of Enlightenment thought: subjectivism, objectivism, positivism, and totalitarianism. In privileging Man and the principle of self, the Enlightenment rationale put man at the centre of the Universe, and turned individuality into individualism. Such subjectivism in turn distanced man from the world. The world became an object of observation and exploration, an alien which was infinitely discoverable. Enlightenment quantified too and generalized the particular, thereby enabling the creation of a total, manageable system. The programme of Enlightenment had to fail however, besieged as it was with inner contradictions:

> The grandiose enterprise that was launched to liberate humanity from the grip of mythological thinking ... collapsed into a new mythology, which is all the worse, since it is still mesmerized by delusions of power ... Before, people were paralyzed by the mythology of superstition; now the reign of reason has produced its own mythology, rationality. In another sense, we are even more helpless now, having been deceived by our best potential.[2]

2. Lambropoulos, p101.

By bringing myth and reason together and the contradictory interplay of knowledge and power, Lambropoulos is able to reveal the circular trajectory of Enlightenment reasoning, argued cohesively in his analyses of Horkheimer and Adorno's Odysseus and their views on the barbarity of anti-Semitism.

Horkheimer and Adorno proposed Judaism, or 'de-Hellenization', or even the complete annihilation of the Greek element from western learning, as a project of 'atonement' for wrongdoing. Their message was: repeat, repent, return. Accordingly, they created a sinister model of Greek thought, representing thirty centuries of western civilization, from Odysseus to Hitler. Horkheimer and Adorno could hardly have been able to create a culture of atonement if it had not been for inventing a mythology of their own. Lambropoulos demystifies the extreme position of Horkheimer and Adorno, and guards against further essentialisms while examining the various perspectives adopted by Lukács, Marx, Bauer, Sartre, Weber, and Derrida.

It is clear that in fashioning distinct identities, the rhetoric of 'otherness' is significantly important since identities are prone to becoming essentialist rather than relational, viewed as they then will be from a position external to the actuality of relationships between cultures or from a privileging epistemology centred in unequal relationships. From this position, the Other is always Hebraic: the essential Other is the Jew who has to qualify for the test of proficiency in Hellenic culture in order to enter into the civic society of interpretive rights. Lambropoulos here skilfully extricates himself from paying homage to either of the two schools. He reaches instead for an area of postmodern interpretation – 'interpretation at its last historical phase' – in which the canon does not matter so long as 'everything is read, treated like text, interpreted, Biblicized'. As Lambropoulos writes: 'Both the separatist and the assimilationist positions, both the humanist and the anti-humanist attitudes find in Hebraism the postmodern universal that asserts the moral superiority of contemplation, the cultural ethics of atonement'. Undoubtedly, this is another transfiguration into pure faith.

Are we to then understand that Lambropoulos extends ultimately the Derridean model? Derrida, too, like Horkheimer and Adorno, blames the Greeks for the overwhelming oppression of Hellenism. As in *Writing and Difference*, he posits:

> The Greek father who still holds us under his sway must be killed; and this is what a Greek – Plato – could never resolve to do, deferring the act into a hallucinatory murder. A hallucination within a hallucination that is already speech. But will a non-Greek ever succeed in doing what a Greek in this case could not do, except by disguising himself as a Greek, by *speaking* Greek, by feigning to speak Greek in order to get near the King?[3]

Derrida must really settle his scores with Heidegger's Greeks than, in fact, with Plato. In other words, Derrida argues that Hebraism is not Judaism but its difference from the Hellenic, and further, that the Hebraic can kill the Greek father only by speaking the language of the Alien.

Towards the end, Lambropoulos asks the question: Can there be a Hebraic culture at all? In Derridean terms, 'the Jew and the Poet' are not circumscribed by the Greek Polis as both can attain the promised land of language. Judaism is on its way to becoming a universal condition: we are all Jews, and all things Greek are anti-Semitic. Or, the authority of theoria is simply eroded. This links up with deconstruction both being and not being a liberating enterprise. It questions authority but in the end, sanctions it, being really an affirmative movement. Deconstruction implies the awareness that interpretation and emancipation, reading and the freedom from it, the Hellenic and the Hebraic turns of culture are all supportive units of the Protestant project of modernity.

Indeed, Lambropoulos' new book sets up a discursive space for cultural politics, while adequately bringing out his optimism that it is not entirely impossible to conceive of a scholarship that neither corrupts history nor is indifferent to human reality.

3. Jacques Derrida, 'Structure, Sign, and Play in the Discourse of the Human Sciences', *Writing and Difference*, trans. Alan Bass, University of Chicago Press, Chicago 1967, p89.

PLUS ÇA CHANGE . . .

N.J. Rengger

Stephen Crook, Jan Pakulski and Malcom Waters, *Postmodernisation: Change in Advanced Society*, Sage, London 1992, 264 pp: £12.95

Discussions of the character and significance of the changes that so-called 'advanced industrial societies' are currently undergoing seem to be one of the few growth industries such societies are still producing. In the last few months, for example, we have had three heavyweight sociologists weighing in with a combined effort (Ulrich Beck, Anthony Giddens and Scott Lash, *Reflexive Modernisation*, together with another related treatment by Lash and his co-author John Urry, *Economies of Signs and Space*, picking up where they left off in *The End of Organised Capitalism*.[1]

1. *Reflexive Modernisation*, Polity Press, Cambridge 1994; *Economies of Signs and Space*, Sage, London 1994; *The End of Organised Capitalism*, Polity Press, Cambridge 1987.

The study currently under review, though predating these by a couple of years, is very much focused on similar questions. Like the above books this one is co-authored and focuses on what might be called the socio-cultural aspects of modern political economy. It also attempts, however, to integrate wider theoretical and philosophical concerns within that framework and concludes that postmodernisation is both a radical change within, and a continuation of, modernisation. The study concentrates on six areas, culture, the state, inequality, politics, work organisations and science and technology, each of which effectively gets a chapter to itself, the whole then being bracketed, as it were, by an introductory chapter on modernisation and postmodernisation and a concluding one entitled 'the dialectics of postmodernisation'.

Unquestionably, the authors are treating serious and important issues. They do so, moreover, in a way that is relatively free of the worst excesses of the linguistic year zero that sometimes appears to have affected other writers working in this area. The accounts of the six basic areas offered are succinct and interesting and while the authors clearly share some assumptions and conclusions with the likes of Giddens, Beck or Lash and Urry their argument is sufficiently different to offer an alternative perspective on most of these points.

Overall then this is unquestionably a worthwhile book on an important subject and therefore deserves a wide readership. However, I also have some problems with the analysis offered by Crook, Pakulski and Waters. To outline what I have in mind here let me start by referring to their opening chapter. The authors offer a general survey of contemporary theories of what they term the 'current transformation'. Two broad approaches are essentially high-lighted: on the one hand, there are views outlined by Habermas (together with some of his collaborators and allies such as Claus Offe), the ubiquitous and aforementioned Lash and Urry and David Harvey, all allegedly linked by a 'determination to save the analytic and normative salience of the idea of modernity (frequently within some variant on marxist themes)' (p30). On the other hand, we have a 'postmodern' approach championed (in different ways) by the likes of Lyotard and Baudrillard (p31).

This dichotomy yields three particularly important theoretical statements about the changes contemporary advanced societies are undergoing, the authors suggest: post-industrialism, disorganisation and postmodernist culture. Obviously, however, each of these is given different emphasis by the various approaches and it is the thesis of Crook, Pakulski and Waters that each is incomplete relative to the others and that a proper account of postmodernisation requires an account of each related to the other in the context of the six areas previously identified. The authors then give the following characterisation of our contemporary situation which it is worth quoting in full:

> The onset of postmodernisation is genuinely explosive as liberated social components diverge rapidly from the central direction of modernity. Postmodernisation is characterized by an unprecedented level of unpredictability and apparent chaos. Action is divorced from underlying material constraints (or rather these constraints disappear) and enters the voluntaristic world taste, choice and preference. As it does so the boundaries between determined social groups disappear. So class, gender and ethnicity decline in social significance and so also do some of their characteristic forms of expression ... the progressive differentiation of culture, society and personality characteristic of modernity involutes so that the very idea of an independent, purely social structural realm no longer makes sense. Rather 'society' must be understood in terms of culture as patterns of signs and symbols penetrate and erode structural boundaries ... The advanced societies of the contemporary world are poised on the cusp of this transformation ... the trend is not irreversible ... however ... a reversal would involve a legitimation crisis of such massive proportions that it would demand either cataclysmic economic decline or extreme coercion or both, on a global scale (p35).

There are a number of points that arise from this characterisation. I shall pass over the use of terms such as 'involute' as a temporary linguistic aberration but I want to concentrate on two points derived from the above argument. First, it seems to me at least, the authors' characterisation can be questioned in a number of ways. Is it really the case that such things as ethnicity and gender (and even class) are becoming less significant? Quite the contrary, I would have said. In so-called 'advanced societies', gender issues are increasingly seen as a central feature of political debate and action. Far from becoming less significant they seem to be becoming much *more* significant. Of course, the authors might suggest that this is what they mean, that in the process of such things as gender and ethnicity declining in importance, contemporary understandings of them must be problematised. However, *gender* as such has an increasingly high-profile and is likely to continue to do so for the foreseeable future, however much particular gender roles or assumptions might disappear.

A similar point can be made with regard to ethnicity. It is clearly not the case that 'ethnicity' has ceased to be a feature of (say) contemporary German politics (Gastarbeiter, Grundgesetz), British politics (Northern Ireland, racial attacks) or – perhaps most obviously of all – the United States (the LA riots, for example). Many similar arguments could be made with regard to other claims the authors make. Must society really now be seen in terms of 'culture', or if it must, how is this different from the way in which anthropologists such as Geertz have suggested that we should always see the relations between society and culture? Moreover, if we are on the 'cusp' of this transformation (as the authors suggest) then presumably a 'reversal' is always possible unless you also assume that the trends they analyse have some kind of determinate logic which is itself irreversible.

This leads on to my second point. The authors clearly veer towards the 'postmodern' side of the debate (as expressed above) – though by no means entirely – and yet they do not really examine the notion enough nor discuss the philosophical and metaphysical claims that such a view might require. Of course, in some ways, this is fair enough; there should be some academic division of labour somewhere. However, it does leave the impression of unfinished business, as it were. In fact, I would argue that the authors quite understandably focus on (post)modernity as socio-cultural form, and they have not provided a sufficiently rich analysis of the postmodern mood which might accompany it. As a result the true implications of their analysis are, I think, obscured.

Despite these disagreements, however, I hope it is clear that I think that the book is an excellent one. Discussions of these questions that are as wide-ranging, as accessible and as stimulating as this one are none too common. One hopes that the authors will take their analysis further.

MODERNITY (AND AFTER)!

N.J. Rengger

David Lyon, *Postmodernity*, Open University Press, Buckingham 1994, 104 pp; £8.99 cloth, £30.00 paper.

People could be forgiven for thinking that the world could profitably do without many more more books on postmodernism, postmodernity and the like, of which, of late, we seem to have had a positive torrent.

I do not share the view, at least not quite. If by it it is meant that we have probably had about enough of allegedly 'postmodern' agonising (or celebration) about our 'radical', 'new' situation, the sort of thing that Gilles Lipovetsky has recently engaged us with in *Le Crepescule du devoir*, for example, then I would probably agree (with a hearty cheer). On the other hand the tendency, especially among many political theorists, to avoid discussing modernity (or its putative 'post') at all I find almost equally worrying. Whether or not we feel that we can agree with any particular theorist of 'postmodernity', to deny its importance as a cultural claim seems perverse. What we need, therefore, is work that attempts to treat questions about modernity and postmodernity in ways that bring out its importance without sounding either messianic or, worse, flippant.

David Lyon's book clearly attempts to pursue this aim and does so I think with commendable clarity and an unusual – though certainly welcome – brevity. The book is manifestly intended as an introduction to this enormously complex area and as such it succeeds extremely well. Divided into six chapters, the book traces the idea of postmodernity through its historical stages, its links with notions of modernity as such, its connection with such ideas as post-industrialism, and, the emphasis that Lyon sees as central for it, the change in the nature of such phenomena as consumerism. In the concluding chapter he also attempts, rightly I think, to relate some of the recent elevations of the pre-modern (MacIntyre, Grant, Milbank) to their postmodern cousins. Overall the book is clearly written, tightly focused and is likely to be an excellent book to put in the hands of students.

Lyon's book is about 'postmodernity' but he clearly sees this in terms of the discussions of both ideas *about* the postmodern and changes *in*, for example, productive forces which are creating a new society. These two aspects of the modernity debate could be seen as, respectively, modernity as mood and modernity as socio-cultural form and Lyon is, I think, quite right to see these two phenomena as linked. However, in my view they are also importantly distinct. Indeed, they need to be held apart *in order* to properly see how they might best be related to one another. For example, there are pronounced changes in the character of consumerism in the late twentieth century created by (to just pick up some themes at random) informational and technological shifts, globalisation, demographic change (as Lyon discusses in some detail in his penultimate chapter). This seems to me to be undeniable. The question is how to assess the significance of such changes.

Here it is the relation of these claims to the more obviously theoretical and philosophical accounts of the 'crisis of representation' (and/or knowledge/and or ethics and/or meaning) that are the leitmotif of 'postmodern thought' (as mood) that is interesting and central with regard to an assessment of whether or not we can legitimately use the term 'postmodernity' to refer to a qualitatively different (or at least changing) society. However, to properly assess this we must have an understanding of the sense of each aspect of the question before we can say how closely one might depend upon the other or even how congruent the two claims are. After all, many thinkers not interested in 'postmodernity' as such would accept that there have been major changes in social or productive forms. To assert that we should see these changes in the way that theses about 'postmodernity' claim is to assert a *particular* relationship between 'postmodern' claims about knowledge/meaning and so on and these socio-economic shifts.

Lyon's book discusses discrete aspects of both modernity as mood and modernity as socio-cultural form very well. However, he sometimes seems to run the two together in a way that I think is problematic in that it runs the risk of hindering, rather than aiding, the task of understanding both. His discussion of consumerism, interesting though it is, has something of this about it as do his reflections on the history of postmodernity as an idea outlined at the beginning of the book.

None of this, however, should detract from Lyon's achievement. The book covers a large amount of territory in a remarkably brief compass, is clearly written and deals with an important issue in an unfussy and illuminating style.

IDENTITY ORGIES

Linda Ruth Williams

Pamela Church Gibson and Roma Gibson (eds), *Dirty Looks: Women Pornography, Power*, BFI Publishing 1993, £12.95 paperback; *Social Text*, 37, Winter 1993.

If feminist debate around pornography and censorship has been at best difficult, the new turn towards interest in the sex industry itself promises to focus a number of problems. What both *Dirty Looks: Women, Pornography, Power* (edited by Pamela Church Gibson and Roma Gibson) and the Winter 1993 edition of *Social Text* (which includes a special section edited by Anne McClintock on the sex trade) have in common, apart from a couple of duplicated essays, is that they evidence a shift not just in feminist attitudes towards the representations of pornography, but in its desire to bridge the gap between analysis of images and the working world of production and consumption, by looking more closely at what sex workers offer their clients (on film or in body), and what the clients want from the sex industry and its images. One basic realignment comes through the ways in which writers in both collections are keen to mark the radical difference between their own positions and those of Andrea Dworkin, Robin Morgan, Catherine MacKinnon, or, in Britain, Catherine Itzin, adding to the burgeoning corpus of challenges to the marriage of certain strains of cultural feminism with right-wing pro-censors. The shift away from fixed models of gender difference is here once again made in a number of ways via a discussion of 'perversion'. Voyeurism, exhibitionism, s/m and b/d activities slide blithely across the gender divide, muddying it in the process; like transvestism for Marjorie Garber in *Vested Interests*, the activities which these texts discuss embody and perform social contradiction.[1] Against the grain of a once-dominant feminist voice, here the pleasures as well as the dangers of pornography and sex work are emphasised, looking towards, at the most extreme point represented in either collection, a feminist 'pornotopia'.[2] Porn is not just an issue around the body (and how bodies are represented), it moves the body (to arousal), just as other low cultural forms provoke tears (melodrama or romance) or screams (horror). The expanding subject area of 'porn studies' (a sexy new academic niche addressed with some irony by Jennifer Wicke in *Dirty Looks*: 'Pornography is sexy, and so is writing about it'[3]) forges connections with others ways of reading genre. Indeed, the potential cross-overs with work on other genres are multiple, not just through the connection made explicitly here with recent work on the identifications of horror cinema (Carol Clover, author of the important 1992 text on horror and gender *Men, Women and Chain Saws,*

1. See in particular Anne McClintock's discussion of Garber in 'Maid to Order: Commercial Fetishism and Gender Power', p98 of *Social Text*.

2. In Gertrude Koch's words – 'The Body's Shadow Realm', in *Dirty Looks*, p42.

3. Jennifer Wicke, 'Through a Gaze Darkly: Pornography's Academic Market', in *Dirty Looks*, p78.

introduces *Dirty Looks*), but with other work on mass-market pleasures and perils. Laura Kipnis reads transvestite self-portraiture alongside the Untitled Film Stills of Cindy Sherman, whilst Lynne Segal's lively discussion of the paucity of concrete evidence linking pornographic consumption with violent sex crime has a strong bearing on the current debate on the behavioural effects (or not) of horror films on their audiences.

The two collections come from different sides of the Atlantic (one is a British Film Institute publication, the other emanates from Duke University), and are inflected rather differently. *Social Text* is centrally concerned with the sex trade, and includes a number of contributions from its workers, whilst the other is a more diverse, but academically focused, set of essays which contain wide discussion of primary 'effects' studies of the relationship between porn consumption and sexual violence, Asian cinema, and the academic obsession with porn itself, as well as a number of readings of different pornographic texts and contexts. By addressing the way in which the primary identifications which psychoanalysis explains are mixed and muddied in the practices the sex trade facilitates, gender theory meets sexual practice in an important way in these collections. Pornography, prostitution, and the sex work associated with these have formed difficult territory for some feminists, upon which some of the bitterest splits in the women's movement have opened up. The battles of pro- and anti-censorship campaigners are well documented, and a number of pieces in the *Social Text* collection also highlight (and condemn) feminist opposition to prostitution as the prime symptom of female false consciousness (the sex worker as, in Laurie Shrage's notorious analogy, a female Uncle Tom), or as female victimage writ large (Dworkin's support only for prostitute groups which highlight the horrors of sex work, such as WHISPER, Women Hurt in Systems of Prostitution Engaged in Revolt). These essays radically depart from the position of anti-pornography campaigners, yet it is ironically here, with this new tone on sexual practice and sexual purchase, that the personal and the political are really being read together again, as escort workers discuss their autonomy, cross-dressers articulate their femininity as clients in s/m scenarios, sociolgoists debate the difficulties of participant observation in the sex trade, and Candida Royalle accounts for the new ways in which sex videos by and for women are being thought and made.

These are diverse positions, coming from a number of countries and rendered in very different first-person voices, a mixed bag perhaps because no formal academic style smoothes over the differences. Whilst the essays of *Social Text* do not *simply* celebrate the pleasures of sex work, they are keen to stress that pleasure and fun are often involved, that this is work like any other, and that all forms of sex work can offer women financial security and independence. (Male sex work is sometimes alluded to, but is not the central concern of either text, although call for more work not just on rent boys but on heterosexual male escorts, as well as on the desires and world of clients, is regularly made here. If there is a primary object which emerges through both books, it is of women as the 'bought' — but often profiting — object in a heterosexual contract).

'Jasmine', a prostitute and activist working for the international decriminalization of sex work, argues that 'women's lib shit' has done nothing for working women, yet emphasises her preference for the collective female support of the whorehouse over the separation of the street, and asks simply that prostitution be included in the 1992 EC Social Charter for Employees. Interviewed by Anne McClintock, Mistress Vena (a New York-based dominatrix) analyses the skills of domination work, the needs of the slave, the ambivalence of control. Robert/'Stella' discusses his long-term paying-partnership with 'Susie', dominatrix women of his dreams. Both of these latter pieces are accompanied by some of Grace Lau's marvellous photo-sequences, of the mistress with her slave, of the man transformed by his rubber femininity in the mirror. Royalle, the prototype 'couples' pornographer, tailoring her products to (her perception of) female desire, casts herself as the capitalist feminist identifying her market niche whilst still somehow gloriously breaking the rules (she is both a woman who 'dare[s] to break with a cultural taboo' and the capitalist who 'recognized and created the market').[4] As Lau writes in her own 'Confessions of a Complete Scopophiliac' in *Dirty Looks*, 'During the 1980s, female desire became a lucrative business'.[5] All voices argue against the image of the sex worker as victim, and not just because she so often controls the scene. Indeed, whilst the differences of women's experiences working across Europe and America as escorts, hookers, masseuses, porn actresses and dominatrixes are evident, one resounding message is clear: the single biggest improvement to prostitutes lives would come if their work were to be properly and universally decriminalised.

In keeping with Lau's title, early theories of the male gaze in cinema are also overtly problematised in both collections, with writers starting from the premise that the look is not intrinsically gendered, that (as Freud argued in the *Three Essays on the Theory of Sexuality*) scopophilia is a primal instinct which plays a role in the sexual dynamics of both genders, of all infants. In 'The Body's Shadow Realm' Gertrude Koch thinks specifically about the pornographic gaze, and problematises the connection which is often made between porn and real acts between real bodies (porn as a substitute for, or a prelude to, 'real' sex or even real violence) by focussing on the way in which it is specifically geared to a solitary voyeurism, enacting 'the ultimate triumph of the eye over the body'.[6] Rather than being a replacement for sex with an absent partner, its pleasures run elsewhere. If two bodies are involved, these are the screen body and the audiences, mediated by the purest voyeurism in cinema, a voyeurism desperate not to be seen to be seeing. And this is the crux: involve another 'real' body here and porn ceases to work in the same way: make the pornographic response a substitute for real sex and you deny its peculiar conditions and pleasures.

Linda Williams' seminal (in more senses than one) text of 1989, *Hard Core: Power, Pleasure, and the 'Frenzy of the Visible'*, is the departure point for many of these essays, particularly its central discussion of the visibility of male pleasure in hard core porn (the money shot) and the (traditional) invisibility of a female pleasure that pornography is nevertheless desperate to represent. In

4. Candida Royalle, 'Porn in the U.S.A.', p24, 32 of *Social Text*.

5. Grace Lau, 'Confessions of a Complete Scopophiliac', in *Dirty Looks*, p205.

6. Koch, p33.

emphasising female sexual performance, and particularly forms of performance which actively obfuscate the division between porn and art, the centrality
of male pleasure as key pornographic spectacle, as well as the certainty of genre
divisions, are both disrupted. The excessive figure of Annie Sprinkle looms
large here. Indeed, her current incarnation as post-porn-modernist
performance artist is the subject of two essays, one by Williams herself ('A
Provoking Agent: The Pornography and Performance Art of Annie Sprinkle',
collected in both texts), the other by Chris Straayer ('The Seduction of
Boundaries: Feminist Fluidity in Annie Sprinkle's Art/Education/Sex', in *Dirty
Looks*). Sprinkle has become such an important focus for debate because her
spectacular transformations, from hooker to porn actress to avant garde film
maker to performance artist, challenge not only the boundaries between
different selves and forms of work, but between the 'high' concerns of
performance and the 'low' concerns of porn. By highlighting the elements of
performance, artifice and pastiche, Sprinkle manages to problematise models
of 'natural' or 'authentic' sexual response whilst also evidently enjoying herself.
In the process, she offers herself and her audiences, in Straayer's words, 'a
virtual identity orgy'.

The identificatory cross-overs which pornography can facilitate are central
to perhaps all of the issues and subjects raised here. The argument which
Clover has made in *Men, Women and Chain Saws*, that the pleasures of horror
and other forms of exploitation cinema involve the audience in a number of
contrary and cross-identifications, with victim, monster, and victim-turned-
killer, have a role to play in the analysis of porn. In *Dirty Looks* Clover returns to
this issue, but it is Williams' first essay here ('Second Thoughts on *Hard Core*:
American Obscenity Law and the Scapegoating of Deviance') that makes the
point most intriguingly and candidly. The piece looks not only at the deviance
of those who militate against porn, but Williams' new willingness to discuss the
pornographies of gay and lesbian, as well as straight, sexualities. *Hard Core*
concentrated on the latter, since, as Williams now puts it, 'I felt I had no right
or authority to analyse gay and lesbian porn'. Her revision resonates with a
wider position on access to diverse images:

> Speaking from what I now recognise to be a false sense of fixed sexual
> identity ... I was unable to see then that what I was learning from the book
> was actually how easy it was to identify with diverse subject positions and to
> desire diverse objects, indeed how polymorphously perverse the genre of
> pornography could be.[7]

7. Linda Williams,
'Second thoughts on
Hard Core: American
Obscenity and the
Scapegoating of
Deviance', *Dirty Looks*,
p56.

8. Lynne Segal, 'Does
Pornography Cause
Violence? The Search
for Evidence', *Dirty
Looks*, p15.

And just as our responses are fluid, so are the objects upon which we choose to
fix pornographically. There is, then, no single dominant image which is intrinsically pornogrpahic and, simple as this sounds, 'Context really does matter'.[8] 'It
is never possible, whatever the image', writes Lynne Segal, 'to isolate it, to fix its
meaning and predict some inevitable pattern of response, independently from
assessing its wider representational context and the particular recreational,

educational or social context in which it is being received'.[9]

Context also matters here, in the way in which the essays are presented, and the moments at which the essays repeat. Williams' piece on Annie Sprinkle appears in both collections, Anne McClintock edits one, and her piece on commercial fetishism appears under slightly different titles in both. The same words are accompanied by rather different illustrations, however, pushing McClintock's essay itself into somewhat different territory. With its British publication comes a flagellation wood-cut from 1718 (risky, but steeped in the authority of an historical artefact), and three coy tabloid cartoons focussed on that peculiarly British phenomenon, Madame Cyn. The photographs which accompany Grace Lau's essay in *Dirty Looks* are somewhat tamer than those of Lau's which are used alongside the American version of McClintock's essay – of a rubber-hooded, mirror-imaged, s/m embrace. This is followed by a diverse collection of dominatrix's calling-cards ('Be my chair if you dare'; 'Make no mistake … She's in control'), common evidence to be found in every city phone box – and many of these essays – that one of the key spectacles of the skin trade is the woman in control of the submissive man. 'The economy of S/M is the economy of conversion' writes McClintock in her succinct Foucaldian discussion of debates around the transgression and reversals of sex games which 'play the world backwards'.

Yet whilst the BFI collection engages in these debates in a more theoretically ground way, *Social Text* contains a number of first-person accounts from workers in the sex trade which offer the testimony of wide practice. 'Nine times out of ten', writes escort worker "Barbara", 'all men want you to do is seduce them. Men are sick, fed up, and tired with taking the sexual initiative'.[10] If, for Freud, gender begins with a set of alignments which sets masculinity alongside activity, voyeurism, domination, sadism (as opposed to passivity, exhibitionism, submission, masochism), and yet men themselves slide towards the 'wrong' side in their sexual practices, what does this do to the models of gender difference with which we are working? That it is the more passive of each of these pairings which is most characteristic of male practice and identification is evidenced in both volumes. For Mistress Vena, the S/M scene is largely about male submission to female discipline: 'As my own slave says, you can get sex anywhere. What men want, and what they are paying for, is a really strong dominant woman. You've got to show them who's boss'.[11] This does not, for McClintock, add up to a feminist utopia, however. If Mistress Vena's control is finally controlled by her client ('they just want you to have the upper hand … The Mistress controls the scene, so they can let go. It's about making them feel safe while exposing them to extreme danger'),[12] then the female power of the dungeon 'is a paradise arranged and organised for male pleasure'.[13] It's a well-rehearsed argument, but in the context of the worker's analyses of *Social Text*, one which is certainly not yet resolved.

Please note that Linda Ruth Williams, the author of this review, is *not* the same person as Linda Williams whose work is under discussion here.

9. Segal, p15, italics original.

10. 'Barbara', 'It's a Pleasure Doing Business with You', *Social Text*, p11.

11. In Anne McClintock, 'Confessions of a Psycho-Mistress: An Interview with Mistress Vena', *Social Text*, p71.

12. P 71.

13. McClintock, p102.

BACK ISSUES

1 **Peter Wollen** on fashion and orientalism / **Denise Riley** on 'women' and feminism / **Dick Hebdige**'s sociology of the sublime / **Laura Marcus** on autobiographies / **John Tagg** should art historians know their place? / **Franco Bianchini** on the GLC's cultural policies / **Homi K. Bhabha, Stephen Feuchtwang** and **Barbara Harlow** on Fanon

2 **Mary Kelly, Elizabeth Cowie** and **Norman Bryson** on Kelly's Interim / **Greil Marcus** on subversive entertainment / **Georgina Born** on modern music culture / **Geoffrey Nowell-Smith** on popular culture / **Ien Ang** on 'progressive television' / **Alan Sinfield** on modernism and English Studies in the Cold War / **Tony Bennett** on Eagleton.

3 *TRAVELLING THEORY* – **Julia Kristeva** on the melancholic imaginary / **David Edgar** on carnival and drama / **Kobena Mercer** black hair – style politics / **Jacques Rancière** on journeys into new worlds / **Peter Hulme**'s Caribbean diary / **Bill Schwarz** on travelling stars / **Ginette Vincendeau** on chanteuses réalistes / **Steve Connor** on Springsteen / **Christopher Norris** on Gasché's Derrida.

4 *CULTURAL TECHNOLOGIES* – **Simon Frith** making sense of jazz in Britain / **Griselda Pollock** on Doré's London / **Colin Mercer** on entertainment / **Tony Bennett**'s exhibitionary complex / **Ian Hunter** setting limits to culture / **David Saunders** on copyright and literature / **Jody Berland** on television.

5 *IDENTITIES* – **Homi K. Bhabha** on the commitment to theory / **Philip Cohen** on Tarzan and the jungle bunnies / **Glenn Bowman** on Palestinian nationalist consciousness / **Kristin Ross** on Rimbaud and spatial history / **Kaja Silverman** on liberty, maternity, commodification / **Adrian Rifkin** on Carmenology / **Margaret**

Sotan's epistemology of the wandering woman / **Andrew Benjamin** on psychoanalysis / **Gill Davies** on heritage / **Les Back** on soundsystems.

6 *THE BLUES* – **Jacqueline Rose** on Margaret Thatcher and Ruth Ellis / **James Donald** how English is it? / **Benita Parry** on Kipling's imperialism / **John Silver** on Carpentier / **Mitra Tabrizian** and **Andy Golding**'s blues / **Barbara Creed** on *Blue Velvet* / **Joseph Bristow** on masculinity / **Graham Murdock** on Moretti's *Bildungsroman* / **Edmond Wright** on post-Humptydumptyism.

7 *MODERNISM/MASOCHISM* – **Victor Burgin**'s Tokyo / **Linda Williams** on feminine masochism and feminist criticism / **John Tagg** on criticism, photography and technological change / **Geoff Bennington** l'arroseur arrosé(e) / **Emilia Steuerman** on Habermas vs Lyotard / **Paul Crowther** on the Kantian sublime, the avant-garde and the postmodern / **Mark Cousins** on Lévi Strauss on Mauss / **Iain Chambers** being 'British' / **Adrian Forty** on lofts and gardens / **Lisa Tickner** on Griselda Pollock.

8 *TECHNO-ECOLOGIES* – **Peter Wollen** cinema: Americanism and the robot / **John Keane** on the liberty of the press / **S.P. Mohanty** on the philosophical basis of political criticism / **David Kazanjian** and **Anahid Kassabian** naming the Armenian genocide / **Paul Théberge** the 'sound' of music / **David Tomas** the technophilic body / **Félix Guattari** the three ecologies / **Margaret Whitford** on Sartre.

9 *ON ENJOYMENT* – **Slavoj Zizek** the undergrowth of enjoyment / **Peter Osborne** aesthetic autonomy and the crisis of theory / **Rachel Bowlby** the judgement of Paris (and the choice of Kristeva) / **Joseph Bristow** being gay: politics, identity, pleasure

Back issues cost £14.99 each
Make cheques payable to *Lawrence & Wishart* and send to:
Lawrence & Wishart, 144a Old South Lambeth Road, London SW8 1XX

PSYCHOANALYSIS AND CULTURE

new formations 26

EDITOR: LESLEY CALDWELL

Along with its origins and its creator, psychoanalysis as a critical practice has become increasingly subject to attack and sceptical investigation, but at the same time its influence in universities has never been more extensive. As a tool of theoretical critique it has arguably become the dominant paradigm in cultural theorising: it has assumed a definite place in the academic curriculum.

PSYCHOANALYSIS AND CULTURE presents examinations and extensions of Freud and Freudian meta-psychology of relevance to the worth of practising psychoanalysis and to discussions of creativity. It returns to the issues of sexual difference and, in the first British publishing of **Jacques Derrida**'s 12,000 word incisive critique of the International Psychoanalytic Association, brings into question the politics of the main regulatory body of psychoanalysis.

Contributors include:

Malcolm Bowie, Jacques Derrida, André Green, Jim Hopkins, Juliet Mitchell, Clare Pajacowska, Joan Raphael-Leff, Joanna Ryan, Dominique Scarfone, Alex Tarnopolsky, Amal Treacher, Margaret Walters, DW Winnicott, Christopher Wintle.

new formations 26
PSYCHOANALYSIS
AND CULTURE

SPECIAL OFFER Just £3.75!

Yes! Why pay nearly £15 for the next exciting issue of *New Formations* when you can pay **just £3.75**? You will receive our PSYCHOANALYSIS AND CULTURE issue featuring a 12,000 word essay by Jacques Derrida (previously unpublished in Britain) on the international regulation of psychoanalytic practice. This is an edition not to be missed, and its yours at **quarter-price!**

This issue is edited by **Lesley Caldwell** with contributors including **DW Winnicott** outlining the psychology of madness, **Juliet Mitchell** revisiting the impact of psychoanalysis on feminist thinking and **Malcolm Bowie** exploring the relationship between memory and desire.

Take out a subscription **now** and you will receive this issue at **quarter-price**, and should you decide to continue your subscription you will **save £15** on the annual bookshop price of three issues of *New Formations*. Return the form below – send no money now, not even a stamp is needed – and you will receive the next issue at a discount price before it is available in the bookshops and libraries.

PS *No need to cut up your issue, photocopies of the form are OK.*

Signs of the Times present

postmodern|times

saturday 1 july 1995

city university
northampton square
london ec1

As traditional cultural, political and social formations disintegrate
what is the significance of those that take their place?

keynote **speakers**
Angela McRobbie author *Postmodernism and Popular Culture*
Frank Mort author *Dangerous Sexualities*
Ali Rattansi co-editor *Racism, Modernity & Identity*
Edward Soja author *Postmodern Geographies*

over **30 papers** *including:*
**Aziz Al-Azmeh, Louise Abbott, Anthony Giddens, Paul Gilroy, George
Lipsitz, Dave Morley, Jan Nederveen Pieterse, Sadie Plant, Ziauddin
Sardar, Kate Soper, Judith Squires, Errollyn Wallen, Wendy Wheeler**

conference **themes**
Birth of the global or the end of the west?
Pop, techno and the poetics of place
Critical sexualities for the new millennium

research **stream**
Towards a postmodern politics

Tickets £16.95 waged / £13.95 low/part-waged / £9.95 students or unwaged (with
evidence of status). Cheques payable to *Signs of the Times*.
From Postmodern Times, 28 Wargrave Avenue, London N15 6UD.
Tel: 0181-809 5068

In association with:

Lawrence & Wishart

new formations

CRITICAL QUARTERLY

Edited by Colin MacCabe

"The only journal to remain faithful to the original spirit of cultural studies.
It mixes 'high' and 'low' culture, criticism and creative writing without losing
sight of political or social questions" *Rosalind Coward*

Forthcoming issues include:
Theory of the City by Patrizia Lombardo
The Voice edited by Simon Frith
David Trotter edits Gay Lives
Colin MacCabe on Britain
Patrizia Lombardo on The End of
Childhood
Jean Binta Breeze on Poetry
Jon Savage's Passion

Fiction and Poetry:
stories by *Adam Mars Jones, Jeanette
Turner Hospital* and *Hanif Kureishi*,
with poems by *Tom Raworth, Mimi
Khalvati* and *Jean Binta Breeze*

ORDER FORM   **CRITICAL QUARTERLY**

Subscription Rates, Volume 37, 1995   ISSN 0011-1562

**Individuals £27.50 UK/Europe, $50.00 N America*, £32.50 Rest of World
Institutions £49.00 UK/Europe, $85.00 N America*, £55.00 Rest of World**

Published quarterly   *Canadian customers please add 7% GST

☐   Please enter my subscription/send me a sample copy
☐   I enclose a cheque/money order payable to Basil Blackwell
☐   Please charge my American Express/Diners Club/Mastercard/Visa account number

_____ Expiry Date_____
Signature _____ Date _____
Name   _____
Address   _____
             _____
             _____ Postcode _____

*E-Mail Address: jnlsamples@cix.compulink.co.uk
(Please include the name of the journal)*

Payment must accompany orders
Please return this form to: Journals Marketing, Blackwell Publishers, 108 Cowley Road, Oxford,
OX4 1JF, England. Or to: Journals Marketing, CRIQ, Blackwell Publishers, 238 Main Street,
Cambridge, MA 02142, USA

Blackwell Publishers   Oxford, UK and Cambridge, USA

POSTGRADUATE OPPORTUNITIES IN THE DEPARTMENT OF MEDIA AND COMMUNICATIONS

MA IN MEDIA AND COMMUNICATIONS STUDIES
MA BY RESEARCH; MPhil/PhD PROGRAMME

Our taught MA course is offered on either full-time or part-time basis. Students will be based in the Department of Media and Communications, but will also be able to take optional courses offered by the Departments of Sociology, English and Anthropology. Students will take a core course in **Media and Communications Theory;** a specialist course in **Methodologies of Communications and Cultural Analysis** and will choose 4 optional courses (a total of 6, 10-week courses, in all). Students will also complete a supervised Dissertation on a subject of their own choice. Among the optional courses which may be available are:

OPTIONAL COURSES (EXAMPLES OF RECENT COURSES)

Reconceptualising the Media Audience; The Media as a Public Sphere; Post-Colonial Criticism; Modernism and Post-modernism in the Arts; Literary History and Historicism; Literature and Popular Culture; Contemporary Cultural Production; Culture, Identity and Difference; Modernity and its Others; Political Communications; British Cinema 1945-65; Subjectivity and Cultural Production; Hollywood Cinema since the 1960's; Gender, Photography and New Technologies; Music, Material Culture and Social Life.

MA MEDIA/ COMMUNICATIONS BY RESEARCH

Students with an undergraduate qualification in Media, Communications or Cultural Studies can also be considered for an MA by Research, where the principal element is a supervised Extended Dissertation, supplemented by teaching in Methodologies of Research.

MPhil/PhD PROGRAMME

The department runs a lively doctoral programme for both full and part-time students. The department is recognised for the receipt of ESRC and British Academy awards. Students may take a range of courses to support their thesis research from the MA programme, together with tailor-made methodology courses, seminars, workshops and support groups.

FACULTY RESEARCH SPECIALISMS

Professor James Curran (The political economy and influence of mass media)
Professor Valerie Walkerdine (Psychology, post-structuralism, feminist theory, children and media)
Dr David Morley, Reader in Media Studies (Audience studies, cultural identities)
Dr Georgina Born (Technologies of cultural production)
Christine Geraghty (Film and Media theory)
Dr Sarah Kember (Photography, subjectivity, technology)
Gareth Stanton (Post-colonial criticism, Third World Cinema, Post-modernist ethnography).

Goldsmiths
UNIVERSITY
OF LONDON

Further information and Admissions

Application forms and further information about the courses can be obtained from The Postgraduate Office in the Registry, Goldsmiths College, New Cross, London SE14 6NW. Telephone: 0171 919 7538 Fax: 0171 919 7509.

Seeking to promote equality of opportunity in all its activities

MA Cultural Studies:
History and Theory

The Department of Cultural Studies at the University of East London has always emphasised the historical study of culture. Our MA extends this emphasis by focusing on the relations between history and theories such as poststructuralism, postcolonial theory, psycho-analysis and feminist theory. Our particular specialism is the psycho-analytic study of history and culture. Though case studies such as fascism, religion and feminism are offered, students are encouraged to maintain existing research interests.

Teaching staff include: Sally Alexander, Susannah Radstone, Bill Schwarz, Barbara Taylor and Couze Venn.

For more information contact Susannah Radstone, MA Course Tutor, Department of Cultural Studies, University of East London, Longbridge Road, Dagenham, Essex, RM8 2AS. Tel: 0181 849 3545. E-mail: Radstone@UEL.AC.UK. Fax: 0181 849 3598.

UNIVERSITY *of*
EAST LONDON

Antisemitism, Misogyny, and the Logic of Cultural Difference

Cesare Lombroso and Mathilde Serao
Nancy A. Harrowitz

Harrowitz explores the connections between misogyny and antisemitism by discussing two Italian authors of the late nineteenth century. The comparison of Lombroso and Serao raises the issues of why their prejudice focuses on women and Jews, since one author is Jewish and the other a women, how prejudice towards different groups can intersect, and the role of the difficult and complex concept of self-hatred. £28.50 hb

Organic Memory

History and the Body in the Late Nineteenth and Early Twentieth Centuries
Laura Otis

Organic Memory surveys the literary and scientific history of an idea that will not go away. Focusing on the years between 1870 and 1918, Otis explores both the origins and the consequences of the idea that memories can be inherited. Otis singles out major authors whose work reinforced or ridiculed belief in organic memory. They include: Thomas Mann, Sigmund Freud, C. G. Jung, Emile Zola, Thomas Hardy, Miguel de Unamuno, Pío Baroja, Emilia Pardo Bazán, and even Sir Arthur Conan Doyle. £35 hb

Finitude's Score

Essays for the End of the Millennium
Avital Ronell

"This collection is stunning. Ronell has achieved a work of thinking at the highest level. She knows the score."
—John P. Leavey Jr.

In *Finitude's Score*, Avital Ronell writes about the demands that reading makes on readers: to pay attention, to follow along and make sense, to take the work seriously. She looks at the limits of the literary and the borders between words, art, and contemporary politics where significance points to matters beyond signs. Suspending the distinction between headline news and high theory, these essays examine diverse figures of finitude in our modern world: war, guerrilla video, trauma TV, AIDS, music, divorce, sadism, electronic tagging, rumor. £32.95 hb

University of Nebraska Press
c/o Academic & University Publishers Group
1 Gower Street
London WC1E 6HA

Whose Art Is It?
Jane Kramer
Introduction by Catherine R. Stimpson

Whose Art Is It? is a lively and accessible introduction to the ongoing debate on representation and private expression in the public sphere.
Public Planet Books
96 pages, 18 b&w photos,
£9.95 pb, £23.95 hb

Fat Art, Thin Art
Eve Kosofsky Sedgwick

Eve Kosofsky Sedgwick's first volume of poetry opens up another dimension of her continuing project of crossing and recrossing the electrified boundaries between theory, lyric, and narrative.
184 pages, £14.95 pb, £43.50 hb

Crimes of Writing
Problems in the Containment of Representation
Susan Stewart

"Stewart, perhaps one of the most brilliant critics of her generation, recognizes that language can never truly capture or completely 'represent' the world . . . The range is wide, daring, and necessary."
–Irving Malin, *Journal of Modern Literature*
368 pages, 12 illus., £15.95 pb

Flame Wars
The Discourse of Cyberculture
Mark Dery, editor

Rallying around Frederic Jameson's call for a cognitive cartography that "seeks to endow the individual subject with some new heightened sense of place in the global system," the contributors to *Flame Wars* have sketched a corner of that map, an outline for a wiring diagram of a terminally wired world. 320 pages, 12 b&w photos, £12.95 pb, £37.95 hb

Postmodernity in Latin America
The Argentine Paradigm
Santiago Colás

This volume contests the prevailing understanding of the relationship between postmodernity and Latin America by focusing on recent developments in Latin American political and literary culture.
Post-Contemporary Interventions
256 pages, £16.95 pb, £42.75 hb

Materialist Feminism
Toril Moi and Janice Radway, editors

Along with the lively "conversation" between Juliet Mitchell and Toril Moi, the essays gathered here remind us that the debate–among feminists themselves–is as feisty as ever.
A Special Issue of SAQ
200 pages, £9.50 pb

Constituting Americans
Cultural Anxiety and Narrative Form
Priscilla Ward

Constituting Americans rethinks the way that certain writers of the mid-nineteenth and early twentieth century contributed to the project of attempting to fix in words precisely what it means to be American.
New Americanists
£16.95 pb, £54.00 hb

Radical Democracy
David Trend, editor

With the ascendence of neoliberalism in the U.S. and the collapse of communism abroad, does socialism still have meaning for groups on the left? Addressing this question is Stanley Aronowitz and eight other diverse left commentators.
A Special Issue of Socialist Review
190 pages, £8.50 pb

The Fate of the Self
German Writers and French Theory
Stanley Corngold

"*The Fate of the Self* is a daring and independent work. . . It brings intellectual history and literary criticism together without slighting either." –Allan Megill, University of Virginia. 312 pages, £16.95 pb

Negotiating Performance
Gender, Sexuality, and Theatricality in Latin/o America
Diana Taylor and Juan Villegas, editors

By redefining performance to include such events as Mayan and AIDS theatre, the Mothers of the Plaza de Mayo, and Argentine drag culture, this energentic volume discusses the dynamics of Latino/a identity politics and the sometime discordant intersections of gender, sexuality, and nationalism.
400 pages, 36 b&w photos, £17.95 pb, £52.50 hb

Asia/Pacific as Space of Cultural Production
Arif Dirik and Rob Wilson, editors

This volume documents the effort of indigenous cultural workers to claim and reimagine Asia/Pacific as a space for their own cultural production. *A Special Issue of* Boundary 2. 236 pages, £11.00 pb

Circuits of Desire
Yukiko Hanawa, editor

Circuits of Desire takes seriously the "queer" mandate to challenge the boundaries of queerness itself by analyzing the theoretical problems that occur when queer theory is transported to non-Anglo American communities.
A Special Issue of positions
240 pages, 4 colour illus., £9.50 pb

DUKE UNIVERSITY PRESS, c/o AUPG, 1 Gower Street, London WC1E 6HA Tel: 0171 580 395